P9-CQV-520

the once and future QUEEN

™

VOLUME ONE: OPENING MOVES

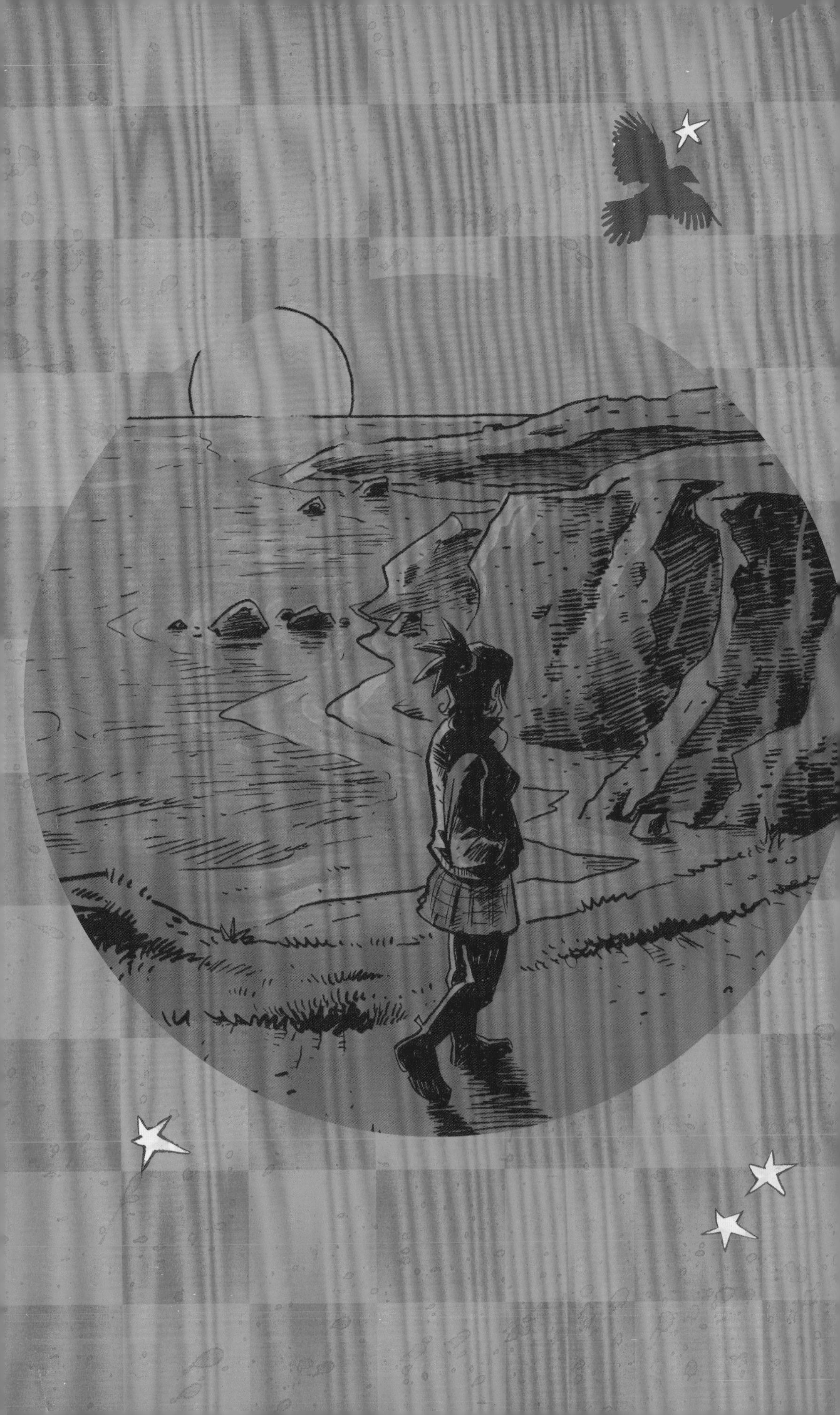

THE ONCE AND FUTURE QUEEN

STORY BY
Adam P. Knave and D.J. Kirkbride

ART AND COVER BY
Nick Brokenshire

LETTERS AND LOGO DESIGN BY
Frank Cvetkovic

DARK HORSE BOOKS

PUBLISHER **Mike Richardson**
EDITOR **Shantel LaRocque**
ASSISTANT EDITOR **Katii O'Brien**
DESIGNER **Anita Magaña**
DIGITAL ART TECHNICIAN **Christianne Goudreau**

SPECIAL THANKS TO HANNAH MEANS-SHANNON.

Neil Hankerson Executive Vice President • Tom Weddle Chief Financial Officer • Randy Stradley Vice President of Publishing • Matt Parkinson Vice President of Marketing • David Scroggy Vice President of Product Development • Dale LaFountain Vice President of Information Technology • Cara Niece Vice President of Production and Scheduling • Nick McWhorter Vice President of Media Licensing • Mark Bernardi Vice President of Book Trade and Digital Sales • Ken Lizzi General Counsel • Dave Marshall Editor in Chief • Davey Estrada Editorial Director • Scott Allie Executive Senior Editor • Chris Warner Senior Books Editor • Cary Grazzini Director of Specialty Projects • Lia Ribacchi Art Director • Vanessa Todd Director of Print Purchasing • Matt Dryer Director of Digital Art and Prepress • Sarah Robertson Director of Product Sales • Michael Gombos Director of International Publishing and Licensing

Published by Dark Horse Books
A division of Dark Horse Comics, Inc.
10956 SE Main Street
Milwaukie, OR 97222

First edition: November 2017
ISBN 978-1-50670-250-6

1 3 5 7 9 10 8 6 4 2
Printed in China

International Licensing: (503) 905-2377
Comic Shop Locator Service: (888) 266-4226

The Once and Future Queen™ © 2017 Adam P. Knave, D.J. Kirkbride, and Nick Brokenshire. Dark Horse Books® and the Dark Horse logo are registered trademarks of Dark Horse Comics, Inc. All rights reserved. No portion of this publication may be reproduced or transmitted, in any form or by any means, without the express written permission of Dark Horse Comics, Inc. Names, characters, places, and incidents featured in this publication either are the product of the author's imagination or are used fictitiously. Any resemblance to actual persons (living or dead), events, institutions, or locales, without satiric intent, is coincidental.

This volume collects *The Once and Future Queen* #1–#5.

Names: Knave, Adam P., 1975- author. | Kirkbride, D. J., author. | Brokenshire, Nick, artist. | Cvetkovic, Frank, letterer.
Title: Opening moves / script by Adam P. Knave & D.J. Kirkbride ; art and cover by Nick Brokenshire ; letters by Frank Cvetkovic.
Description: First edition. | Milwaukie, OR : Dark Horse Books, 2017. | Series: The once and future queen | "This volume collects The Once and Future Queen #1-#5"
Identifiers: LCCN 2017018758 | ISBN 9781506702506 (paperback)
Subjects: LCSH: Comic books, strips, etc. | BISAC: COMICS & GRAPHIC NOVELS / Fantasy. | COMICS & GRAPHIC NOVELS / Gay & Lesbian. | COMICS & GRAPHIC NOVELS / General.
Classification: LCC PN6728.O496 K63 2017 | DDC 741.5/973--dc23
LC record available at https://lccn.loc.gov/2017018758

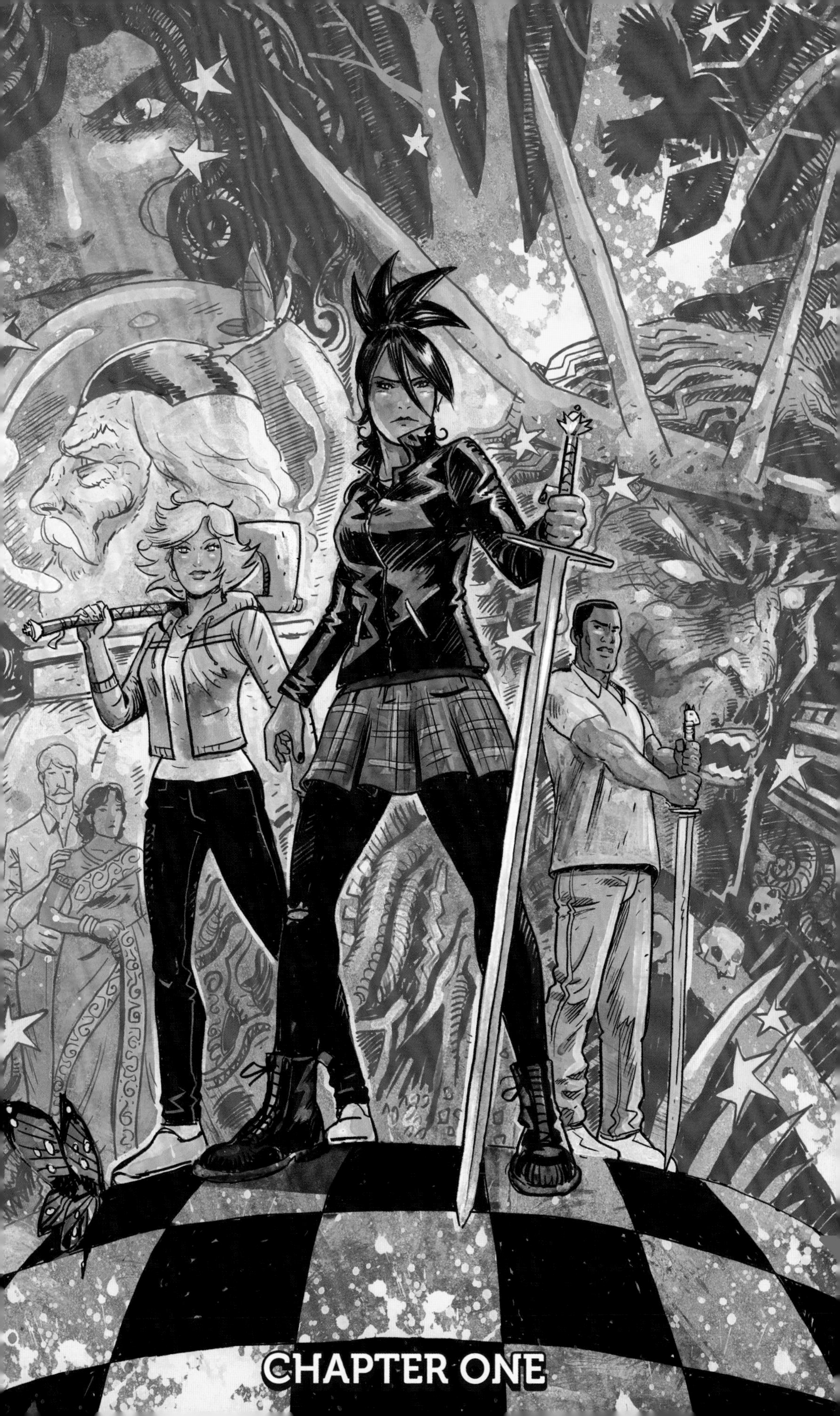

CHAPTER ONE

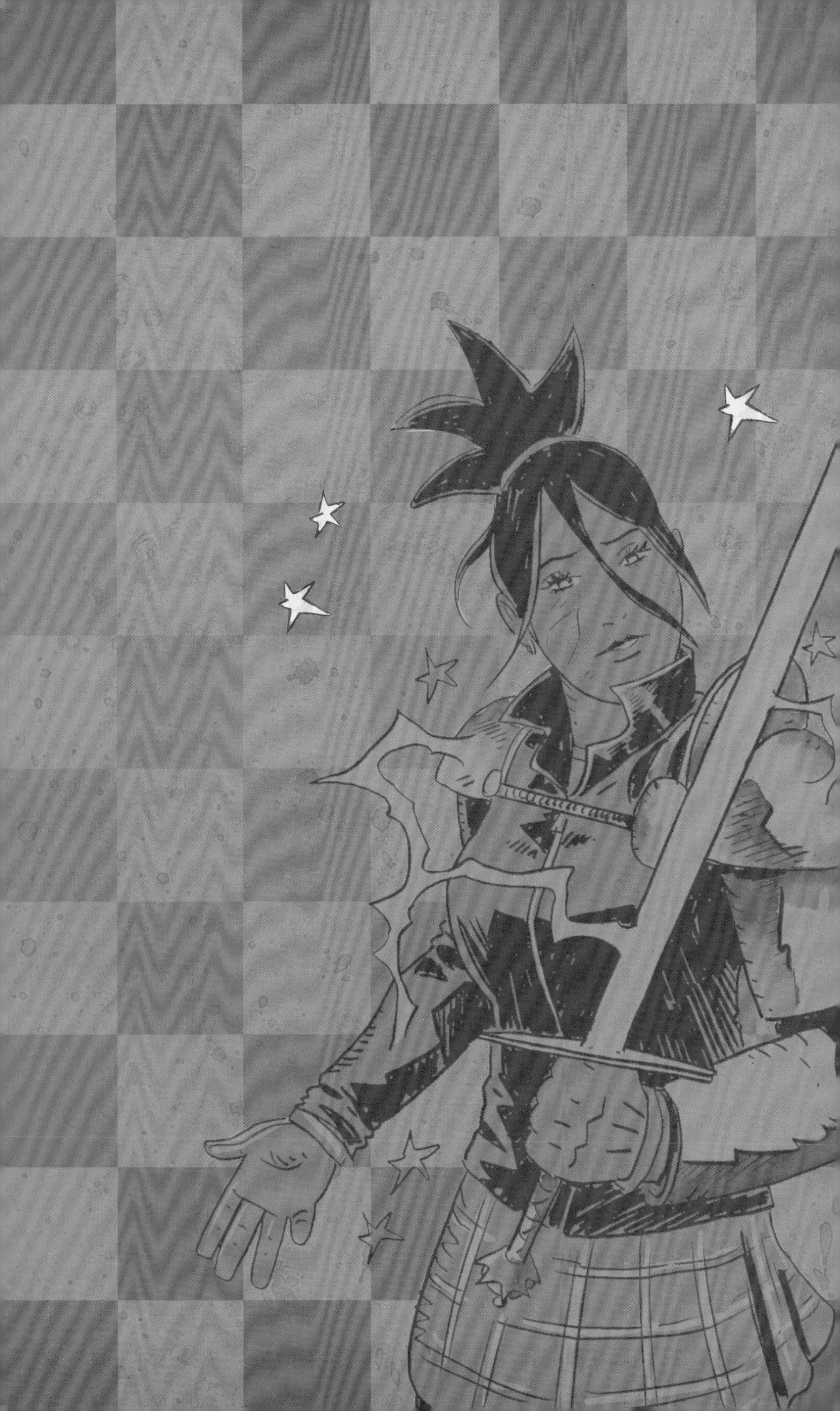

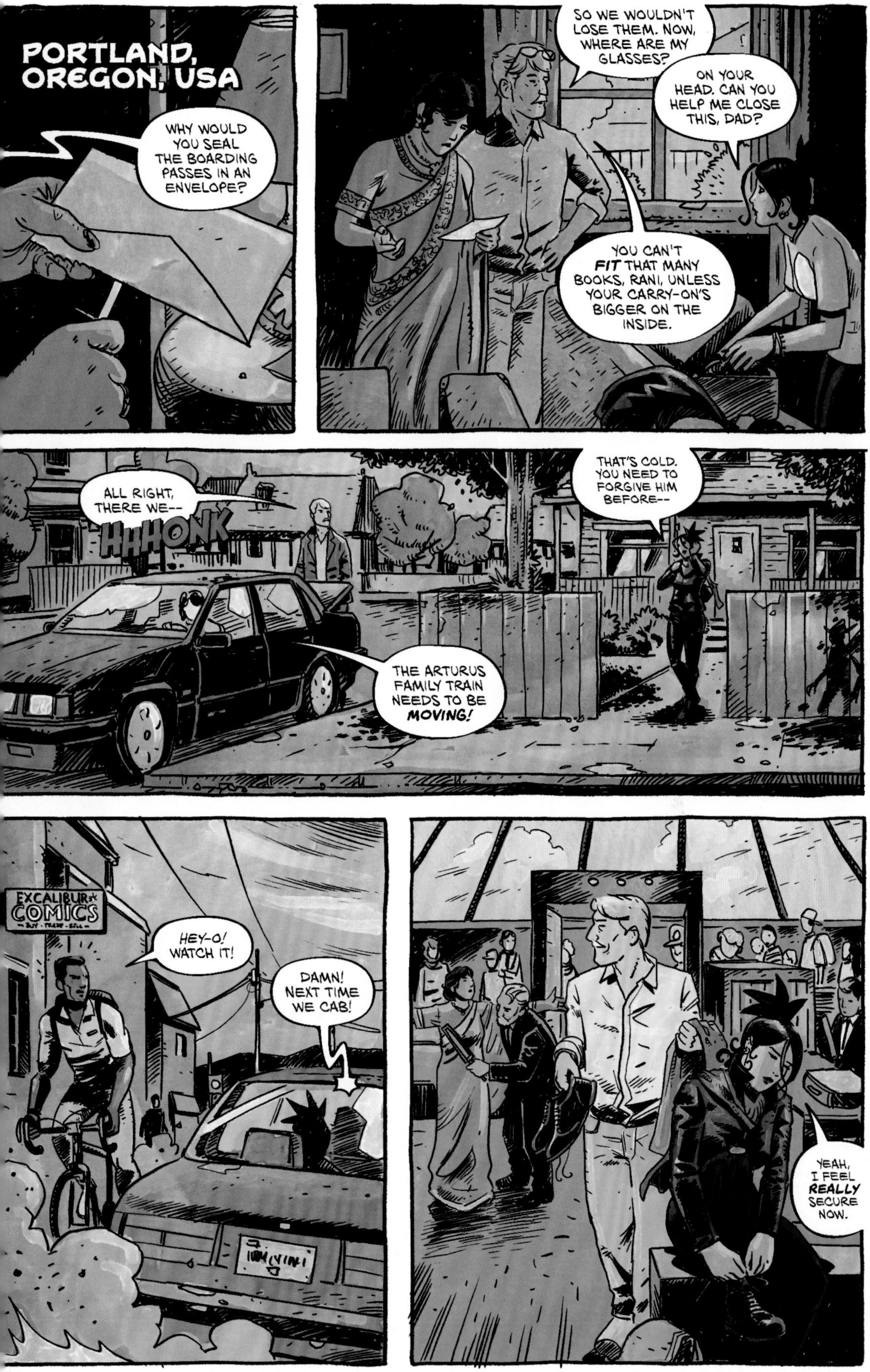

PORTLAND, OREGON, USA
WHY WOULD YOU SEAL THE BOARDING PASSES IN AN ENVELOPE?
SO WE WOULDN'T LOSE THEM. NOW, WHERE ARE MY GLASSES?
ON YOUR HEAD. CAN YOU HELP ME CLOSE THIS, DAD?
YOU CAN'T FIT THAT MANY BOOKS, RANI, UNLESS YOUR CARRY-ON'S BIGGER ON THE INSIDE.
ALL RIGHT, THERE WE--
HHHONK
THAT'S COLD. YOU NEED TO FORGIVE HIM BEFORE--
THE ARTURUS FAMILY TRAIN NEEDS TO BE MOVING!
EXCALIBUR COMICS
HEY-O! WATCH IT!
DAMN! NEXT TIME WE CAB!
YEAH, I FEEL REALLY SECURE NOW.

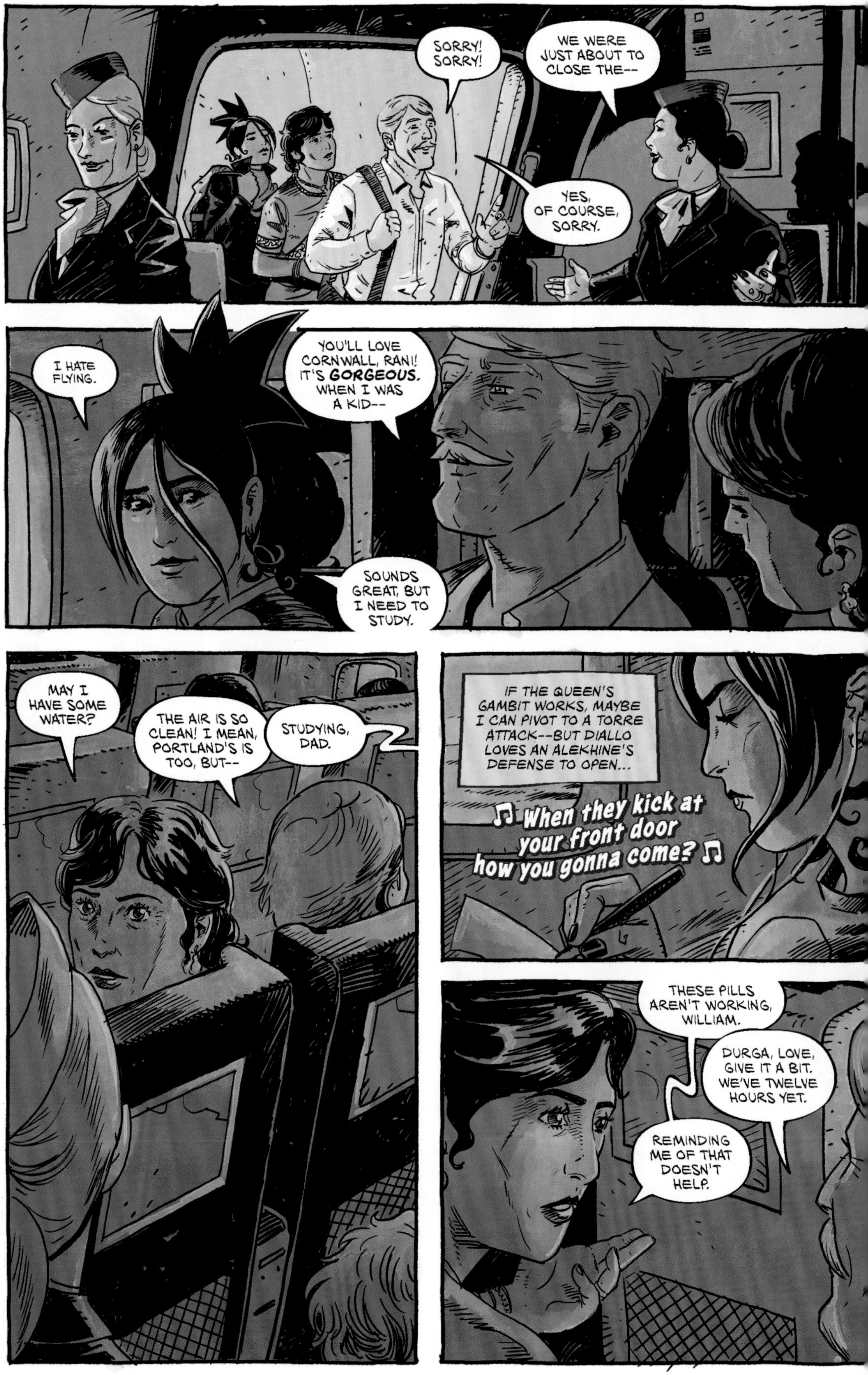
SORRY! SORRY!
WE WERE JUST ABOUT TO CLOSE THE--
YES, OF COURSE, SORRY.
I HATE FLYING.
YOU'LL LOVE CORNWALL, RANI! IT'S **GORGEOUS.** WHEN I WAS A KID--
SOUNDS GREAT, BUT I NEED TO STUDY.
MAY I HAVE SOME WATER?
THE AIR IS SO CLEAN! I MEAN, PORTLAND'S IS TOO, BUT--
STUDYING, DAD.
IF THE QUEEN'S GAMBIT WORKS, MAYBE I CAN PIVOT TO A TORRE ATTACK--BUT DIALLO LOVES AN ALEKHINE'S DEFENSE TO OPEN...
♫ When they kick at your front door how you gonna come? ♫
THESE PILLS AREN'T WORKING, WILLIAM.
DURGA, LOVE, GIVE IT A BIT. WE'VE TWELVE HOURS YET.
REMINDING ME OF THAT DOESN'T HELP.

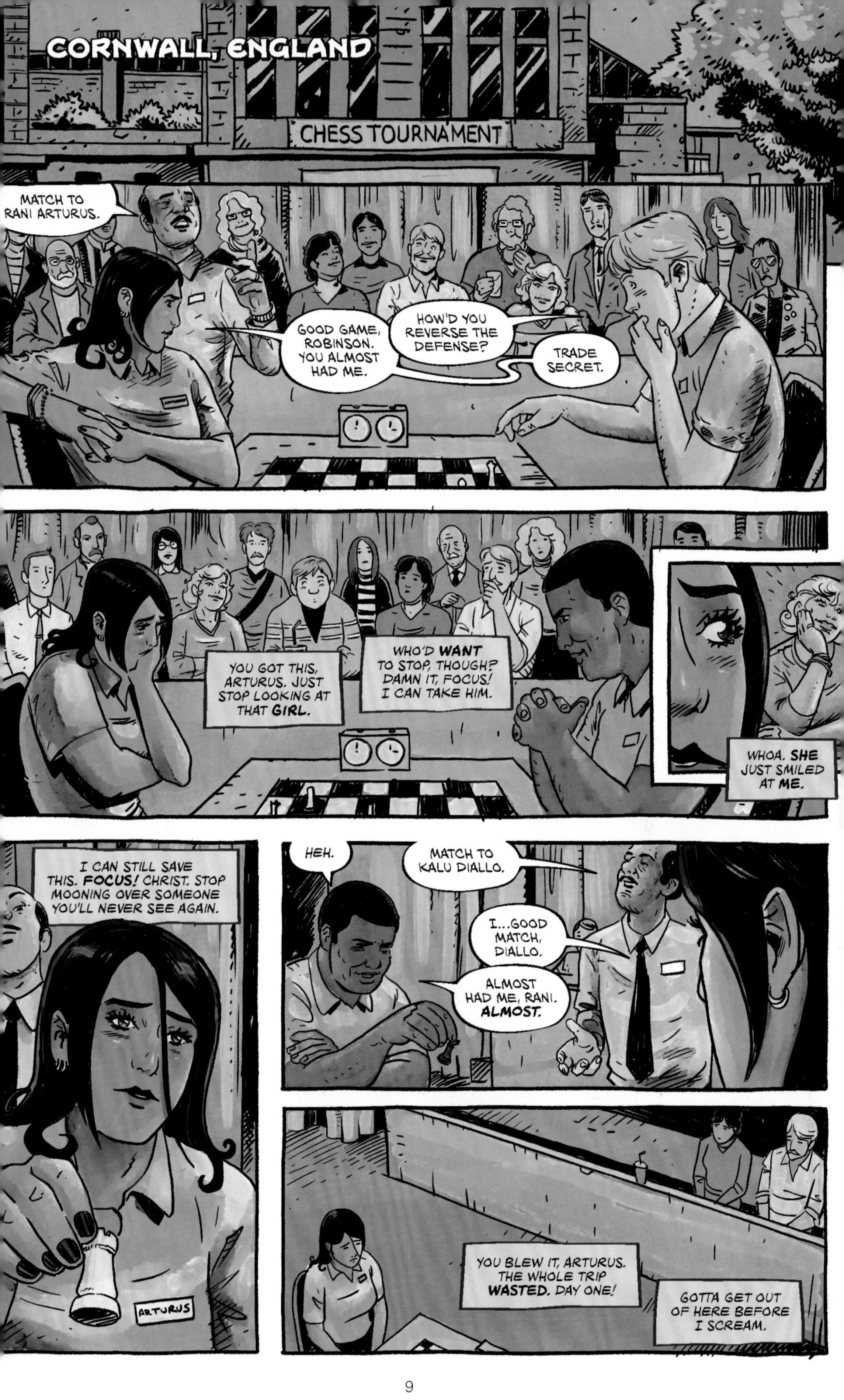
CORNWALL, ENGLAND
CHESS TOURNAMENT
MATCH TO RANI ARTURUS.
GOOD GAME, ROBINSON. YOU ALMOST HAD ME.
HOW'D YOU REVERSE THE DEFENSE?
TRADE SECRET.
YOU GOT THIS, ARTURUS. JUST STOP LOOKING AT THAT GIRL.
WHO'D WANT TO STOP, THOUGH? DAMN IT, FOCUS! I CAN TAKE HIM.
WHOA. SHE JUST SMILED AT ME.
I CAN STILL SAVE THIS. FOCUS! CHRIST. STOP MOONING OVER SOMEONE YOU'LL NEVER SEE AGAIN.
ARTURUS
HEH.
MATCH TO KALU DIALLO.
I...GOOD MATCH, DIALLO.
ALMOST HAD ME, RANI. ALMOST.
YOU BLEW IT, ARTURUS. THE WHOLE TRIP WASTED. DAY ONE!
GOTTA GET OUT OF HERE BEFORE I SCREAM.

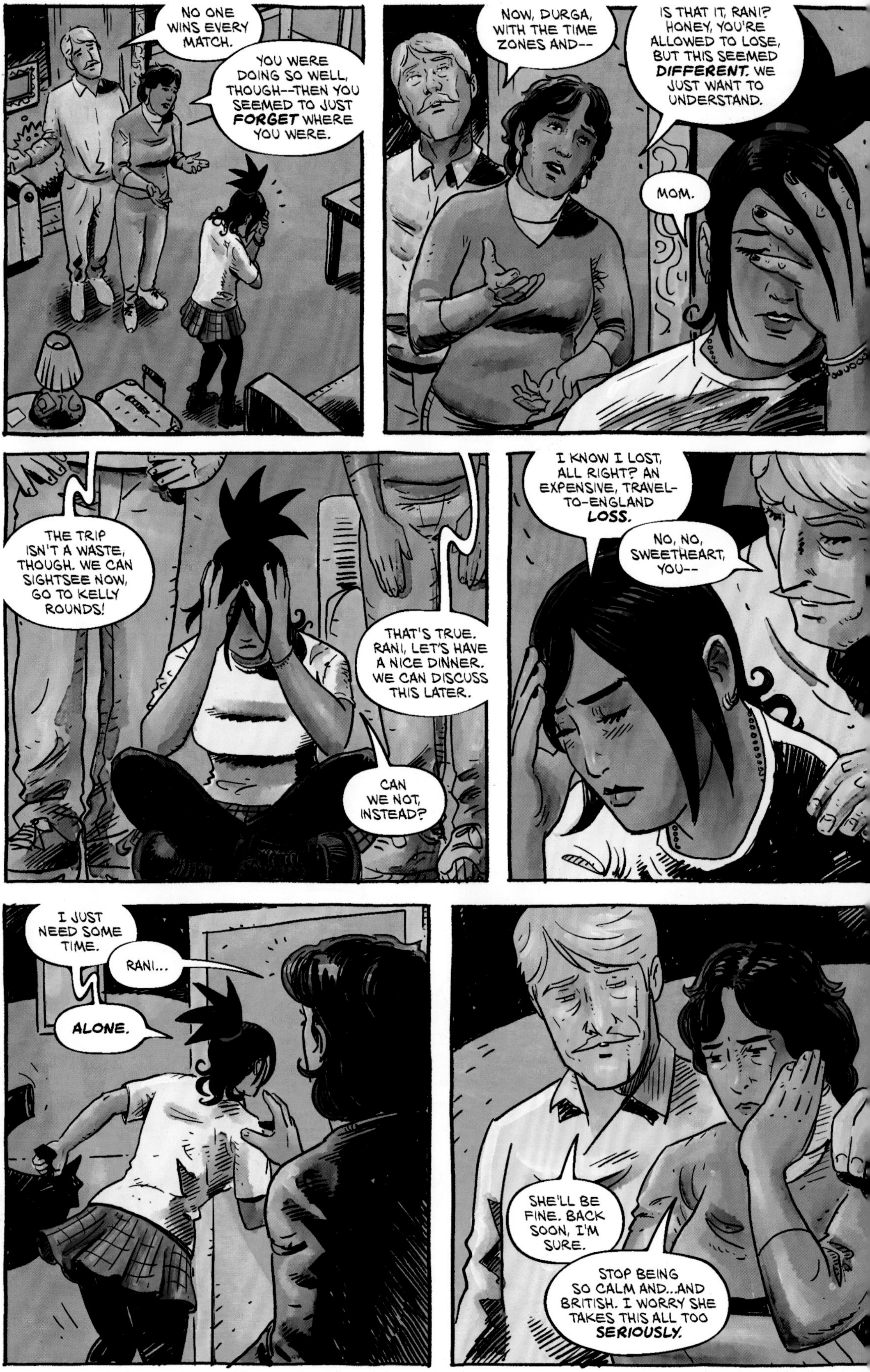
NO ONE WINS EVERY MATCH.
YOU WERE DOING SO WELL, THOUGH--THEN YOU SEEMED TO JUST **FORGET** WHERE YOU WERE.
NOW, DURGA, WITH THE TIME ZONES AND--
IS THAT IT, RANI? HONEY, YOU'RE ALLOWED TO LOSE, BUT THIS SEEMED **DIFFERENT.** WE JUST WANT TO UNDERSTAND.
MOM.
THE TRIP ISN'T A WASTE, THOUGH. WE CAN SIGHTSEE NOW, GO TO KELLY ROUNDS!
THAT'S TRUE. RANI, LET'S HAVE A NICE DINNER. WE CAN DISCUSS THIS LATER.
CAN WE NOT, INSTEAD?
I KNOW I LOST, ALL RIGHT? AN EXPENSIVE, TRAVEL-TO-ENGLAND **LOSS.**
NO, NO, SWEETHEART, YOU--
I JUST NEED SOME TIME.
RANI...
ALONE.
SHE'LL BE FINE. BACK SOON, I'M SURE.
STOP BEING SO CALM AND...AND BRITISH. I WORRY SHE TAKES THIS ALL TOO **SERIOUSLY.**

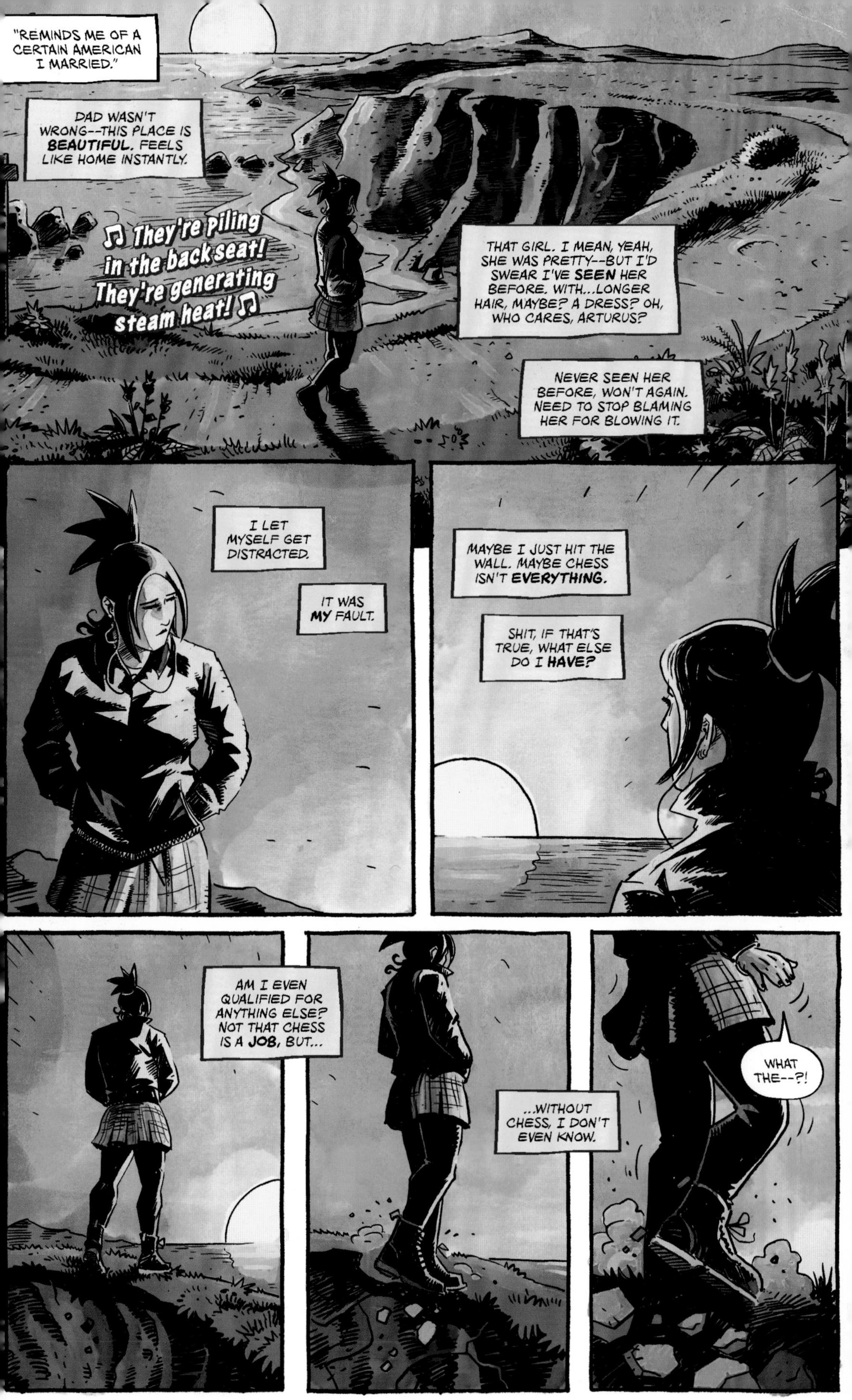
"REMINDS ME OF A CERTAIN AMERICAN I MARRIED."
DAD WASN'T WRONG--THIS PLACE IS **BEAUTIFUL.** FEELS LIKE HOME INSTANTLY.
♫ They're piling in the back seat! They're generating steam heat! ♫
THAT GIRL. I MEAN, YEAH, SHE WAS PRETTY--BUT I'D SWEAR I'VE **SEEN** HER BEFORE. WITH...LONGER HAIR, MAYBE? A DRESS? OH, WHO CARES, ARTURUS?
NEVER SEEN HER BEFORE, WON'T AGAIN. NEED TO STOP BLAMING HER FOR BLOWING IT.
I LET MYSELF GET DISTRACTED.
IT WAS **MY** FAULT.
MAYBE I JUST HIT THE WALL. MAYBE CHESS ISN'T **EVERYTHING.**
SHIT, IF THAT'S TRUE, WHAT ELSE DO I **HAVE?**
AM I EVEN QUALIFIED FOR ANYTHING ELSE? NOT THAT CHESS IS A **JOB,** BUT...
...WITHOUT CHESS, I DON'T EVEN KNOW.
WHAT THE--?!

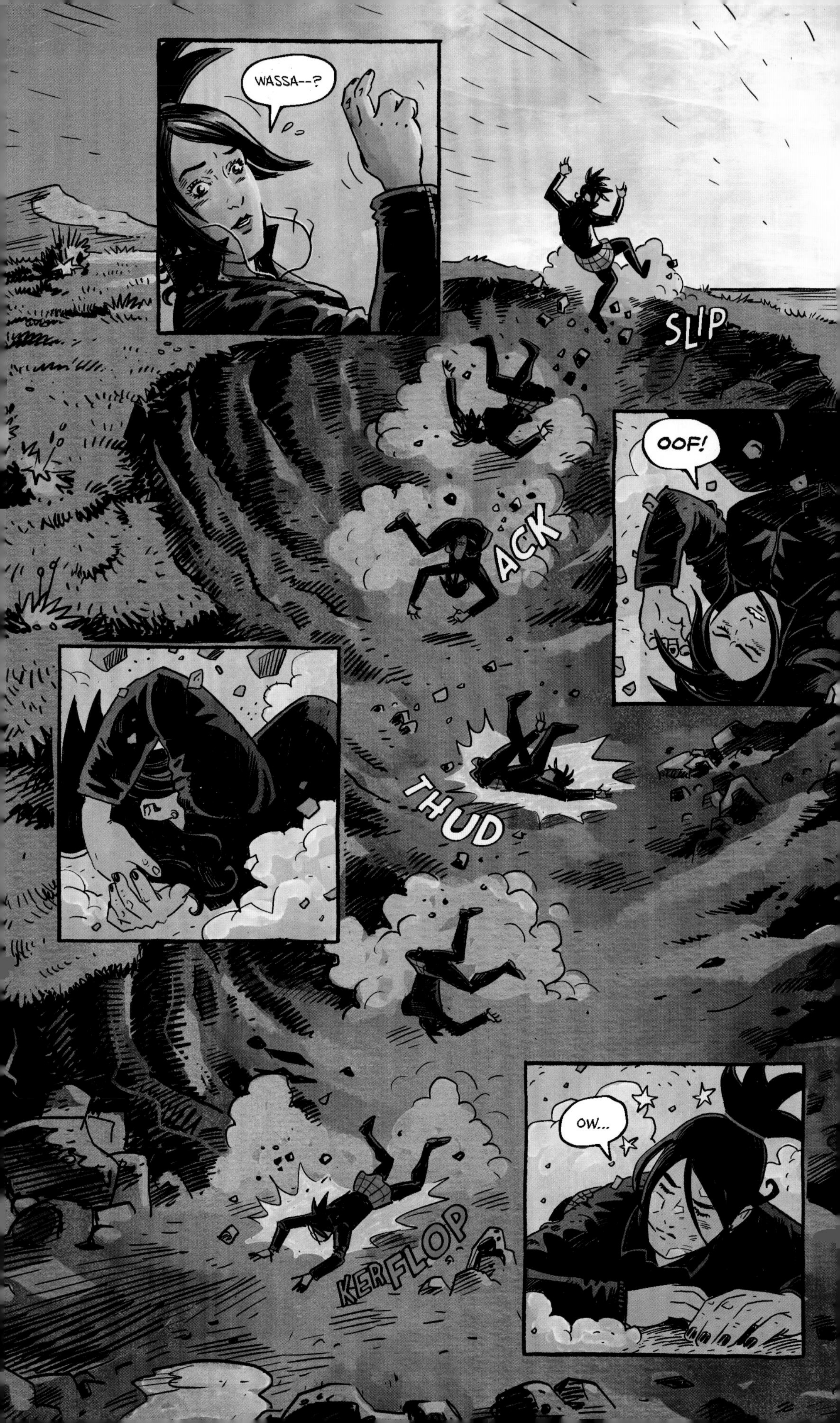
WASSA--?
SLIP
ACK
OOF!
THUD
KERFLOP
OW...

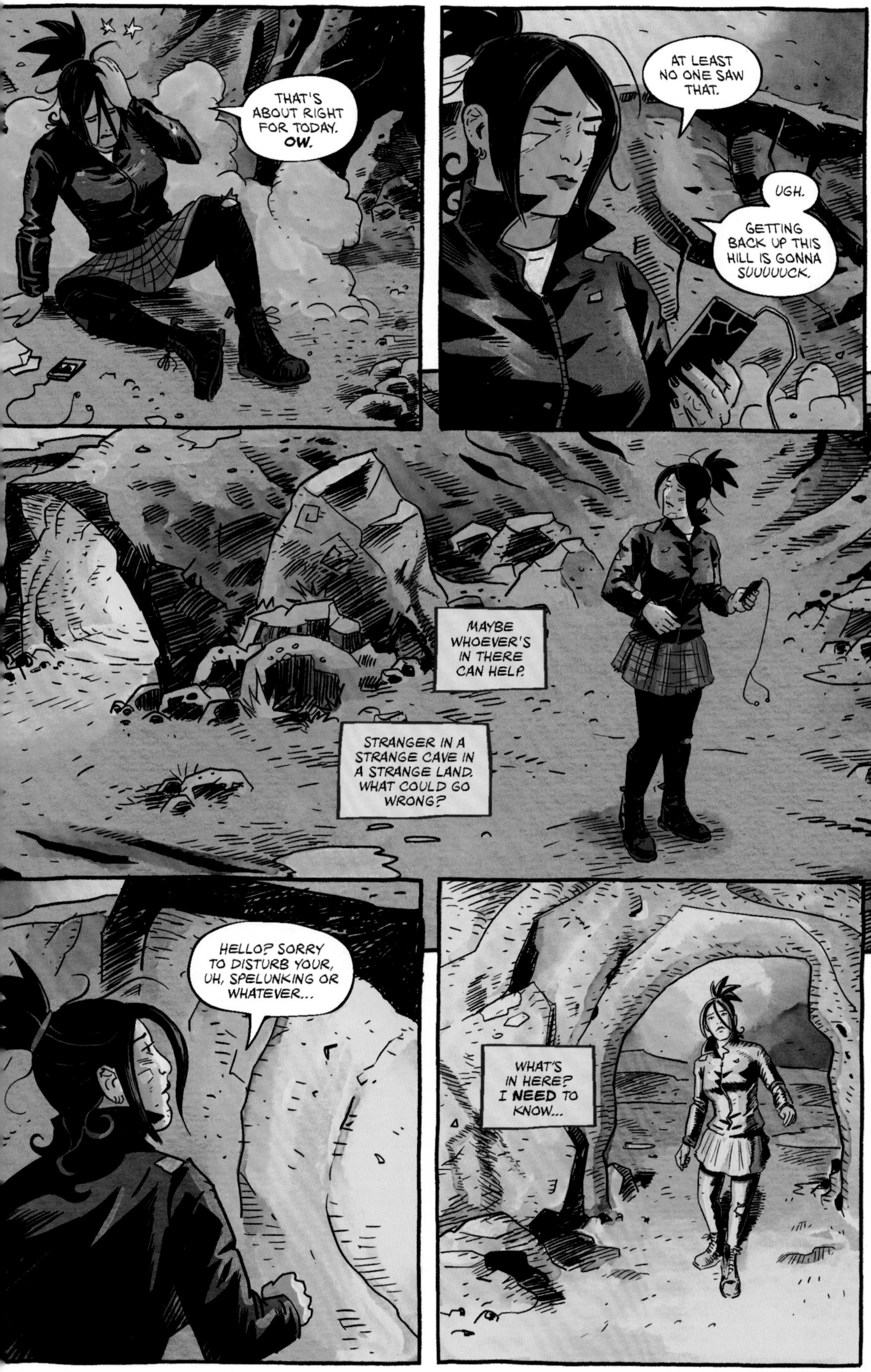
THAT'S ABOUT RIGHT FOR TODAY. OW.
AT LEAST NO ONE SAW THAT.
UGH.
GETTING BACK UP THIS HILL IS GONNA SUUUUUCK.
MAYBE WHOEVER'S IN THERE CAN HELP.
STRANGER IN A STRANGE CAVE IN A STRANGE LAND. WHAT COULD GO WRONG?
HELLO? SORRY TO DISTURB YOUR, UH, SPELUNKING OR WHATEVER...
WHAT'S IN HERE? I NEED TO KNOW...

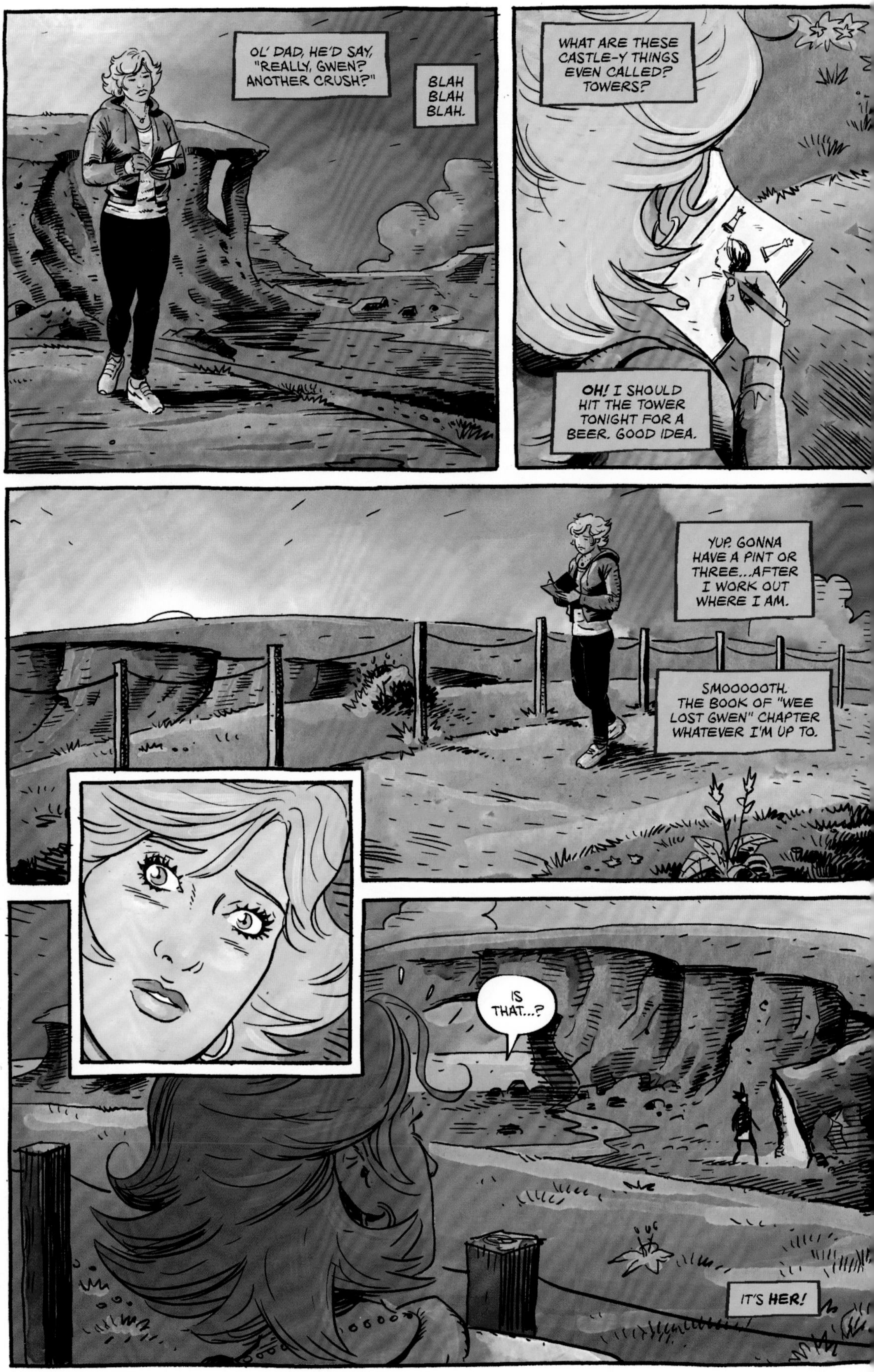

OL' DAD, HE'D SAY, "REALLY, GWEN? ANOTHER CRUSH?"
BLAH BLAH BLAH.
WHAT ARE THESE CASTLE-Y THINGS EVEN CALLED? TOWERS?
OH! I SHOULD HIT THE TOWER TONIGHT FOR A BEER. GOOD IDEA.
YUP. GONNA HAVE A PINT OR THREE...AFTER I WORK OUT WHERE I AM.
SMOOOOOTH. THE BOOK OF "WEE LOST GWEN" CHAPTER WHATEVER I'M UP TO.
IS THAT...?
IT'S HER!

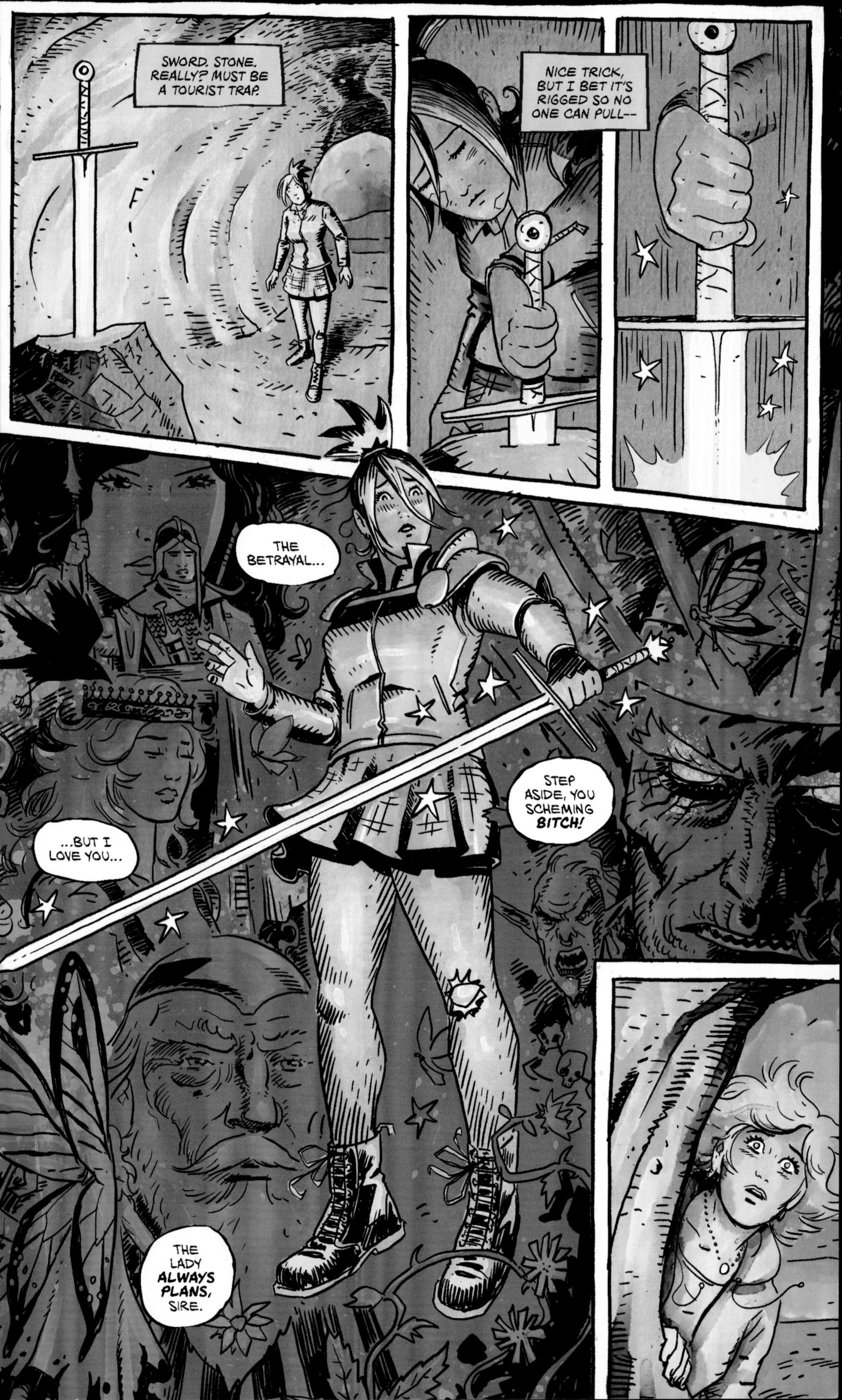
SWORD. STONE. REALLY? MUST BE A TOURIST TRAP.
NICE TRICK, BUT I BET IT'S RIGGED SO NO ONE CAN PULL--
THE BETRAYAL...
STEP ASIDE, YOU SCHEMING **BITCH!**
...BUT I LOVE YOU...
THE LADY **ALWAYS PLANS,** SIRE.

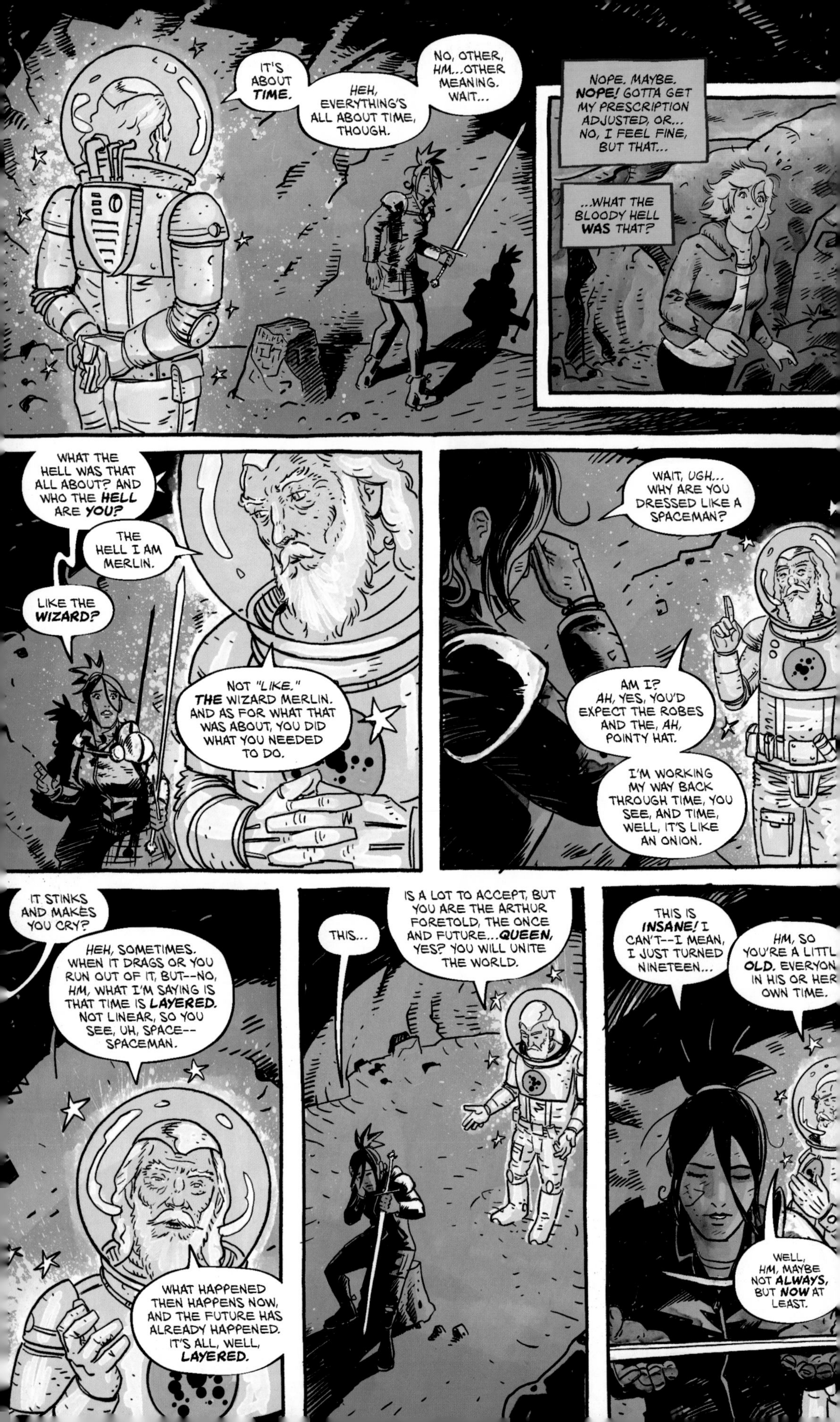

IT'S ABOUT TIME.
HEH, EVERYTHING'S ALL ABOUT TIME, THOUGH.
NO, OTHER, HM...OTHER MEANING. WAIT...
NOPE. MAYBE. NOPE! GOTTA GET MY PRESCRIPTION ADJUSTED, OR... NO, I FEEL FINE, BUT THAT...
...WHAT THE BLOODY HELL WAS THAT?
WHAT THE HELL WAS THAT ALL ABOUT? AND WHO THE HELL ARE YOU?
THE HELL I AM MERLIN.
LIKE THE WIZARD?
NOT "LIKE." THE WIZARD MERLIN. AND AS FOR WHAT THAT WAS ABOUT, YOU DID WHAT YOU NEEDED TO DO.
WAIT, UGH... WHY ARE YOU DRESSED LIKE A SPACEMAN?
AM I? AH, YES, YOU'D EXPECT THE ROBES AND THE, AH, POINTY HAT.
I'M WORKING MY WAY BACK THROUGH TIME, YOU SEE, AND TIME, WELL, IT'S LIKE AN ONION.
IT STINKS AND MAKES YOU CRY?
HEH, SOMETIMES. WHEN IT DRAGS OR YOU RUN OUT OF IT, BUT--NO, HM, WHAT I'M SAYING IS THAT TIME IS LAYERED. NOT LINEAR, SO YOU SEE, UH, SPACE-- SPACEMAN.
WHAT HAPPENED THEN HAPPENS NOW, AND THE FUTURE HAS ALREADY HAPPENED. IT'S ALL, WELL, LAYERED.
THIS...
IS A LOT TO ACCEPT, BUT YOU ARE THE ARTHUR FORETOLD, THE ONCE AND FUTURE...QUEEN, YES? YOU WILL UNITE THE WORLD.
THIS IS INSANE! I CAN'T--I MEAN, I JUST TURNED NINETEEN...
HM, SO YOU'RE A LITTL OLD. EVERYON IN HIS OR HER OWN TIME.
WELL, HM, MAYBE NOT ALWAYS, BUT NOW AT LEAST.

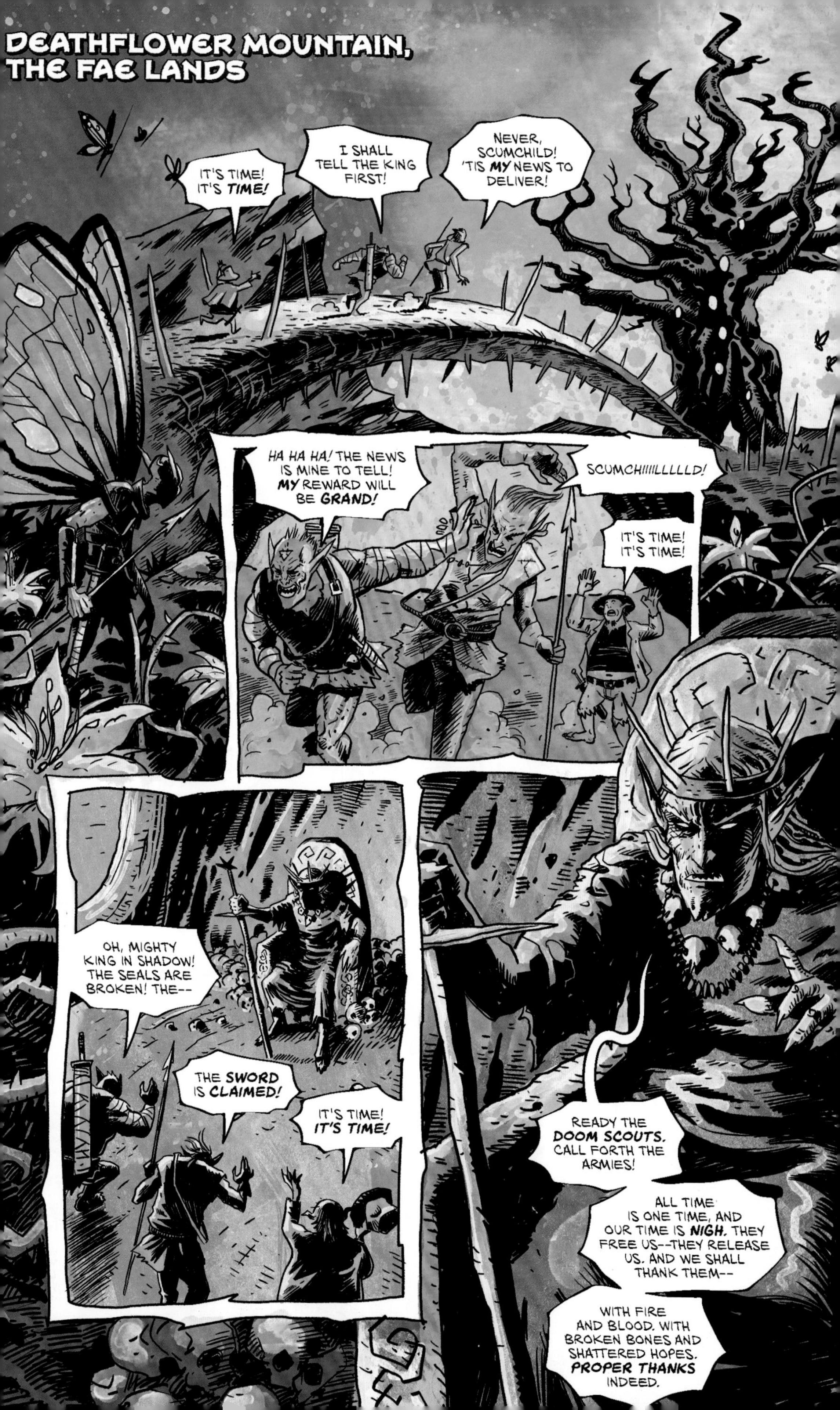
DEATHFLOWER MOUNTAIN, THE FAE LANDS
IT'S TIME! IT'S TIME!
I SHALL TELL THE KING FIRST!
NEVER, SCUMCHILD! 'TIS MY NEWS TO DELIVER!
HA HA HA! THE NEWS IS MINE TO TELL! MY REWARD WILL BE GRAND!
SCUMCHIIIIILLLLLLD!
IT'S TIME! IT'S TIME!
OH, MIGHTY KING IN SHADOW! THE SEALS ARE BROKEN! THE--
THE SWORD IS CLAIMED!
IT'S TIME! IT'S TIME!
READY THE DOOM SCOUTS. CALL FORTH THE ARMIES!
ALL TIME IS ONE TIME, AND OUR TIME IS NIGH. THEY FREE US--THEY RELEASE US. AND WE SHALL THANK THEM--
WITH FIRE AND BLOOD. WITH BROKEN BONES AND SHATTERED HOPES. PROPER THANKS INDEED.

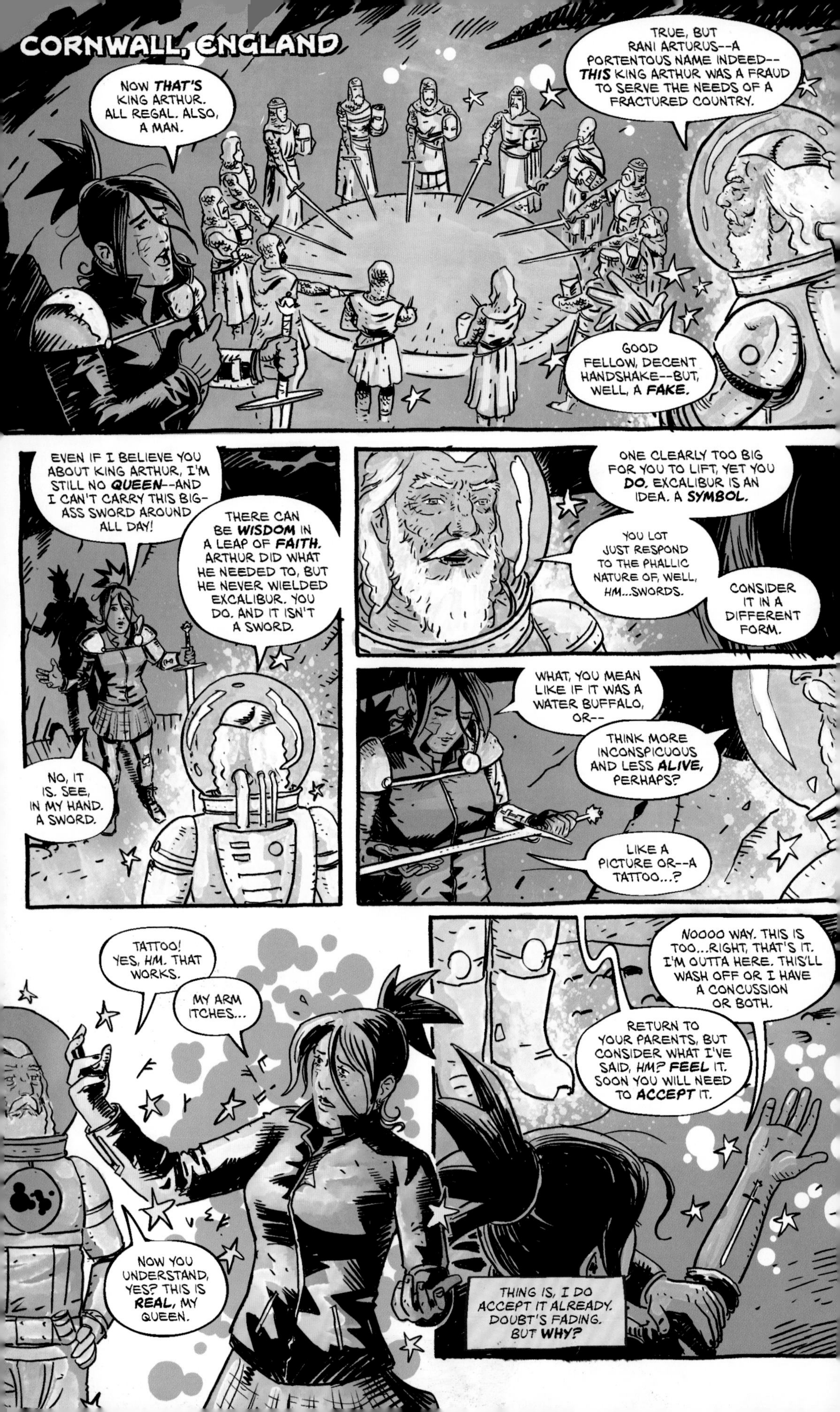
CORNWALL, ENGLAND
NOW THAT'S KING ARTHUR. ALL REGAL. ALSO, A MAN.
TRUE, BUT RANI ARTURUS--A PORTENTOUS NAME INDEED--THIS KING ARTHUR WAS A FRAUD TO SERVE THE NEEDS OF A FRACTURED COUNTRY.
GOOD FELLOW, DECENT HANDSHAKE--BUT, WELL, A FAKE.
EVEN IF I BELIEVE YOU ABOUT KING ARTHUR, I'M STILL NO QUEEN--AND I CAN'T CARRY THIS BIG-ASS SWORD AROUND ALL DAY!
THERE CAN BE WISDOM IN A LEAP OF FAITH. ARTHUR DID WHAT HE NEEDED TO, BUT HE NEVER WIELDED EXCALIBUR. YOU DO. AND IT ISN'T A SWORD.
NO, IT IS. SEE, IN MY HAND. A SWORD.
ONE CLEARLY TOO BIG FOR YOU TO LIFT, YET YOU DO. EXCALIBUR IS AN IDEA. A SYMBOL.
YOU LOT JUST RESPOND TO THE PHALLIC NATURE OF, WELL, HM...SWORDS.
CONSIDER IT IN A DIFFERENT FORM.
WHAT, YOU MEAN LIKE IF IT WAS A WATER BUFFALO, OR--
THINK MORE INCONSPICUOUS AND LESS ALIVE, PERHAPS?
LIKE A PICTURE OR--A TATTOO...?
TATTOO! YES, HM. THAT WORKS.
MY ARM ITCHES...
NOOOO WAY. THIS IS TOO...RIGHT, THAT'S IT. I'M OUTTA HERE. THIS'LL WASH OFF OR I HAVE A CONCUSSION OR BOTH.
RETURN TO YOUR PARENTS, BUT CONSIDER WHAT I'VE SAID, HM? FEEL IT. SOON YOU WILL NEED TO ACCEPT IT.
NOW YOU UNDERSTAND, YES? THIS IS REAL, MY QUEEN.
THING IS, I DO ACCEPT IT ALREADY. DOUBT'S FADING. BUT WHY?

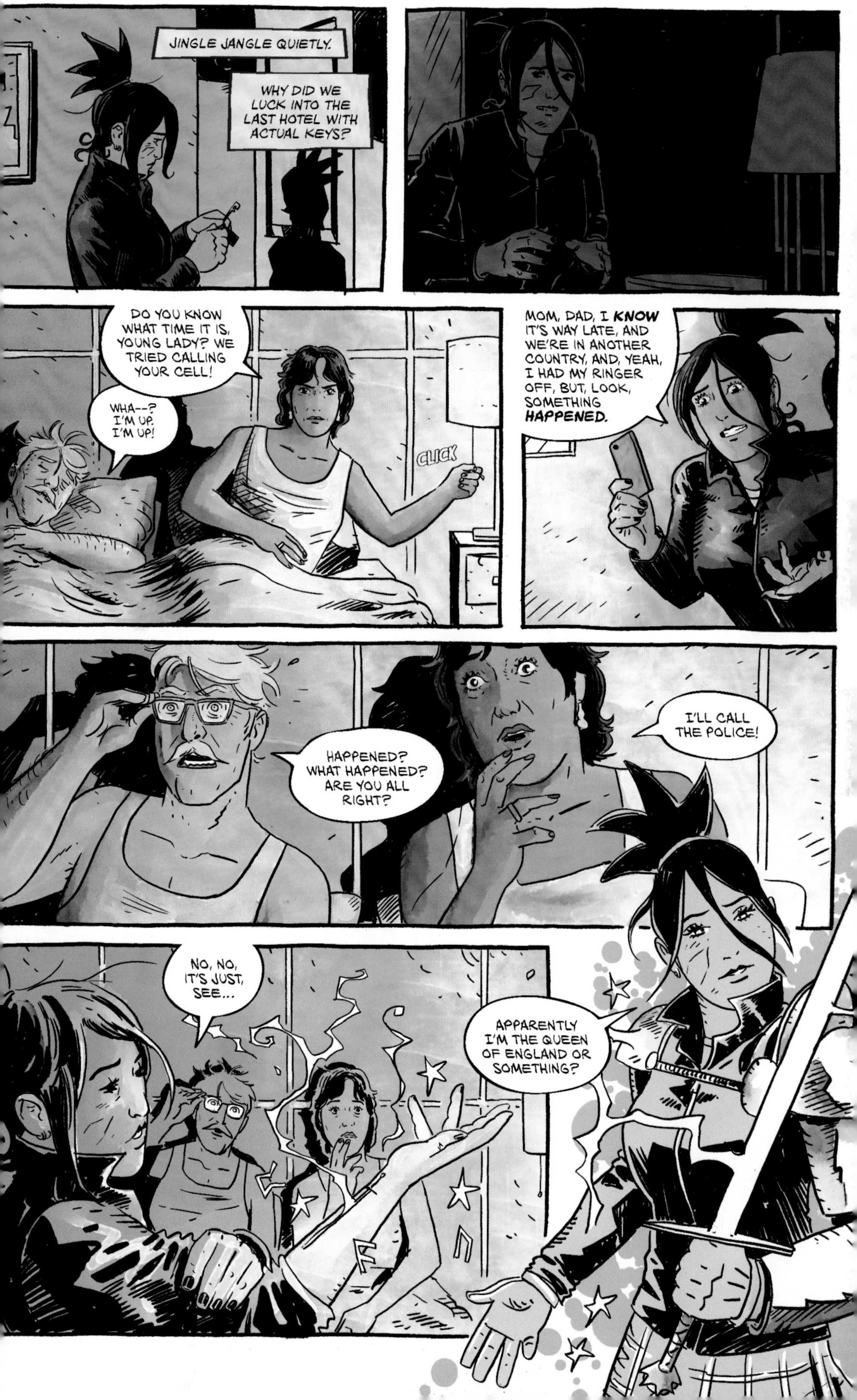
JINGLE JANGLE QUIETLY.
WHY DID WE LUCK INTO THE LAST HOTEL WITH ACTUAL KEYS?
DO YOU KNOW WHAT TIME IT IS, YOUNG LADY? WE TRIED CALLING YOUR CELL!
WHA--? I'M UP. I'M UP!
CLICK
MOM, DAD, I KNOW IT'S WAY LATE, AND WE'RE IN ANOTHER COUNTRY, AND, YEAH, I HAD MY RINGER OFF, BUT, LOOK, SOMETHING HAPPENED.
HAPPENED? WHAT HAPPENED? ARE YOU ALL RIGHT?
I'LL CALL THE POLICE!
NO, NO, IT'S JUST, SEE...
APPARENTLY I'M THE QUEEN OF ENGLAND OR SOMETHING?

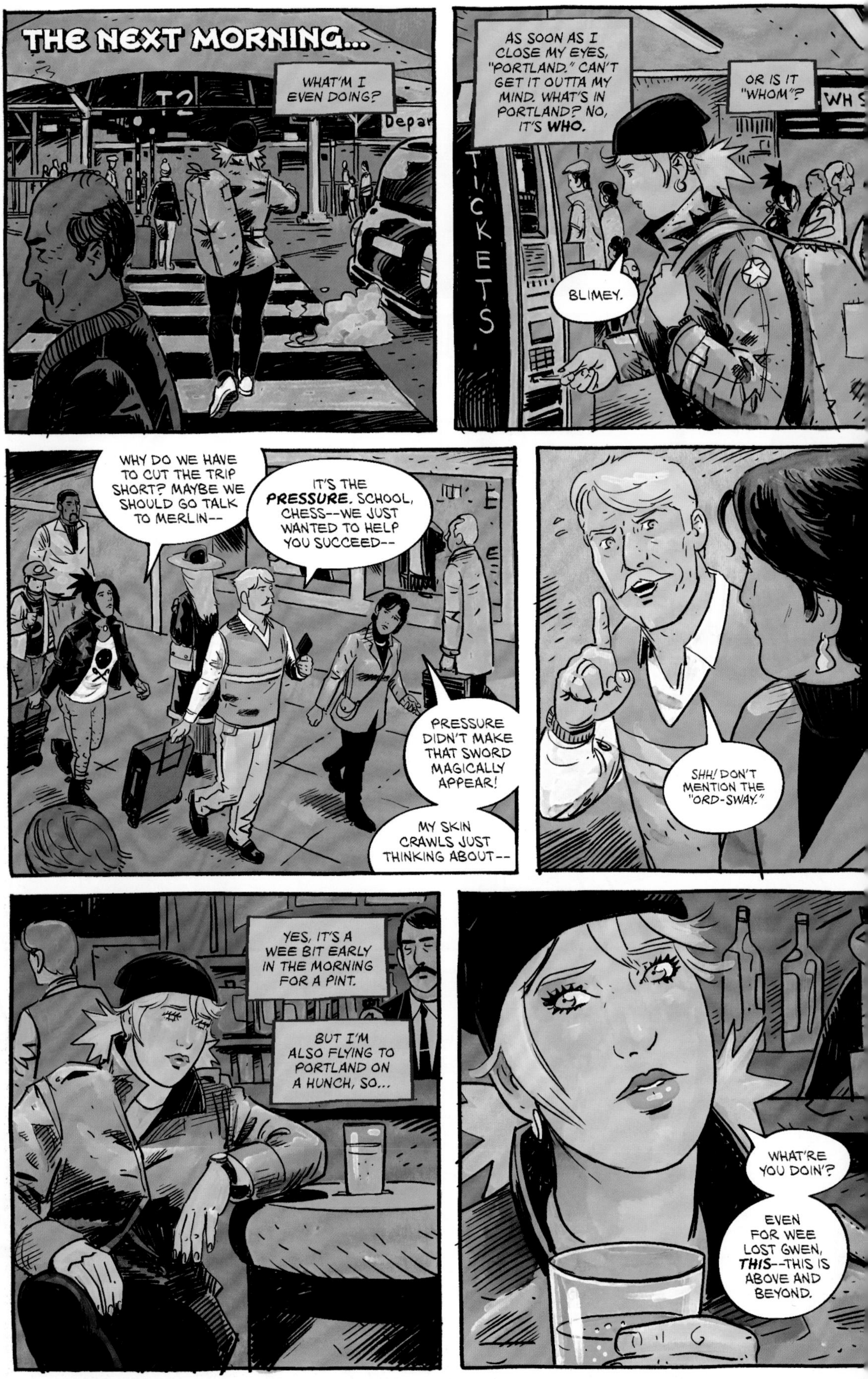
THE NEXT MORNING...
WHAT'M I EVEN DOING?
T2
Depar
AS SOON AS I CLOSE MY EYES, "PORTLAND." CAN'T GET IT OUTTA MY MIND. WHAT'S IN PORTLAND? NO, IT'S WHO.
OR IS IT "WHOM"?
TICKETS
BLIMEY.
WHY DO WE HAVE TO CUT THE TRIP SHORT? MAYBE WE SHOULD GO TALK TO MERLIN--
IT'S THE PRESSURE. SCHOOL, CHESS--WE JUST WANTED TO HELP YOU SUCCEED--
PRESSURE DIDN'T MAKE THAT SWORD MAGICALLY APPEAR!
MY SKIN CRAWLS JUST THINKING ABOUT--
SHH! DON'T MENTION THE "ORD-SWAY."
YES, IT'S A WEE BIT EARLY IN THE MORNING FOR A PINT.
BUT I'M ALSO FLYING TO PORTLAND ON A HUNCH, SO...
WHAT'RE YOU DOIN'?
EVEN FOR WEE LOST GWEN, THIS--THIS IS ABOVE AND BEYOND.

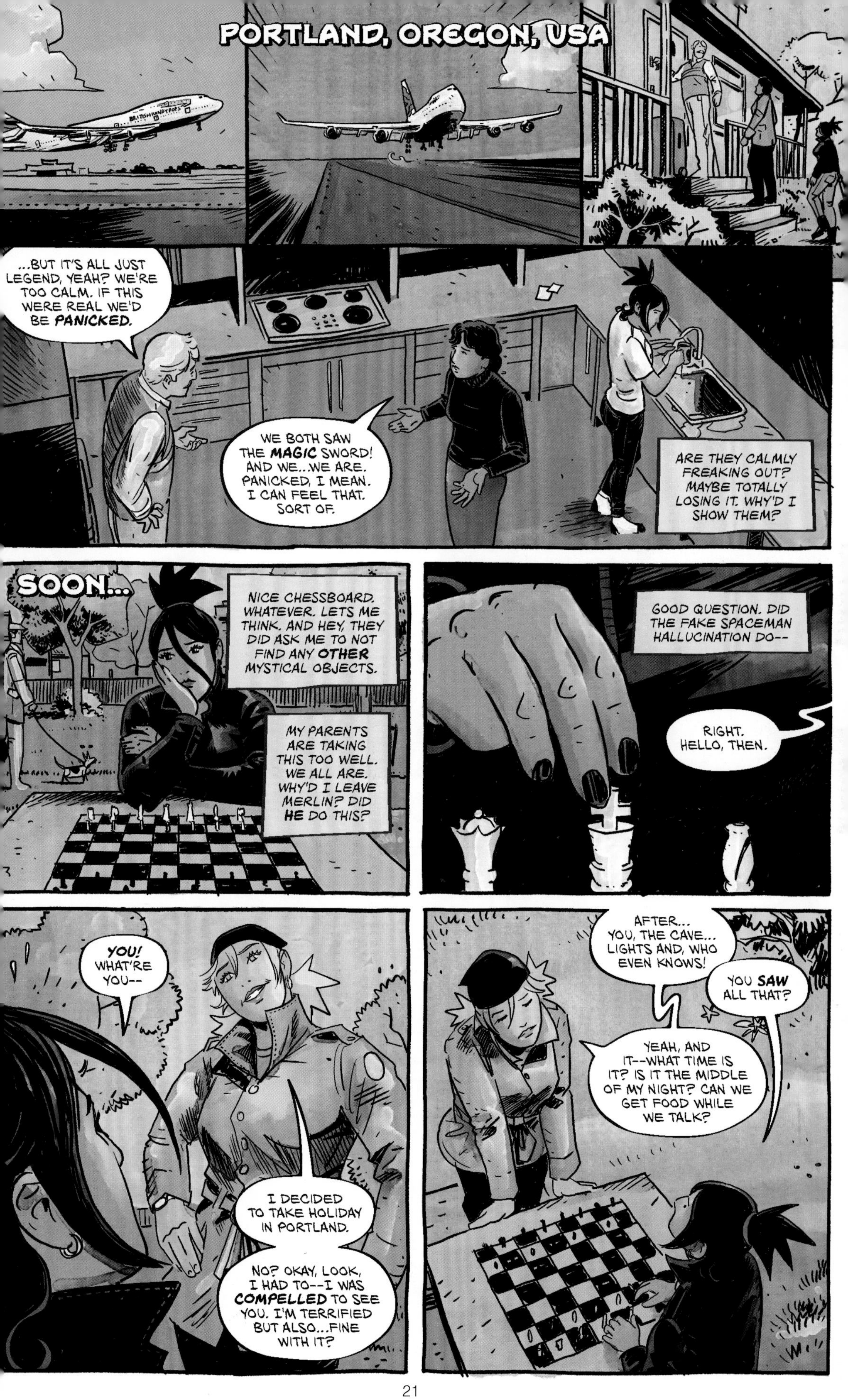
PORTLAND, OREGON, USA
BRITISH HANDYPOPS
...BUT IT'S ALL JUST LEGEND, YEAH? WE'RE TOO CALM. IF THIS WERE REAL WE'D BE PANICKED.
WE BOTH SAW THE MAGIC SWORD! AND WE...WE ARE. PANICKED, I MEAN. I CAN FEEL THAT. SORT OF.
ARE THEY CALMLY FREAKING OUT? MAYBE TOTALLY LOSING IT. WHY'D I SHOW THEM?
SOON...
NICE CHESSBOARD. WHATEVER. LETS ME THINK. AND HEY, THEY DID ASK ME TO NOT FIND ANY OTHER MYSTICAL OBJECTS.
MY PARENTS ARE TAKING THIS TOO WELL. WE ALL ARE. WHY'D I LEAVE MERLIN? DID HE DO THIS?
GOOD QUESTION. DID THE FAKE SPACEMAN HALLUCINATION DO--
RIGHT. HELLO, THEN.
YOU! WHAT'RE YOU--
I DECIDED TO TAKE HOLIDAY IN PORTLAND.
NO? OKAY, LOOK, I HAD TO--I WAS COMPELLED TO SEE YOU. I'M TERRIFIED BUT ALSO...FINE WITH IT?
AFTER... YOU, THE CAVE... LIGHTS AND, WHO EVEN KNOWS!
YOU SAW ALL THAT?
YEAH, AND IT--WHAT TIME IS IT? IS IT THE MIDDLE OF MY NIGHT? CAN WE GET FOOD WHILE WE TALK?

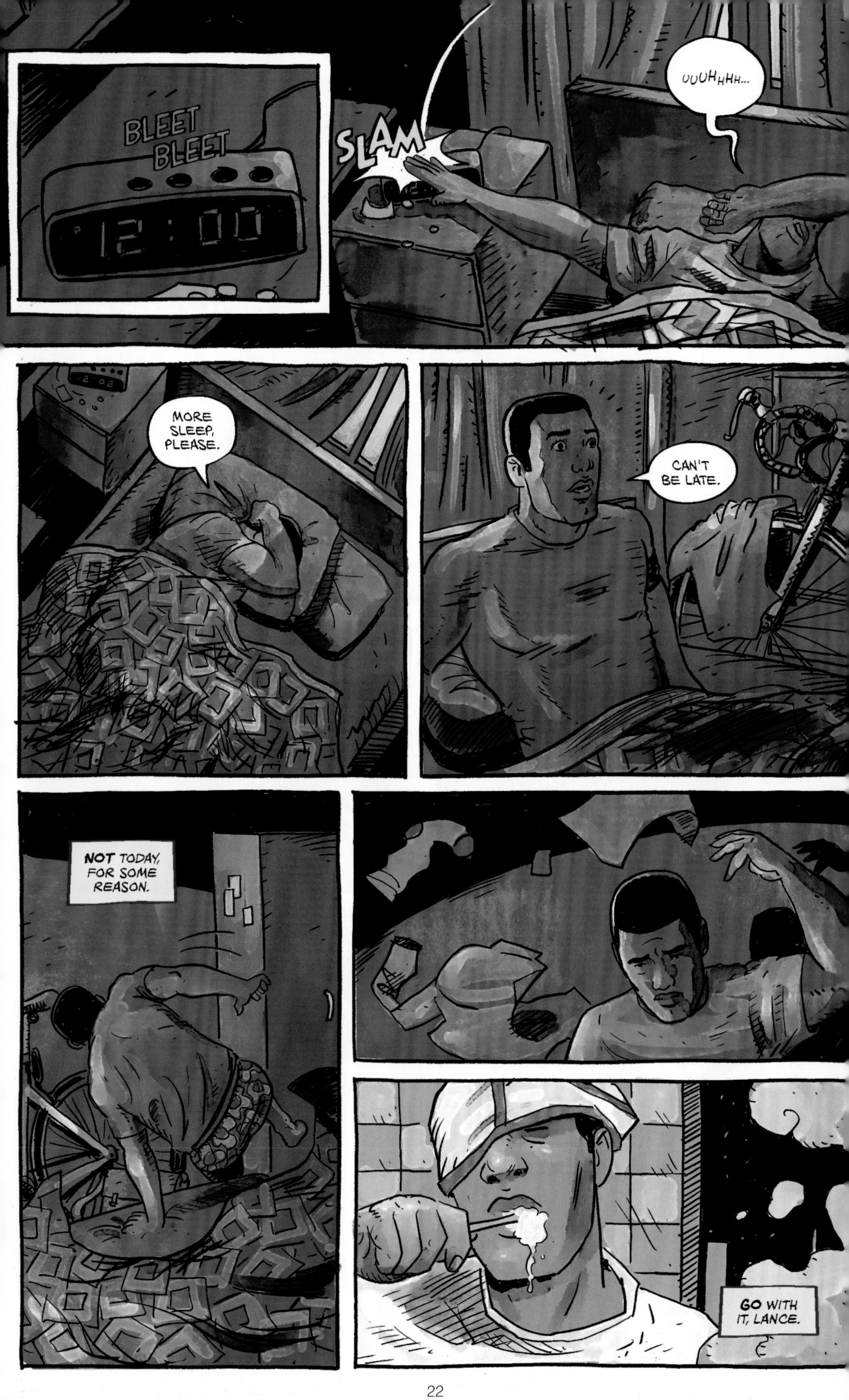
BLEET BLEET
SLAM
UUUHHHH...
MORE SLEEP, PLEASE.
CAN'T BE LATE.
NOT TODAY, FOR SOME REASON.
GO WITH IT, LANCE.

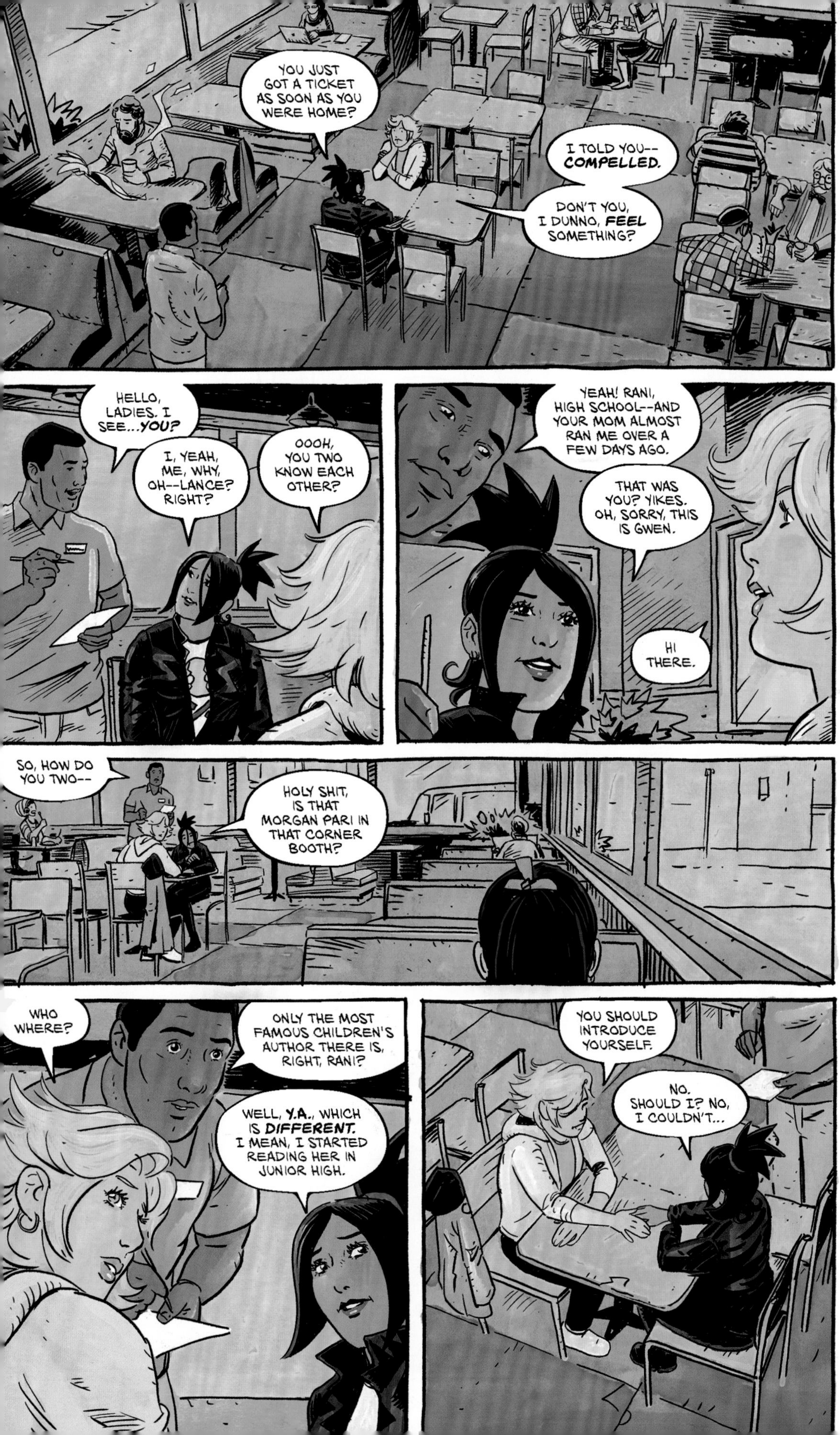

YOU JUST GOT A TICKET AS SOON AS YOU WERE HOME?
I TOLD YOU-- COMPELLED.
DON'T YOU, I DUNNO, FEEL SOMETHING?
HELLO, LADIES. I SEE... YOU?
I, YEAH, ME, WHY, OH--LANCE? RIGHT?
OOOH, YOU TWO KNOW EACH OTHER?
YEAH! RANI, HIGH SCHOOL--AND YOUR MOM ALMOST RAN ME OVER A FEW DAYS AGO.
THAT WAS YOU? YIKES. OH, SORRY, THIS IS GWEN.
HI THERE.
SO, HOW DO YOU TWO--
HOLY SHIT, IS THAT MORGAN PARI IN THAT CORNER BOOTH?
WHO WHERE?
ONLY THE MOST FAMOUS CHILDREN'S AUTHOR THERE IS, RIGHT, RANI?
WELL, Y.A., WHICH IS DIFFERENT. I MEAN, I STARTED READING HER IN JUNIOR HIGH.
YOU SHOULD INTRODUCE YOURSELF.
NO. SHOULD I? NO, I COULDN'T...

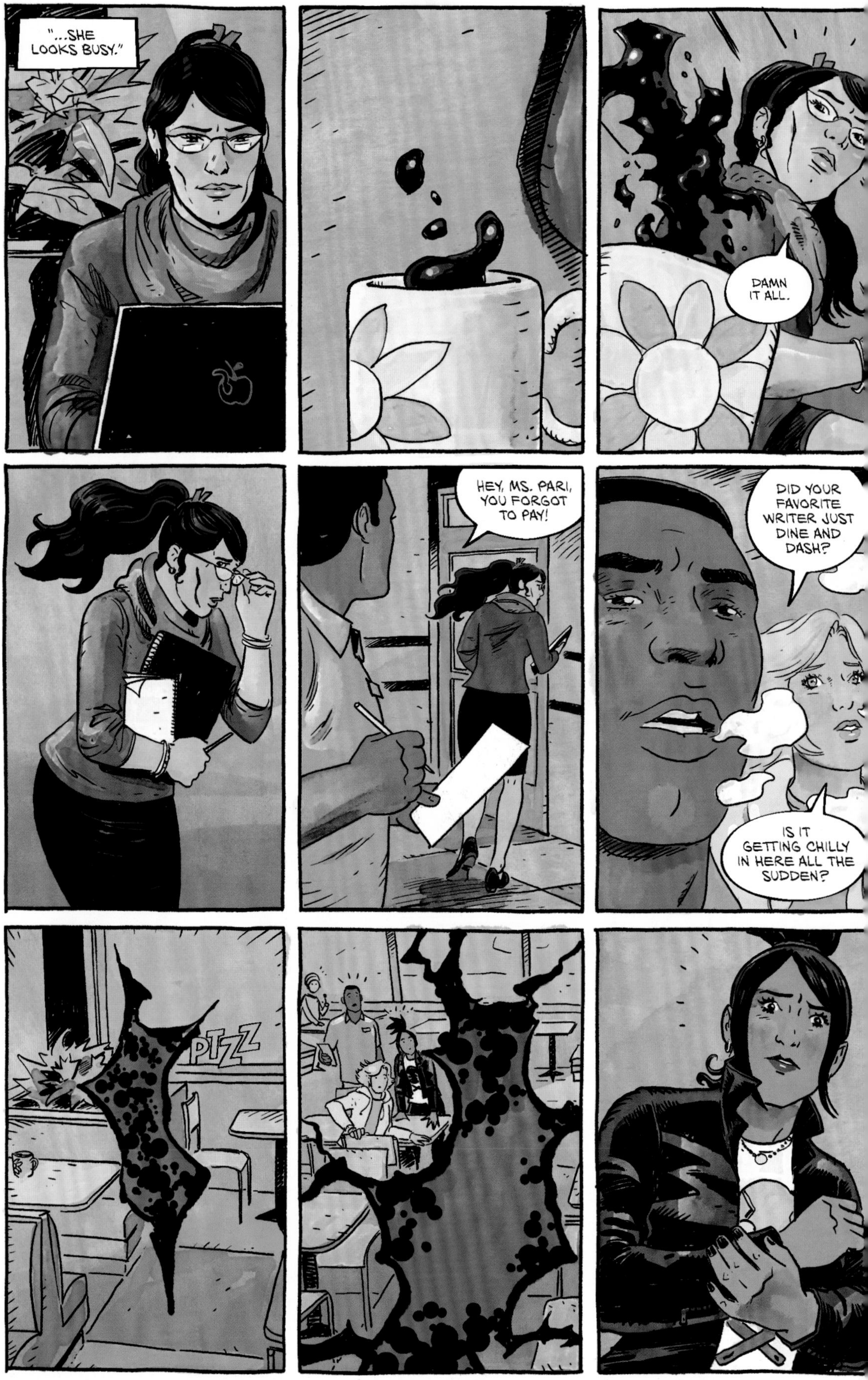
"...SHE LOOKS BUSY."
DAMN IT ALL.
HEY, MS. PARI, YOU FORGOT TO PAY!
DID YOUR FAVORITE WRITER JUST DINE AND DASH?
IS IT GETTING CHILLY IN HERE ALL THE SUDDEN?
PTZZ

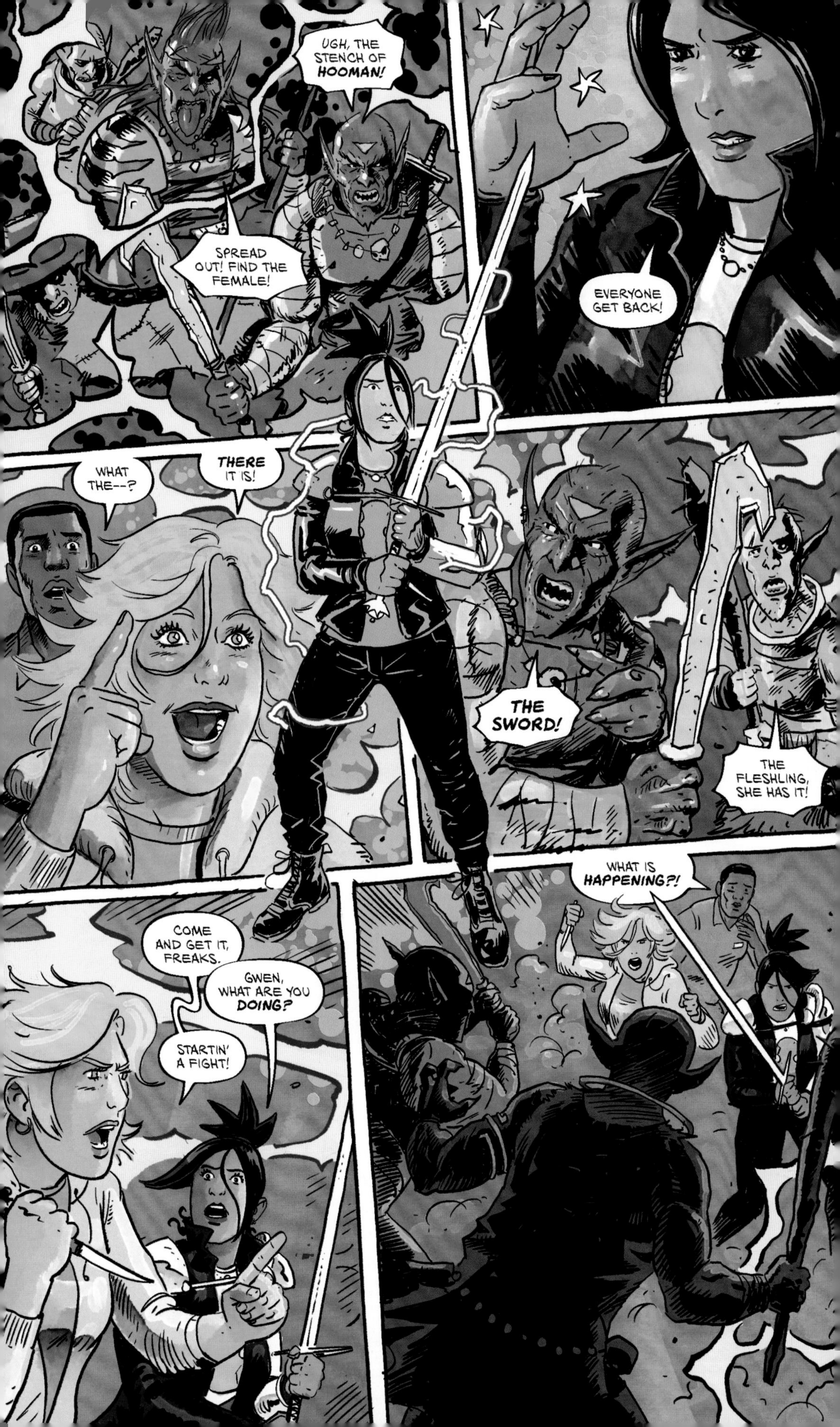
UGH, THE STENCH OF **HOOMAN!**
SPREAD OUT! FIND THE FEMALE!
EVERYONE GET BACK!
WHAT THE--?
THERE IT IS!
THE SWORD!
THE FLESHLING, SHE HAS IT!
COME AND GET IT, FREAKS.
GWEN, WHAT ARE YOU **DOING?**
STARTIN' A FIGHT!
WHAT IS **HAPPENING?!**

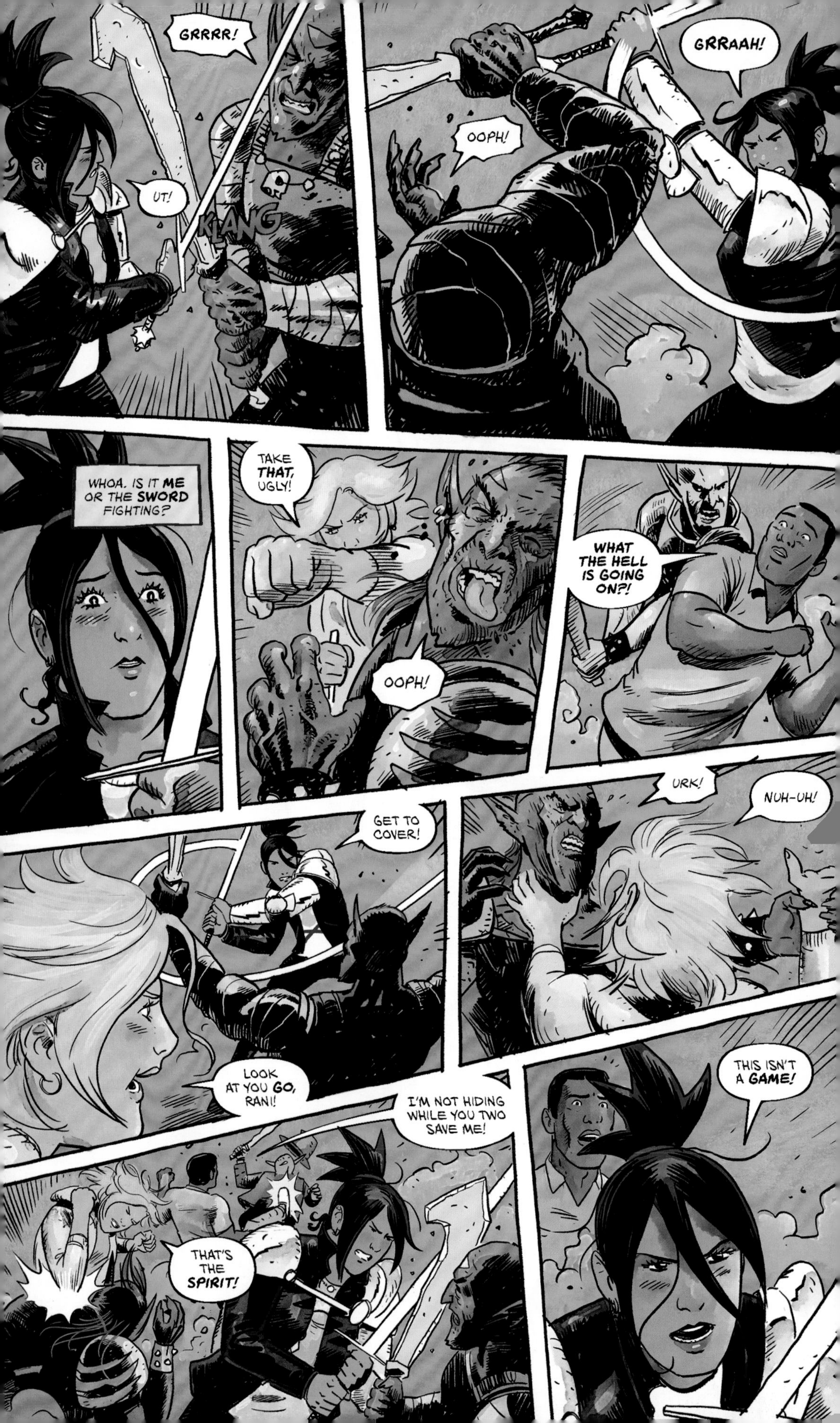
GRRRR!
UT!
KLANG
GRRAAH!
OOPH!
WHOA. IS IT ME OR THE SWORD FIGHTING?
TAKE THAT, UGLY!
OOPH!
WHAT THE HELL IS GOING ON?!
GET TO COVER!
LOOK AT YOU GO, RANI!
URK!
NUH-UH!
I'M NOT HIDING WHILE YOU TWO SAVE ME!
THAT'S THE SPIRIT!
THIS ISN'T A GAME!

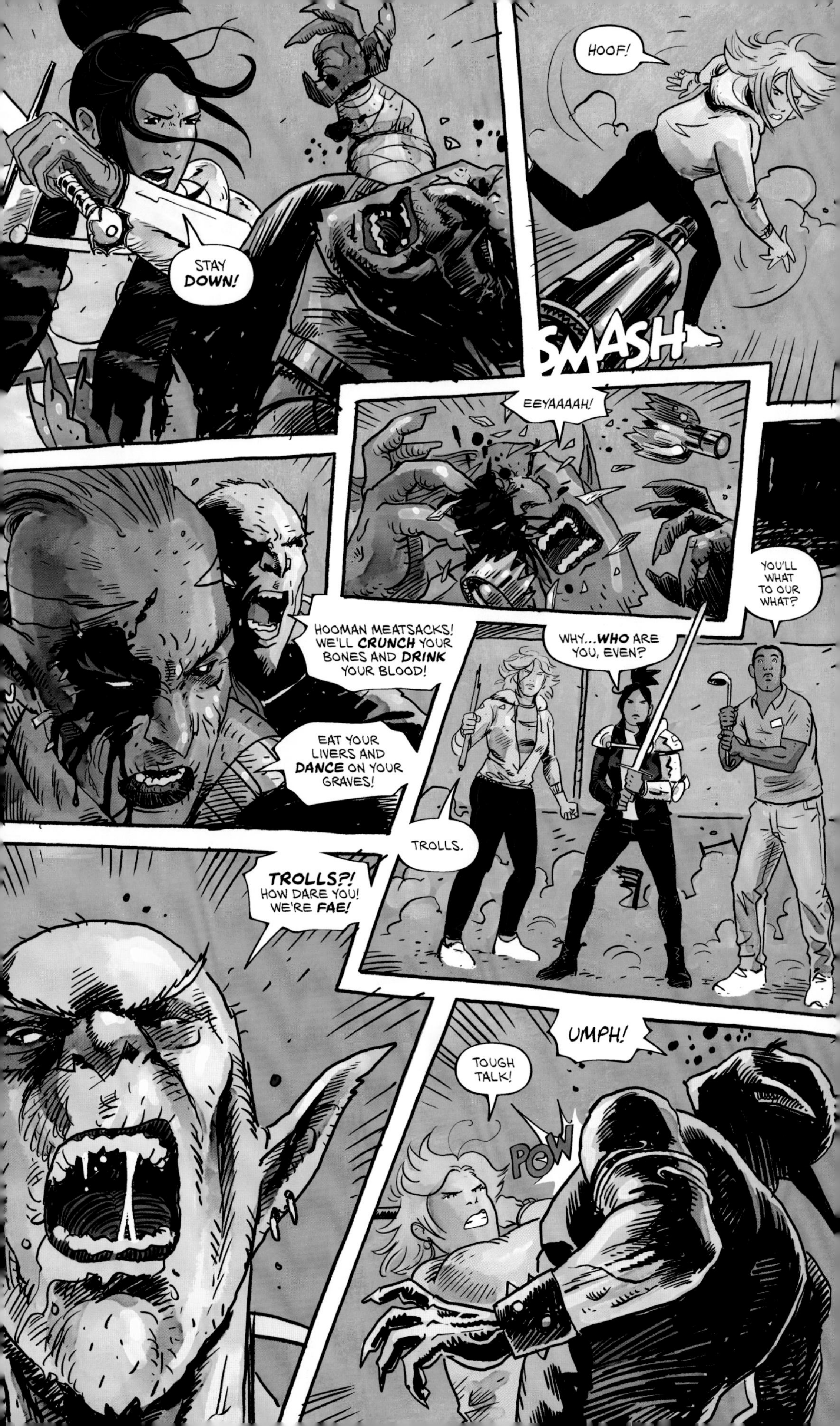
STAY DOWN!
HOOF!
SMASH
EEYAAAAH!
HOOMAN MEATSACKS! WE'LL CRUNCH YOUR BONES AND DRINK YOUR BLOOD!
EAT YOUR LIVERS AND DANCE ON YOUR GRAVES!
WHY...WHO ARE YOU, EVEN?
YOU'LL WHAT TO OUR WHAT?
TROLLS.
TROLLS?! HOW DARE YOU! WE'RE FAE!
UMPH!
TOUGH TALK!
POW

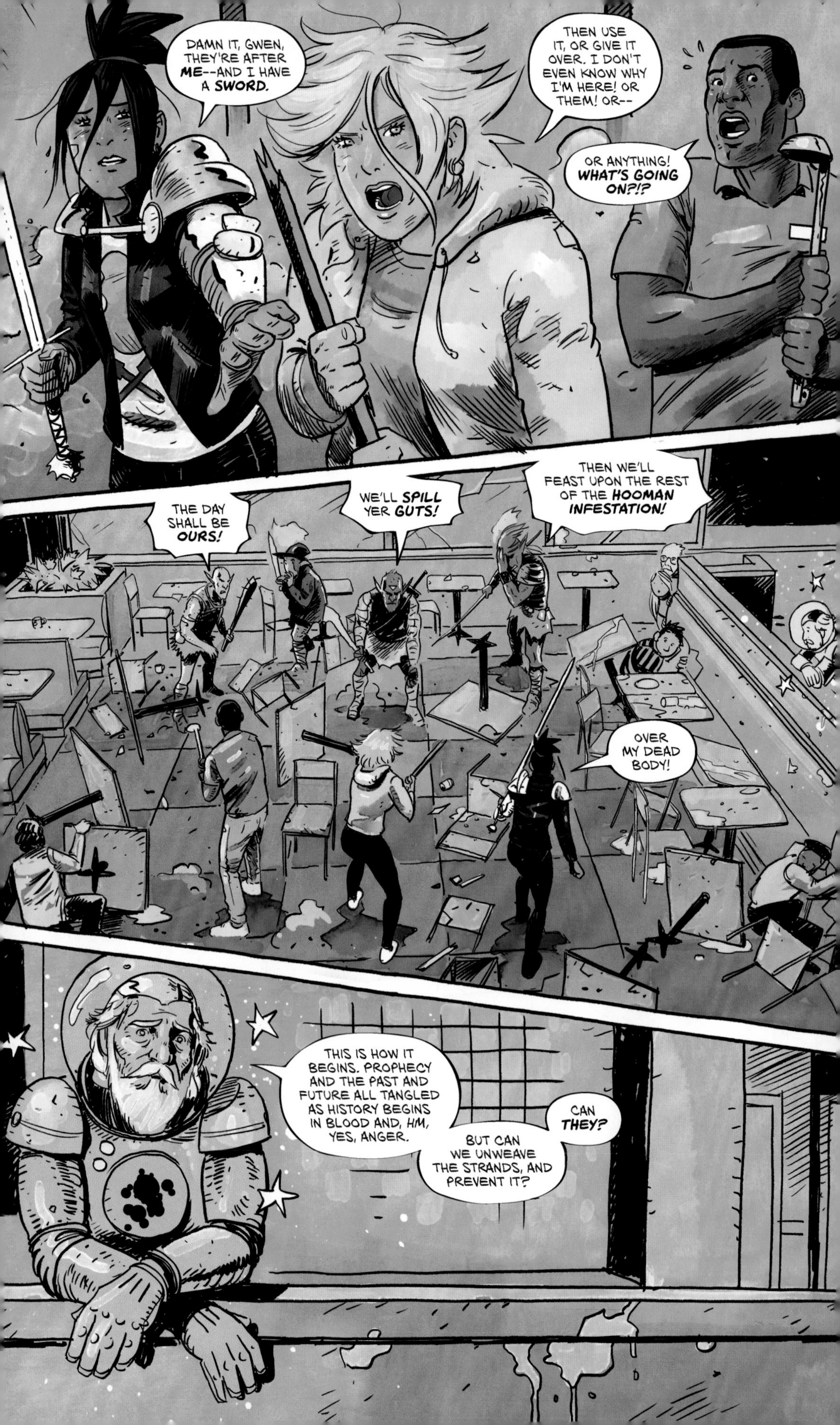
DAMN IT, GWEN, THEY'RE AFTER **ME**--AND I HAVE A **SWORD.**
THEN USE IT, OR GIVE IT OVER. I DON'T EVEN KNOW WHY I'M HERE! OR THEM! OR--
OR ANYTHING! **WHAT'S GOING ON?!?**
THE DAY SHALL BE **OURS!**
WE'LL **SPILL** YER **GUTS!**
THEN WE'LL FEAST UPON THE REST OF THE **HOOMAN INFESTATION!**
OVER MY DEAD BODY!
THIS IS HOW IT BEGINS. PROPHECY AND THE PAST AND FUTURE ALL TANGLED AS HISTORY BEGINS IN BLOOD AND, *HM*, YES, ANGER.
BUT CAN WE UNWEAVE THE STRANDS, AND PREVENT IT?
CAN **THEY?**

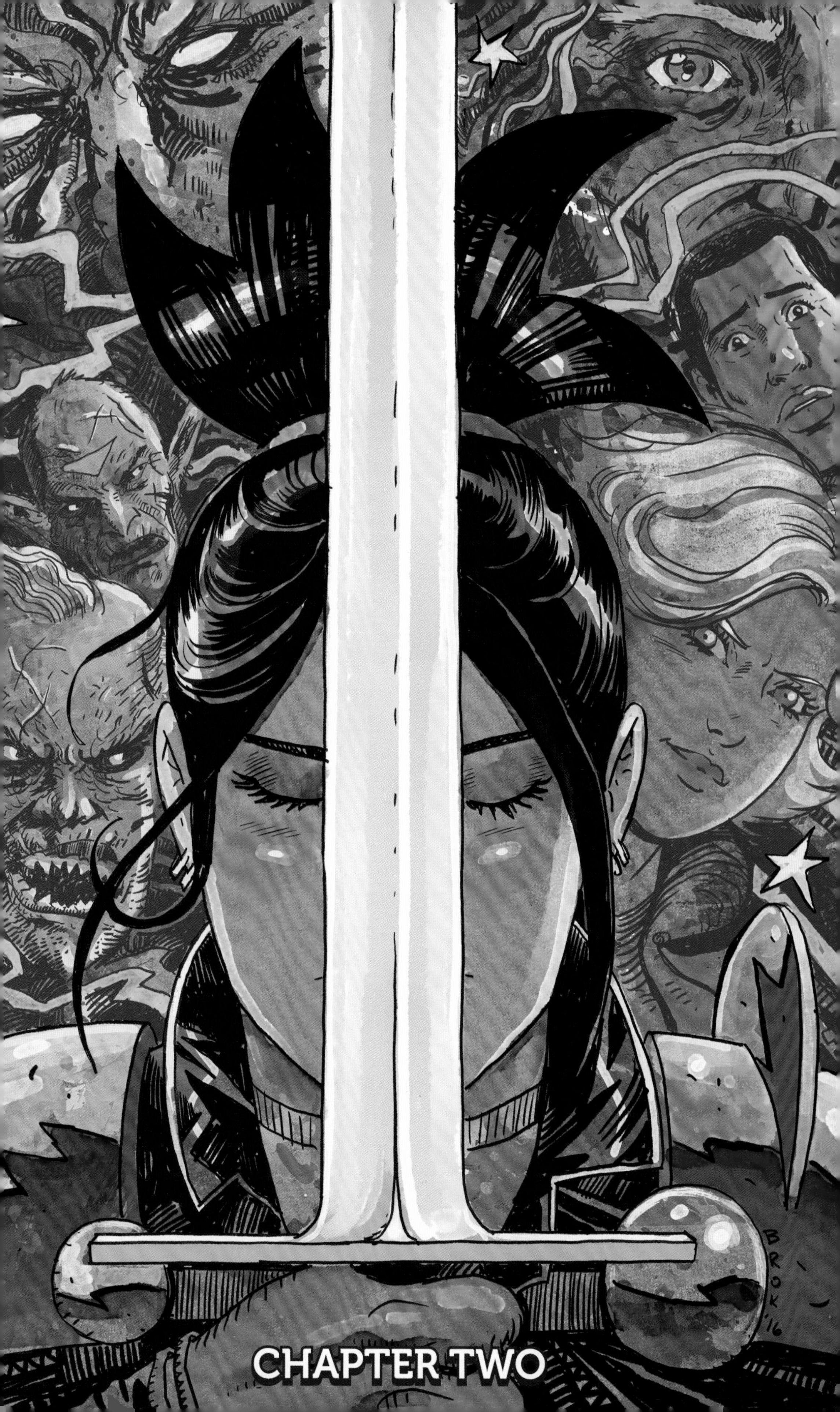
BROK '16

CHAPTER TWO

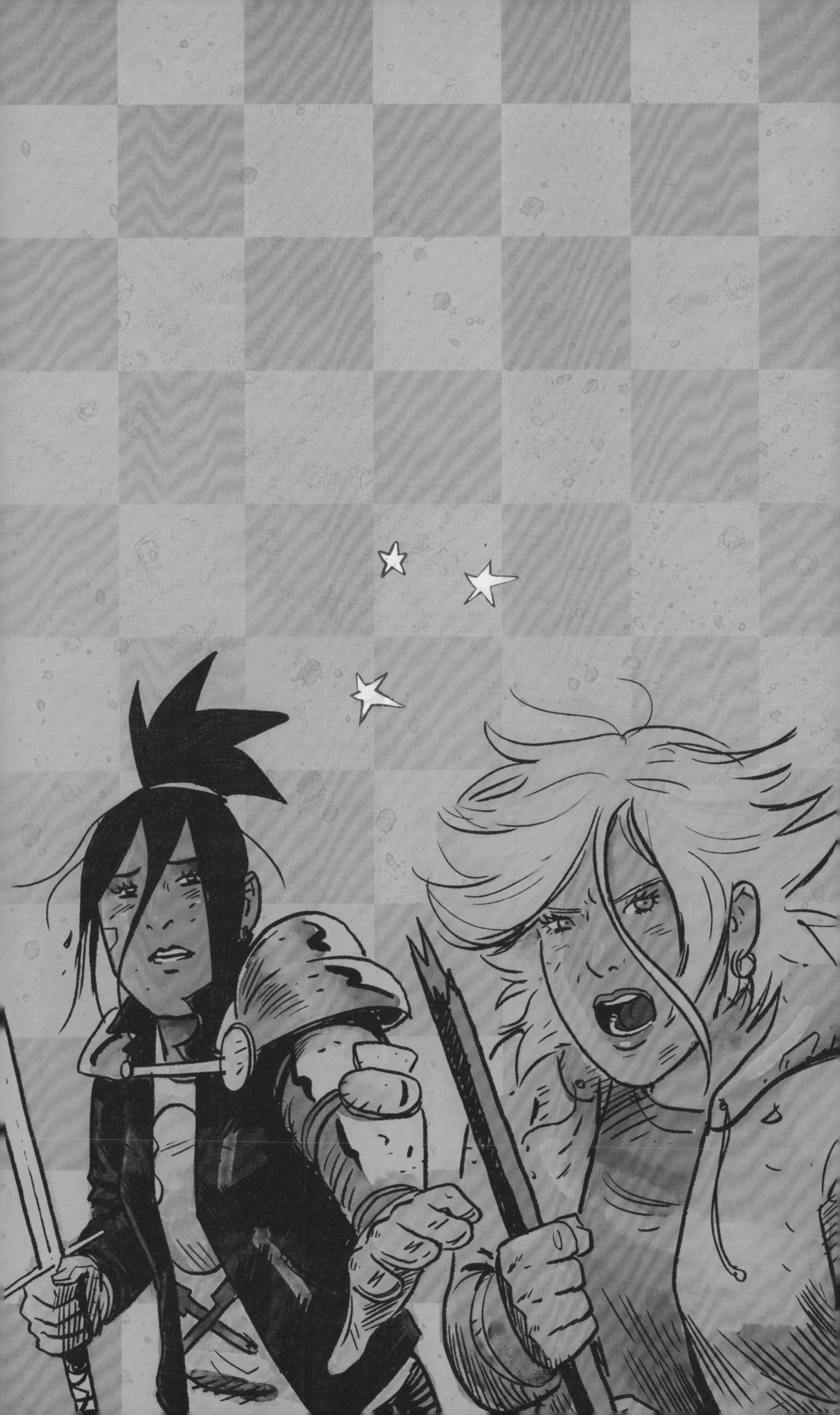

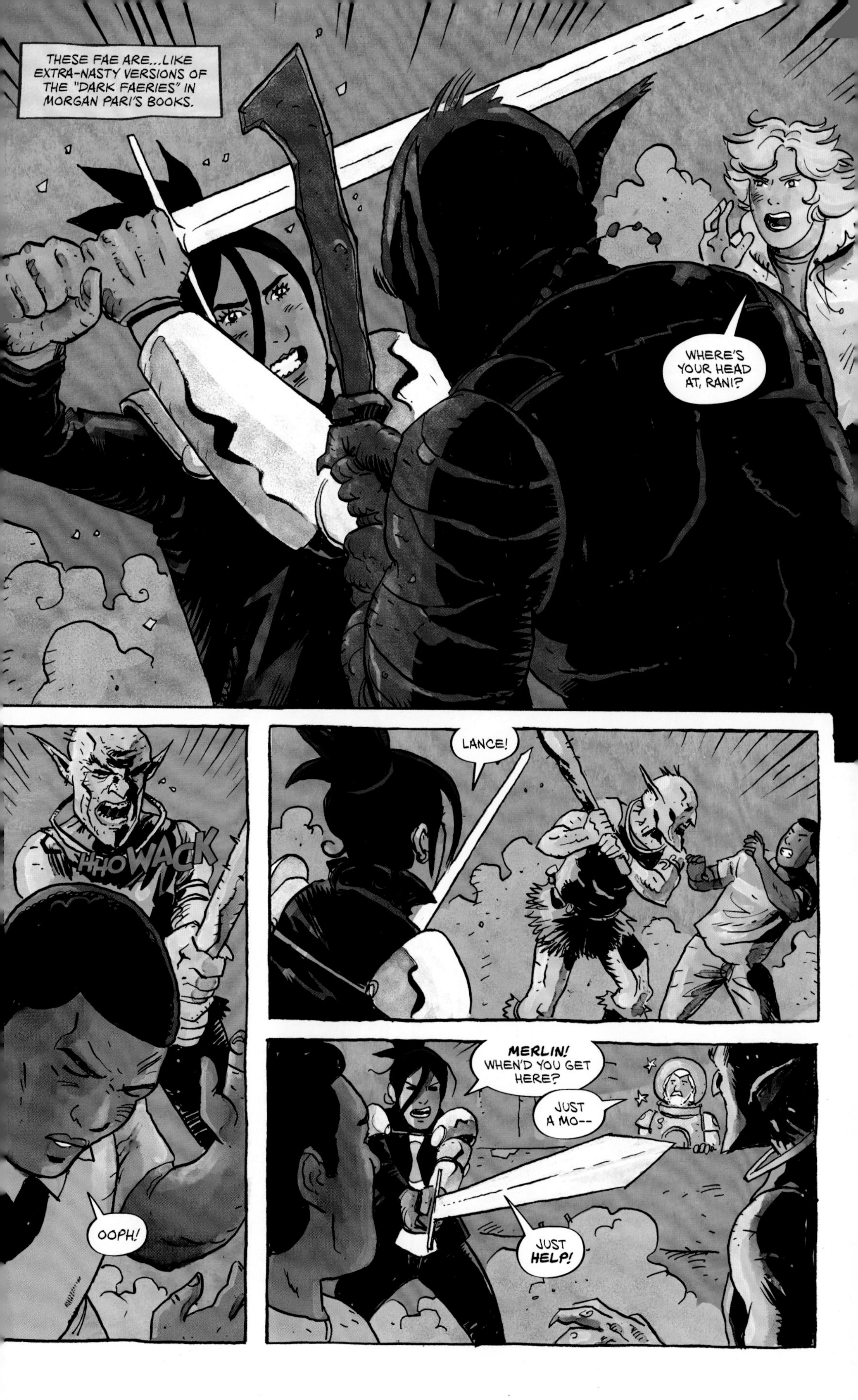
THESE FAE ARE... LIKE EXTRA-NASTY VERSIONS OF THE "DARK FAERIES" IN MORGAN PARI'S BOOKS.
WHERE'S YOUR HEAD AT, RANI?
HHOWACK
OOPH!
LANCE!
MERLIN! WHEN'D YOU GET HERE?
JUST A MO--
JUST HELP!

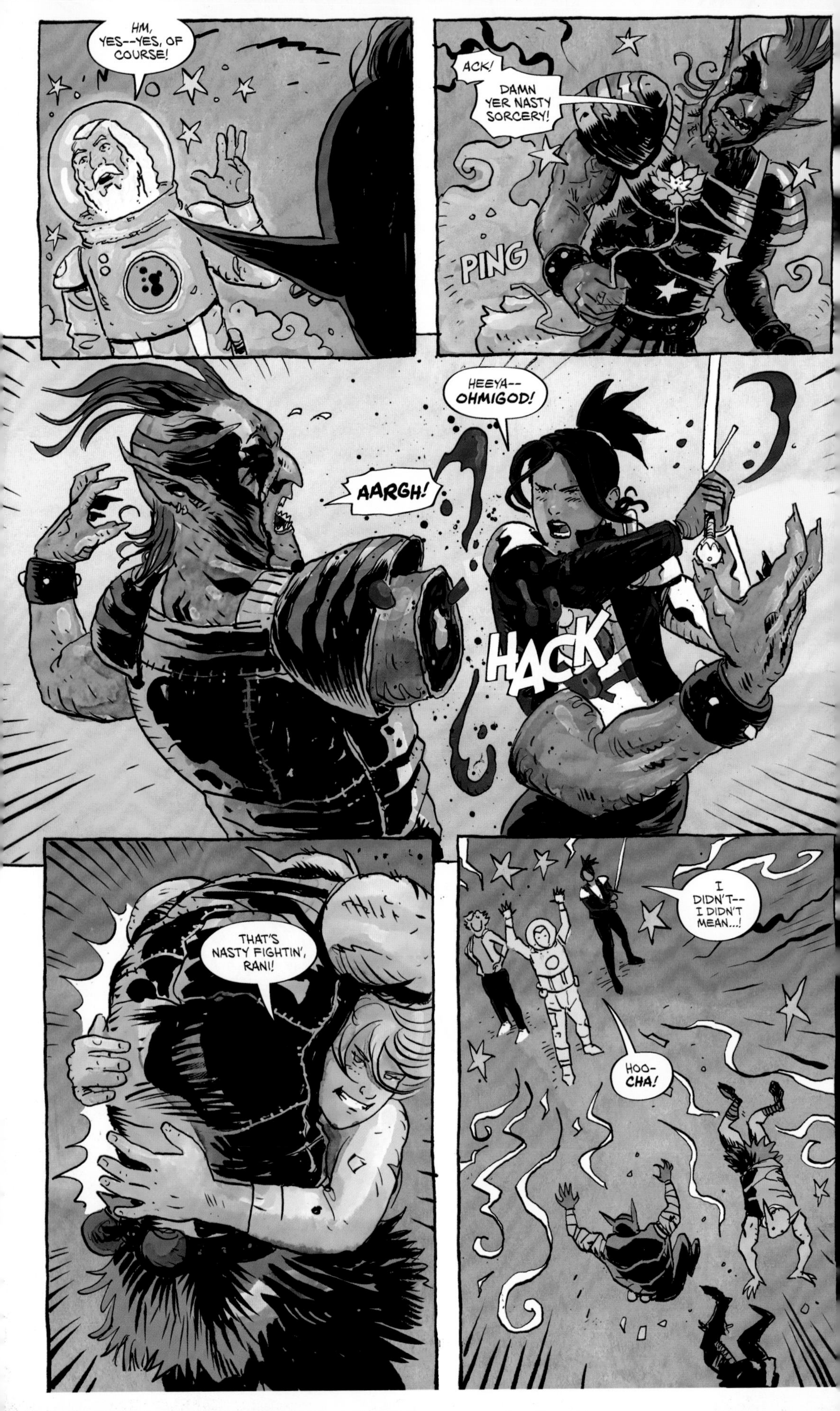
HM, YES--YES, OF COURSE!
ACK!
DAMN YER NASTY SORCERY!
PING
HEEYA-- OHMIGOD!
AARGH!
HACK
THAT'S NASTY FIGHTIN', RANI!
I DIDN'T-- I DIDN'T MEAN...!
HOO-CHA!

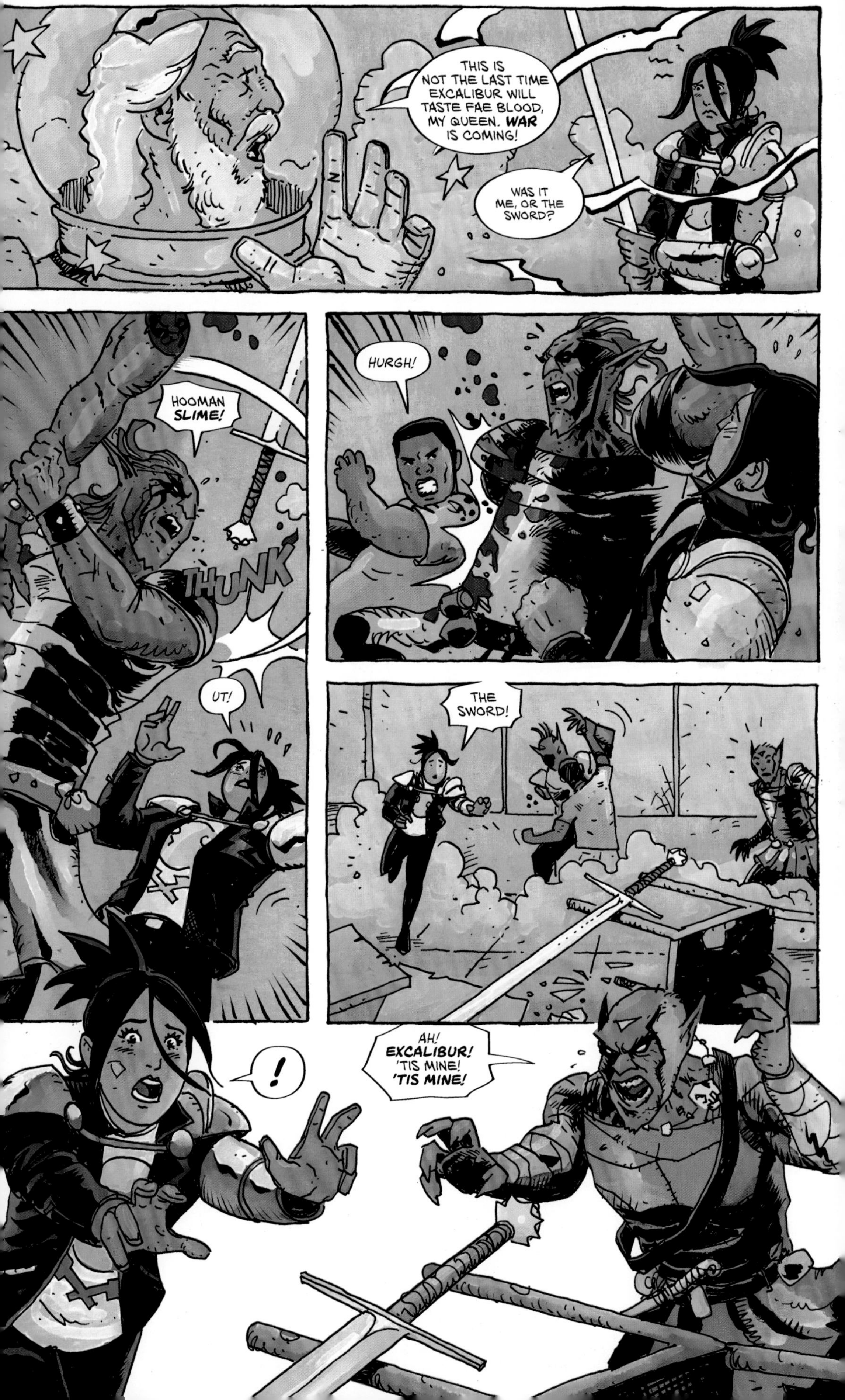

THIS IS NOT THE LAST TIME EXCALIBUR WILL TASTE FAE BLOOD, MY QUEEN. **WAR** IS COMING!
WAS IT ME, OR THE SWORD?
HOOMAN **SLIME!**
THUNK
UT!
HURGH!
THE SWORD!
!
AH! **EXCALIBUR!** 'TIS MINE! **'TIS MINE!**

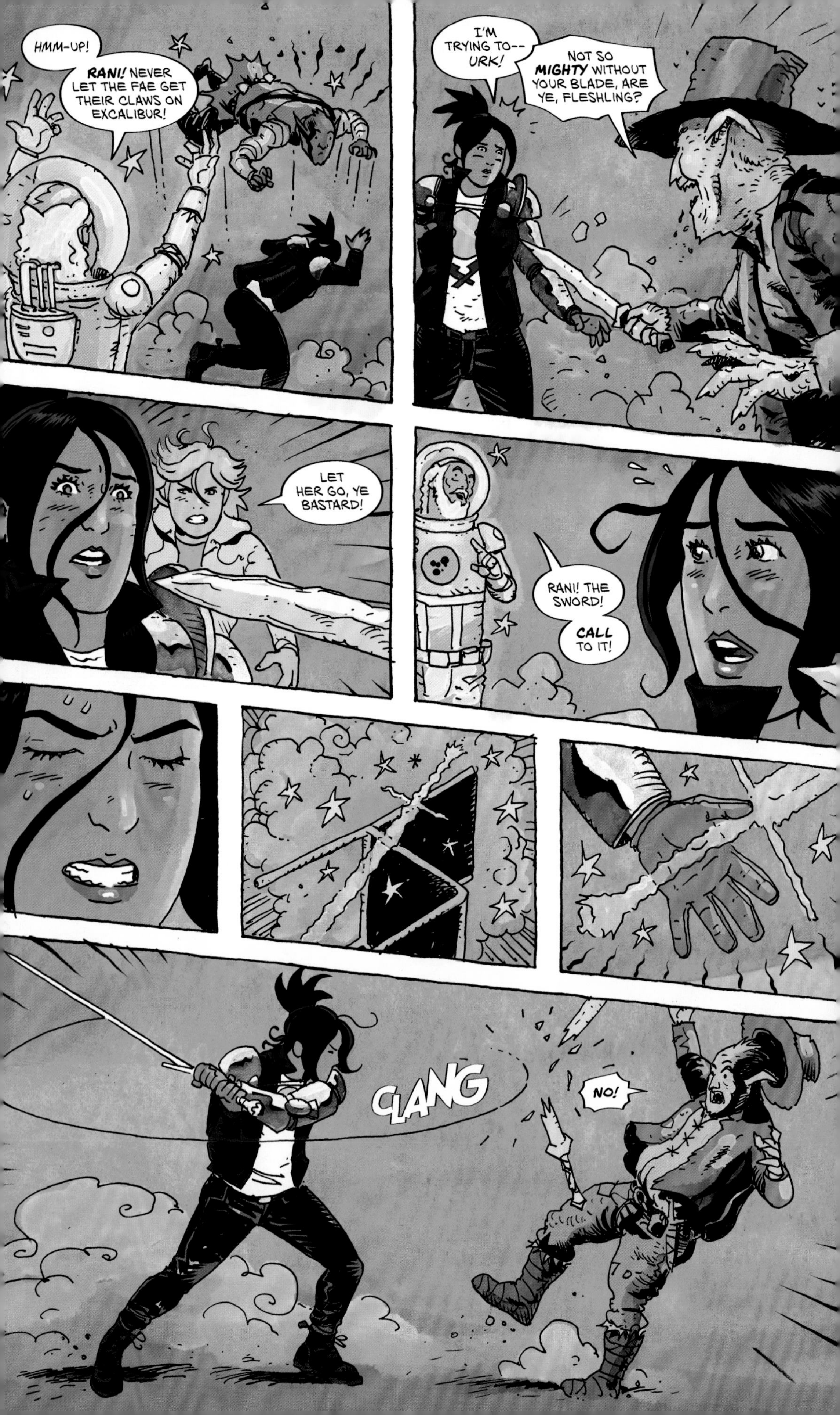
HMM-UP!
RANI! NEVER LET THE FAE GET THEIR CLAWS ON EXCALIBUR!
I'M TRYING TO-- URK!
NOT SO MIGHTY WITHOUT YOUR BLADE, ARE YE, FLESHLING?
LET HER GO, YE BASTARD!
RANI! THE SWORD!
CALL TO IT!
CLANG
NO!

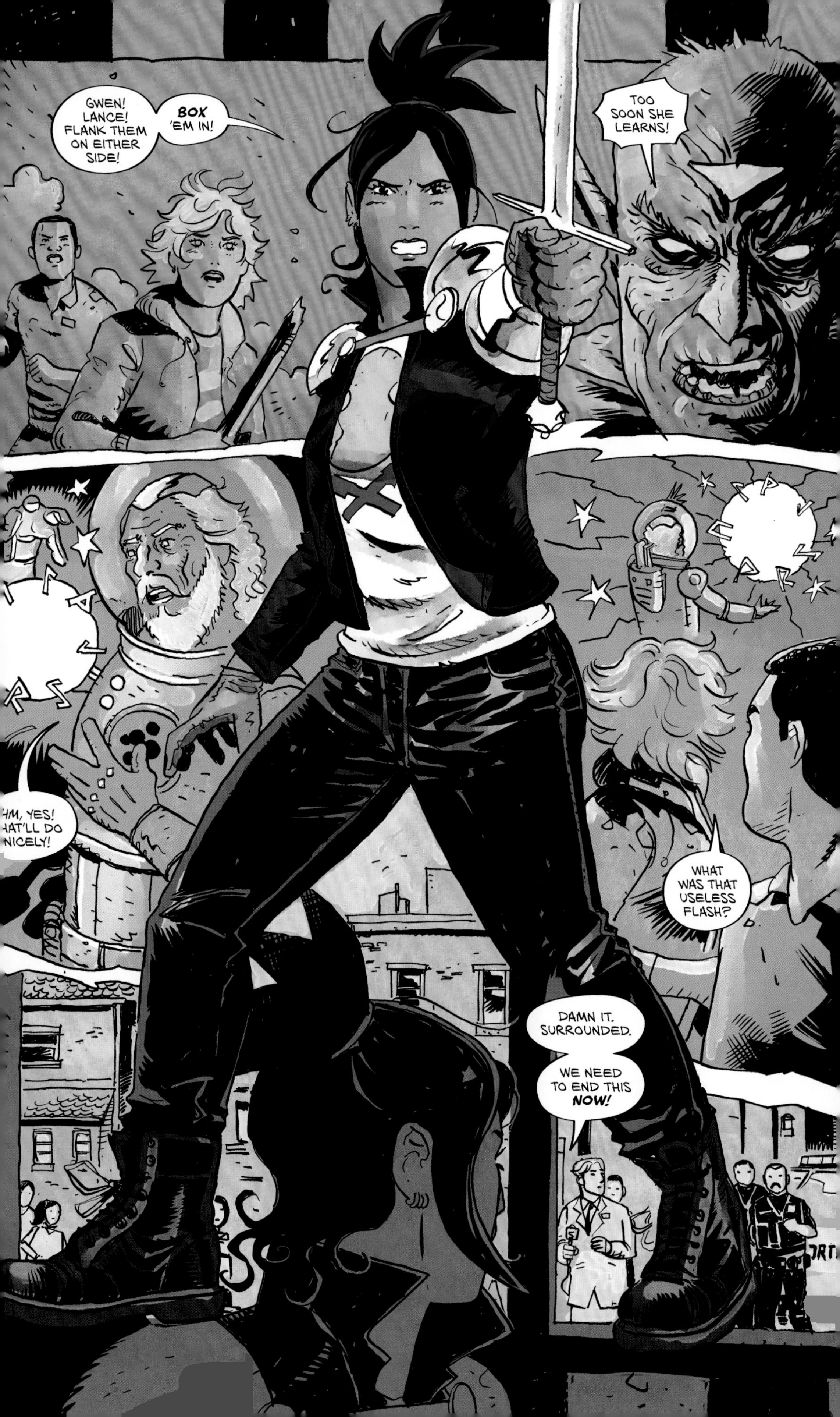
GWEN! LANCE! FLANK THEM ON EITHER SIDE!
BOX 'EM IN!
TOO SOON SHE LEARNS!
HM, YES! THAT'LL DO NICELY!
WHAT WAS THAT USELESS FLASH?
DAMN IT. SURROUNDED.
WE NEED TO END THIS NOW!

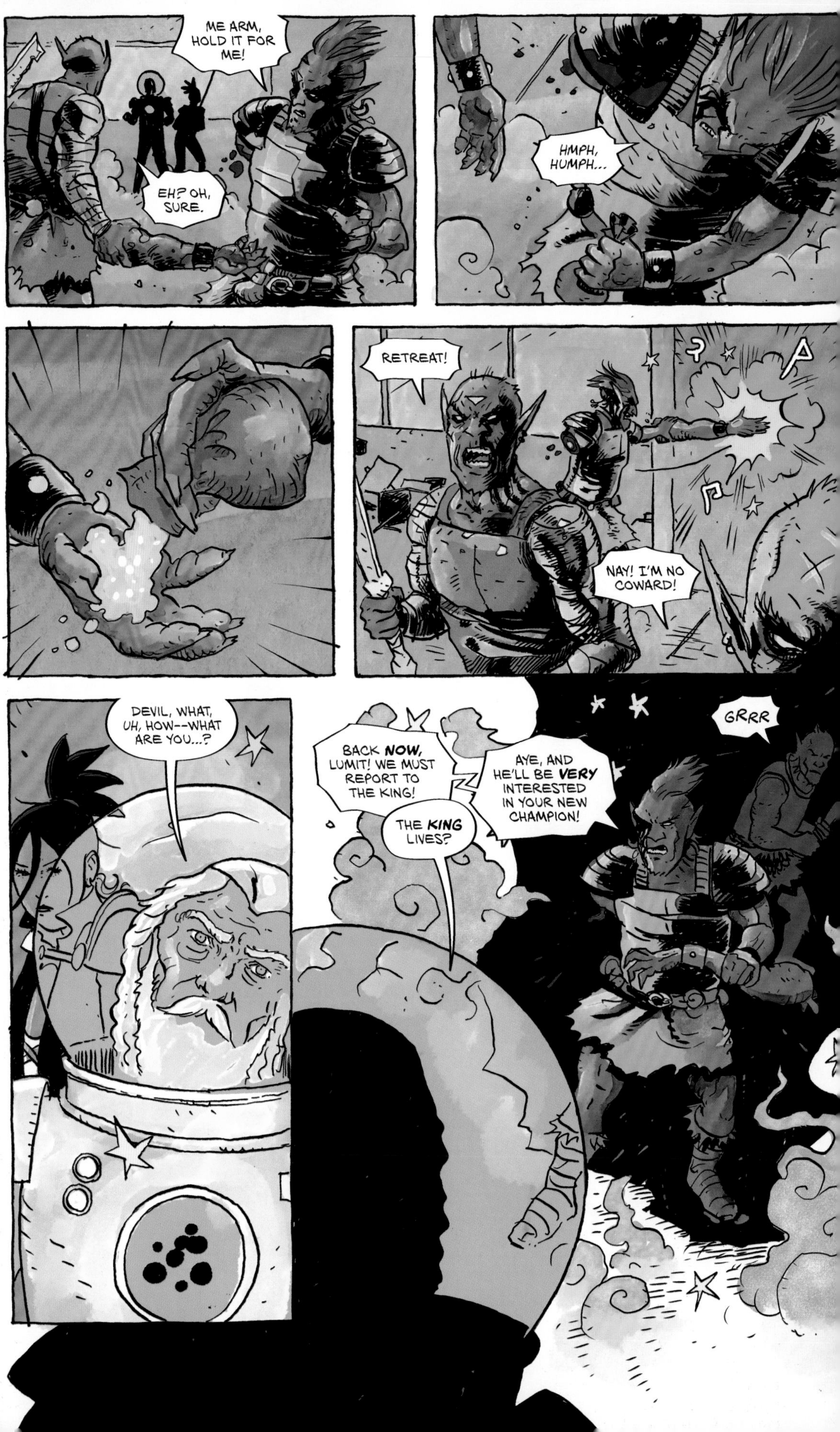
ME ARM, HOLD IT FOR ME!
EH? OH, SURE.
HMPH, HUMPH...
RETREAT!
NAY! I'M NO COWARD!
DEVIL, WHAT, UH, HOW--WHAT ARE YOU...?
BACK NOW, LUMIT! WE MUST REPORT TO THE KING!
AYE, AND HE'LL BE VERY INTERESTED IN YOUR NEW CHAMPION!
THE KING LIVES?
GRRR

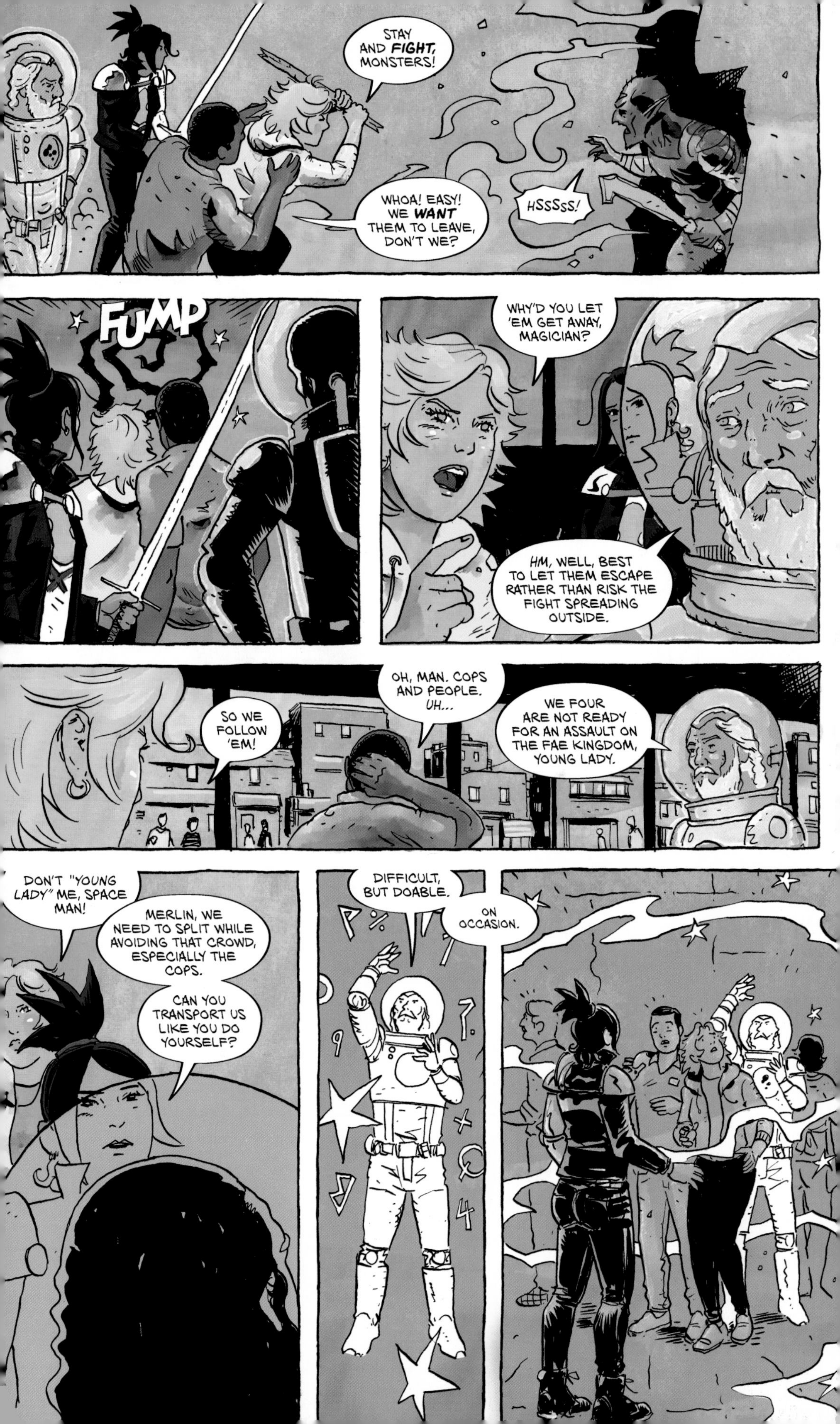
STAY AND FIGHT, MONSTERS!
WHOA! EASY! WE WANT THEM TO LEAVE, DON'T WE?
HSSSSS!
FUMP
WHY'D YOU LET 'EM GET AWAY, MAGICIAN?
HM, WELL, BEST TO LET THEM ESCAPE RATHER THAN RISK THE FIGHT SPREADING OUTSIDE.
SO WE FOLLOW 'EM!
OH, MAN. COPS AND PEOPLE. UH...
WE FOUR ARE NOT READY FOR AN ASSAULT ON THE FAE KINGDOM, YOUNG LADY.
DON'T "YOUNG LADY" ME, SPACE MAN!
MERLIN, WE NEED TO SPLIT WHILE AVOIDING THAT CROWD, ESPECIALLY THE COPS.
CAN YOU TRANSPORT US LIKE YOU DO YOURSELF?
DIFFICULT, BUT DOABLE.
ON OCCASION.

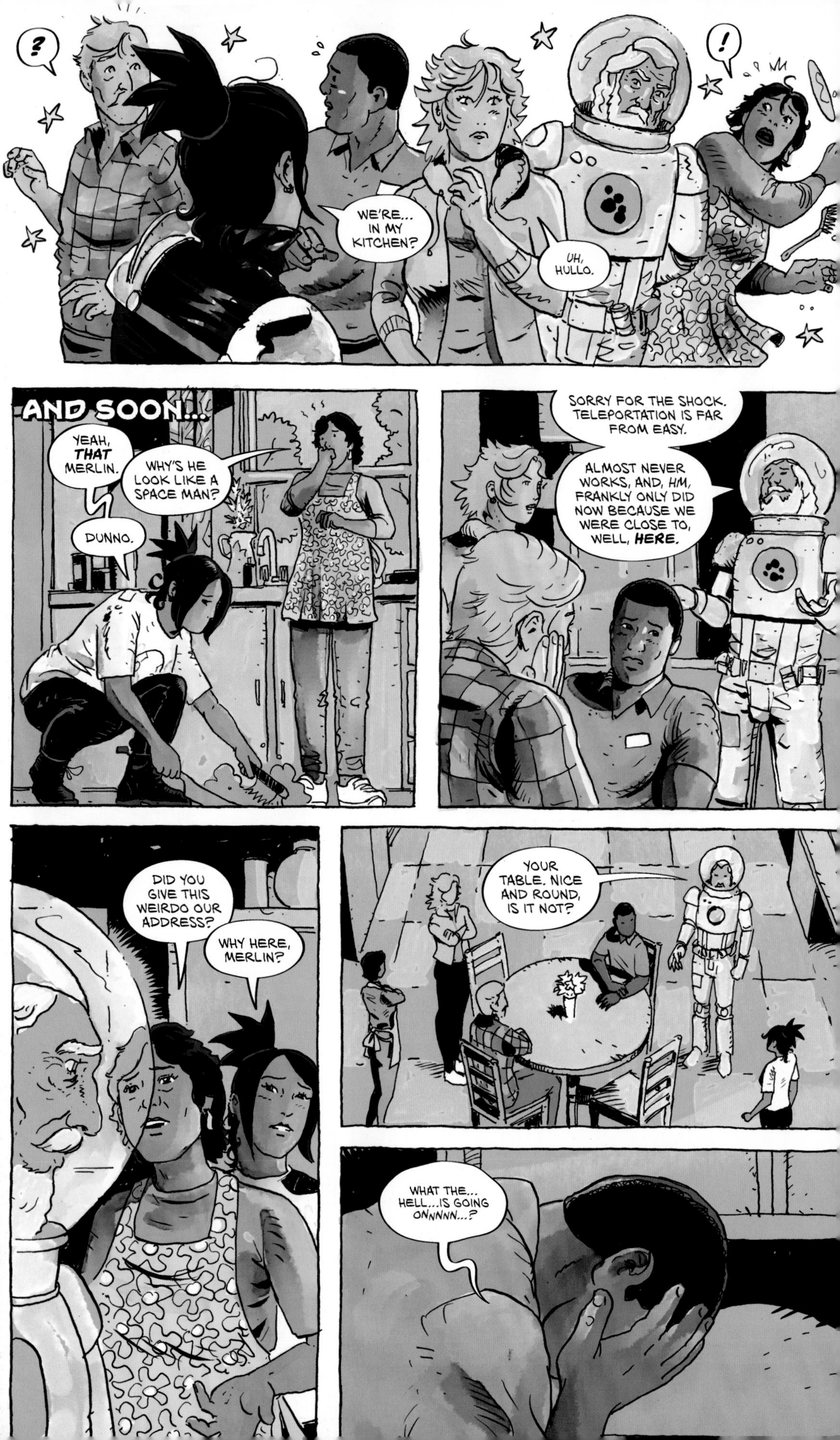
?
!
WE'RE... IN MY KITCHEN?
UH, HULLO.
AND SOON...
YEAH, THAT MERLIN.
WHY'S HE LOOK LIKE A SPACE MAN?
DUNNO.
SORRY FOR THE SHOCK. TELEPORTATION IS FAR FROM EASY.
ALMOST NEVER WORKS, AND, HM, FRANKLY ONLY DID NOW BECAUSE WE WERE CLOSE TO, WELL, HERE.
DID YOU GIVE THIS WEIRDO OUR ADDRESS?
WHY HERE, MERLIN?
YOUR TABLE. NICE AND ROUND, IS IT NOT?
WHAT THE... HELL...IS GOING ONNNNN...?

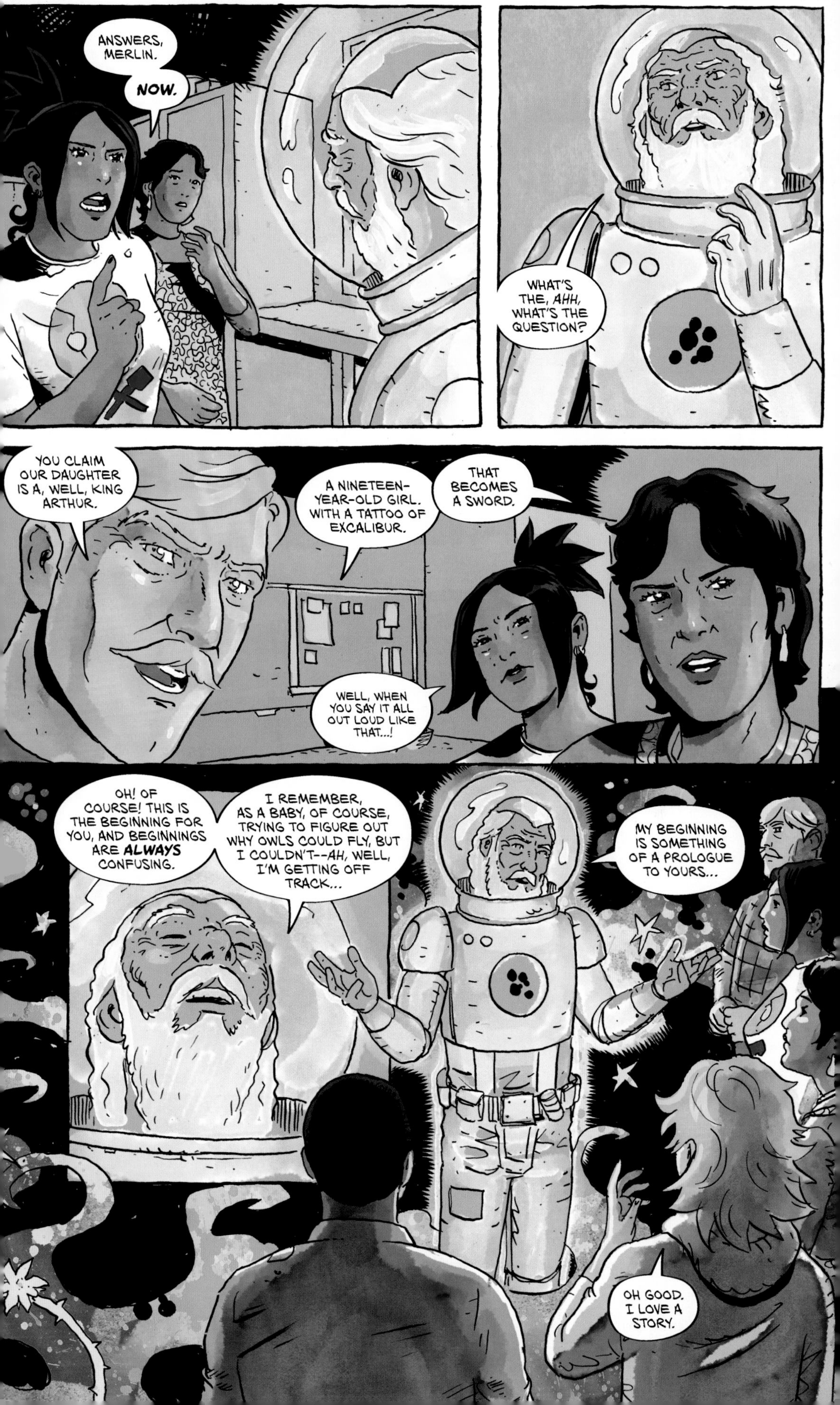
ANSWERS, MERLIN.
NOW.
WHAT'S THE, AHH, WHAT'S THE QUESTION?
YOU CLAIM OUR DAUGHTER IS A, WELL, KING ARTHUR.
A NINETEEN-YEAR-OLD GIRL. WITH A TATTOO OF EXCALIBUR.
THAT BECOMES A SWORD.
WELL, WHEN YOU SAY IT ALL OUT LOUD LIKE THAT...!
OH! OF COURSE! THIS IS THE BEGINNING FOR YOU, AND BEGINNINGS ARE ALWAYS CONFUSING.
I REMEMBER, AS A BABY, OF COURSE, TRYING TO FIGURE OUT WHY OWLS COULD FLY, BUT I COULDN'T--AH, WELL, I'M GETTING OFF TRACK...
MY BEGINNING IS SOMETHING OF A PROLOGUE TO YOURS...
OH GOOD. I LOVE A STORY.

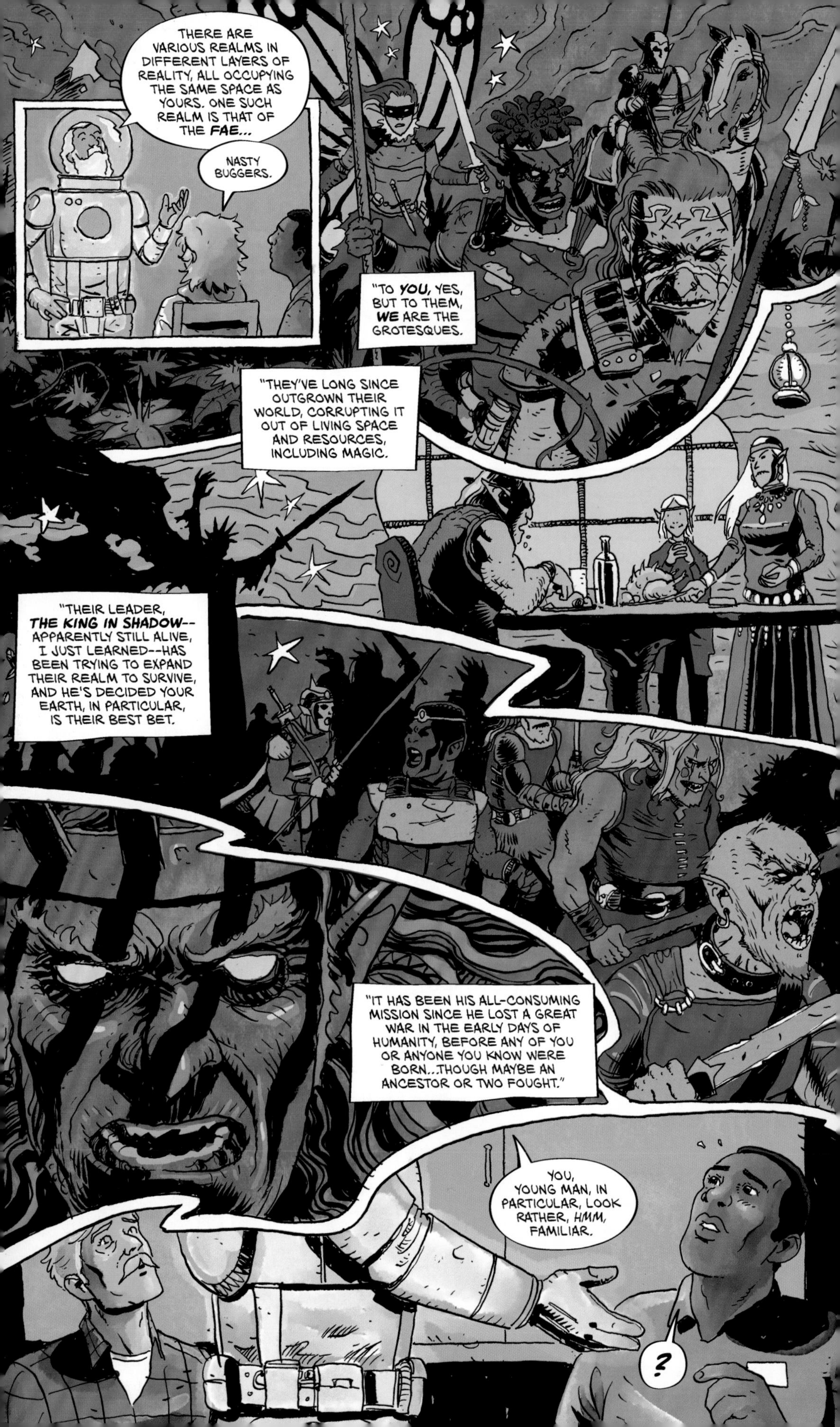

THERE ARE VARIOUS REALMS IN DIFFERENT LAYERS OF REALITY, ALL OCCUPYING THE SAME SPACE AS YOURS. ONE SUCH REALM IS THAT OF THE FAE...
NASTY BUGGERS.
"TO YOU, YES, BUT TO THEM, WE ARE THE GROTESQUES.
"THEY'VE LONG SINCE OUTGROWN THEIR WORLD, CORRUPTING IT OUT OF LIVING SPACE AND RESOURCES, INCLUDING MAGIC.
"THEIR LEADER, THE KING IN SHADOW--APPARENTLY STILL ALIVE, I JUST LEARNED--HAS BEEN TRYING TO EXPAND THEIR REALM TO SURVIVE, AND HE'S DECIDED YOUR EARTH, IN PARTICULAR, IS THEIR BEST BET.
"IT HAS BEEN HIS ALL-CONSUMING MISSION SINCE HE LOST A GREAT WAR IN THE EARLY DAYS OF HUMANITY, BEFORE ANY OF YOU OR ANYONE YOU KNOW WERE BORN...THOUGH MAYBE AN ANCESTOR OR TWO FOUGHT."
YOU, YOUNG MAN, IN PARTICULAR, LOOK RATHER, HMM, FAMILIAR.
?

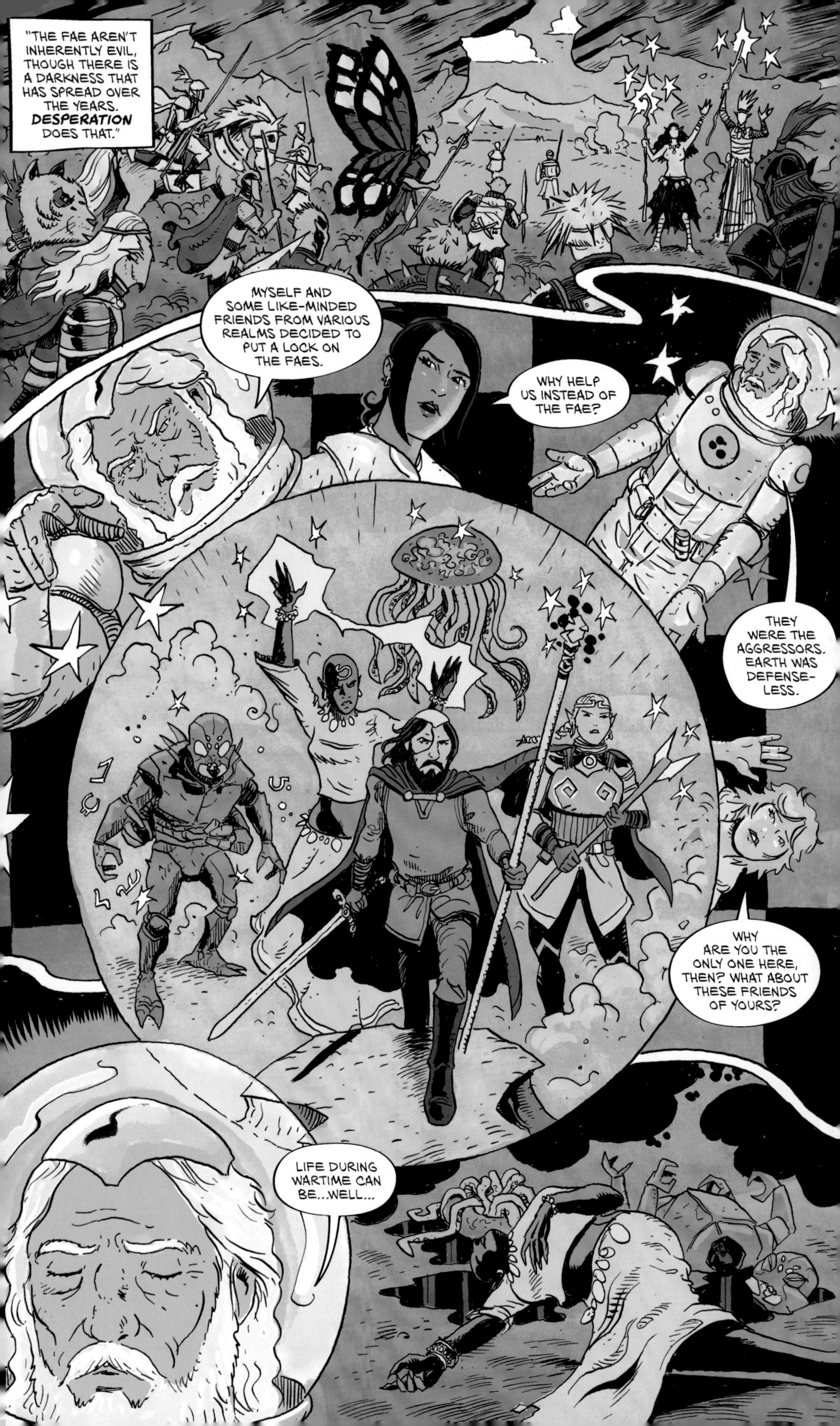
"THE FAE AREN'T INHERENTLY EVIL, THOUGH THERE IS A DARKNESS THAT HAS SPREAD OVER THE YEARS. **DESPERATION** DOES THAT."
MYSELF AND SOME LIKE-MINDED FRIENDS FROM VARIOUS REALMS DECIDED TO PUT A LOCK ON THE FAES.
WHY HELP US INSTEAD OF THE FAE?
THEY WERE THE AGGRESSORS. EARTH WAS DEFENSE-LESS.
WHY ARE YOU THE ONLY ONE HERE, THEN? WHAT ABOUT THESE FRIENDS OF YOURS?
LIFE DURING WARTIME CAN BE...WELL...

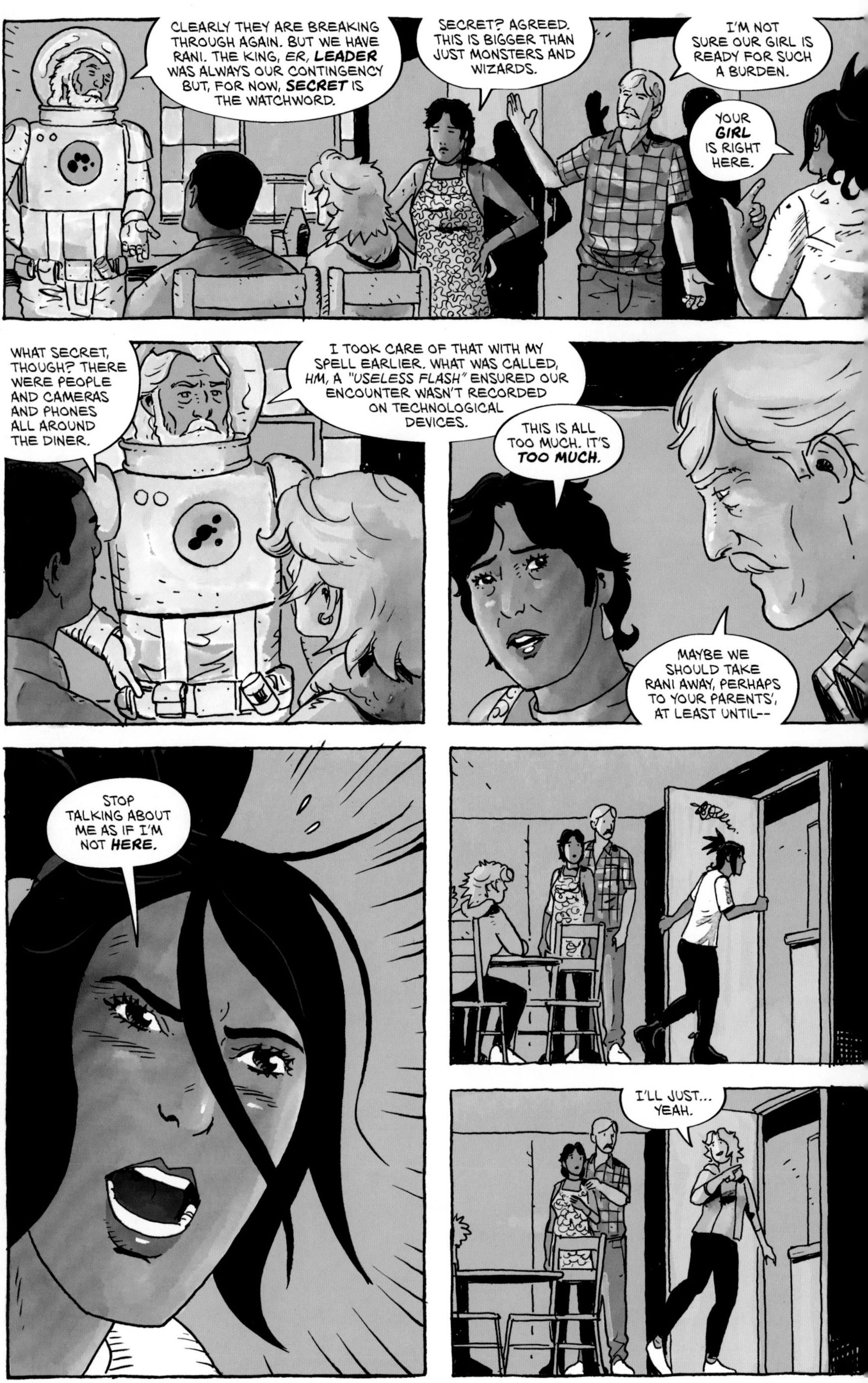
CLEARLY THEY ARE BREAKING THROUGH AGAIN. BUT WE HAVE RANI. THE KING, ER, LEADER WAS ALWAYS OUR CONTINGENCY BUT, FOR NOW, SECRET IS THE WATCHWORD.
SECRET? AGREED. THIS IS BIGGER THAN JUST MONSTERS AND WIZARDS.
I'M NOT SURE OUR GIRL IS READY FOR SUCH A BURDEN.
YOUR GIRL IS RIGHT HERE.
WHAT SECRET, THOUGH? THERE WERE PEOPLE AND CAMERAS AND PHONES ALL AROUND THE DINER.
I TOOK CARE OF THAT WITH MY SPELL EARLIER. WHAT WAS CALLED, HM, A "USELESS FLASH" ENSURED OUR ENCOUNTER WASN'T RECORDED ON TECHNOLOGICAL DEVICES.
THIS IS ALL TOO MUCH. IT'S TOO MUCH.
MAYBE WE SHOULD TAKE RANI AWAY, PERHAPS TO YOUR PARENTS', AT LEAST UNTIL--
STOP TALKING ABOUT ME AS IF I'M NOT HERE.
I'LL JUST... YEAH.

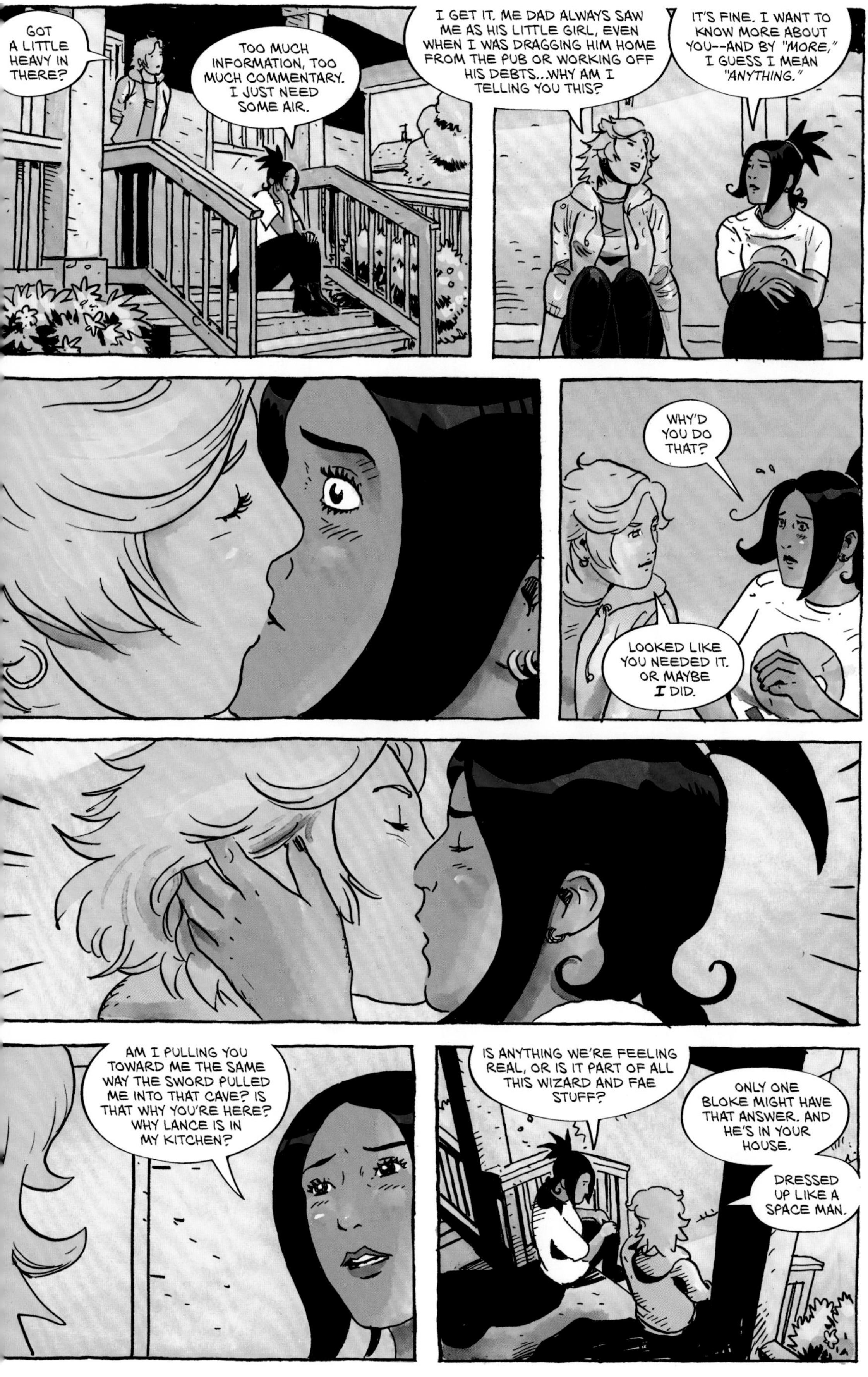
GOT A LITTLE HEAVY IN THERE?
TOO MUCH INFORMATION, TOO MUCH COMMENTARY. I JUST NEED SOME AIR.
I GET IT. ME DAD ALWAYS SAW ME AS HIS LITTLE GIRL, EVEN WHEN I WAS DRAGGING HIM HOME FROM THE PUB OR WORKING OFF HIS DEBTS...WHY AM I TELLING YOU THIS?
IT'S FINE. I WANT TO KNOW MORE ABOUT YOU--AND BY "MORE," I GUESS I MEAN "ANYTHING."
WHY'D YOU DO THAT?
LOOKED LIKE YOU NEEDED IT. OR MAYBE I DID.
AM I PULLING YOU TOWARD ME THE SAME WAY THE SWORD PULLED ME INTO THAT CAVE? IS THAT WHY YOU'RE HERE? WHY LANCE IS IN MY KITCHEN?
IS ANYTHING WE'RE FEELING REAL, OR IS IT PART OF ALL THIS WIZARD AND FAE STUFF?
ONLY ONE BLOKE MIGHT HAVE THAT ANSWER. AND HE'S IN YOUR HOUSE.
DRESSED UP LIKE A SPACE MAN.

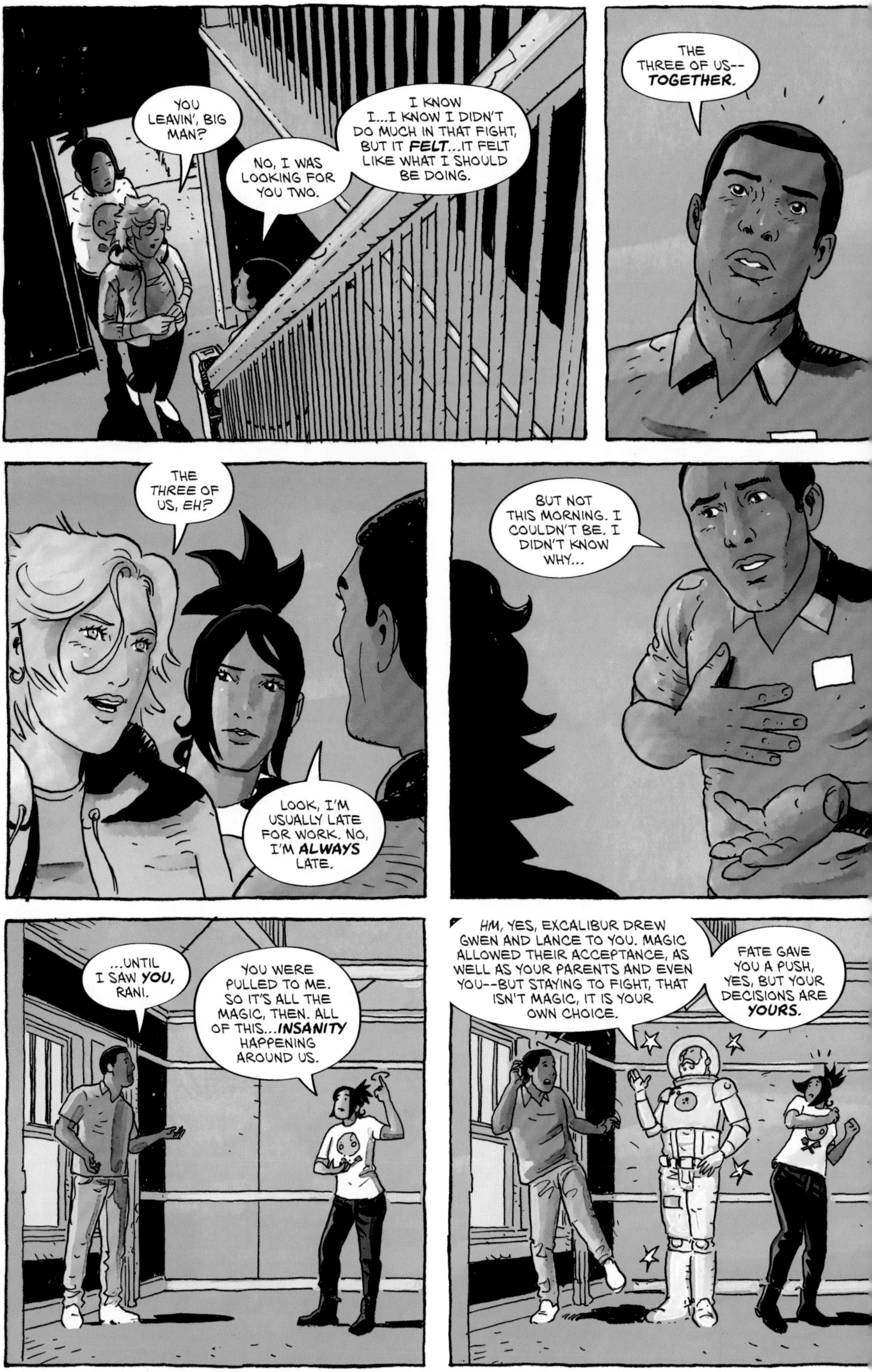
YOU LEAVIN', BIG MAN?
NO, I WAS LOOKING FOR YOU TWO.
I KNOW I...I KNOW I DIDN'T DO MUCH IN THAT FIGHT, BUT IT FELT...IT FELT LIKE WHAT I SHOULD BE DOING.
THE THREE OF US-- TOGETHER.
THE THREE OF US, EH?
LOOK, I'M USUALLY LATE FOR WORK. NO, I'M ALWAYS LATE.
BUT NOT THIS MORNING. I COULDN'T BE. I DIDN'T KNOW WHY...
...UNTIL I SAW YOU, RANI.
YOU WERE PULLED TO ME. SO IT'S ALL THE MAGIC, THEN. ALL OF THIS...INSANITY HAPPENING AROUND US.
HM, YES, EXCALIBUR DREW GWEN AND LANCE TO YOU. MAGIC ALLOWED THEIR ACCEPTANCE, AS WELL AS YOUR PARENTS AND EVEN YOU--BUT STAYING TO FIGHT, THAT ISN'T MAGIC, IT IS YOUR OWN CHOICE.
FATE GAVE YOU A PUSH, YES, BUT YOUR DECISIONS ARE YOURS.

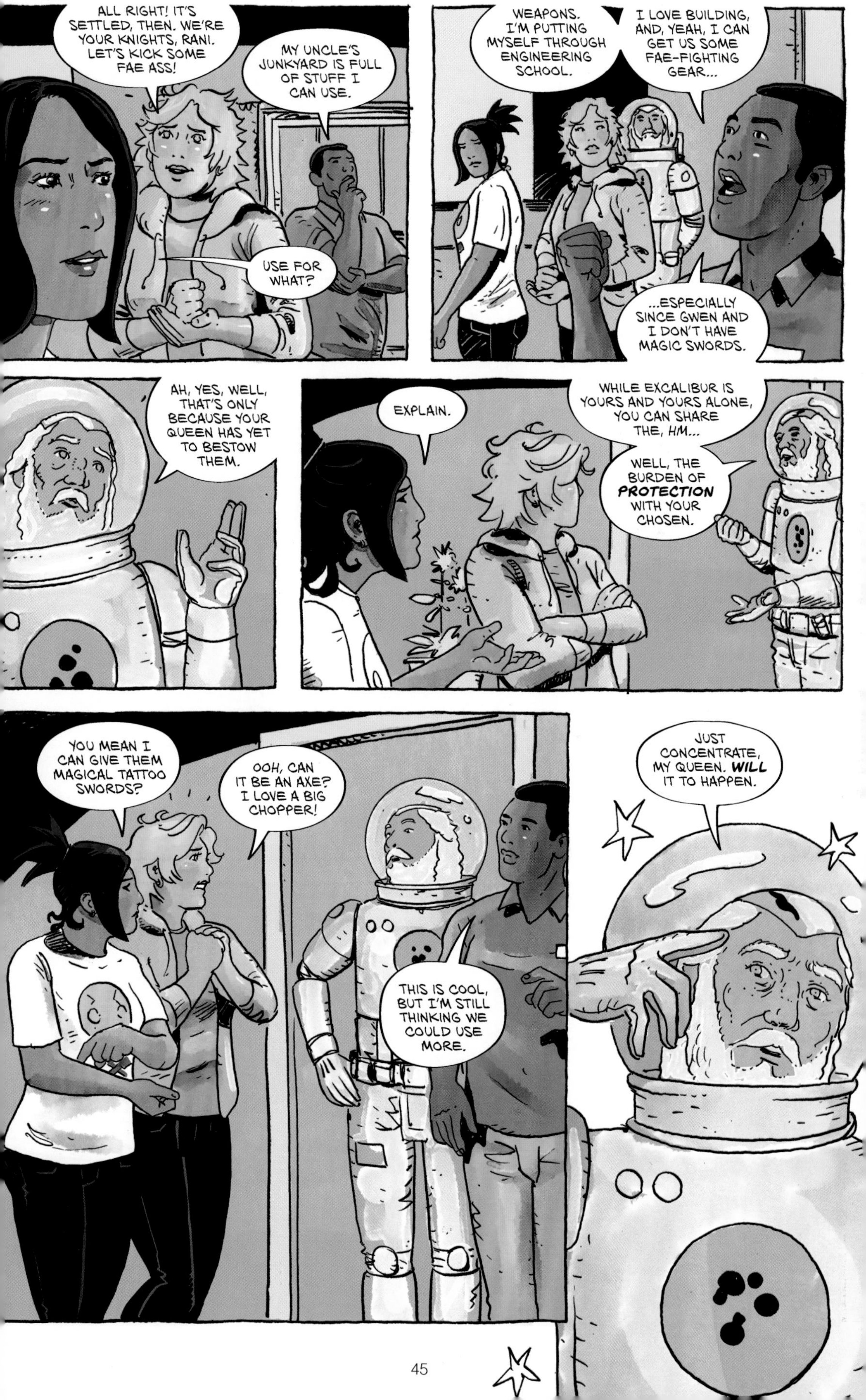

ALL RIGHT! IT'S SETTLED, THEN. WE'RE YOUR KNIGHTS, RANI. LET'S KICK SOME FAE ASS!
MY UNCLE'S JUNKYARD IS FULL OF STUFF I CAN USE.
USE FOR WHAT?
WEAPONS. I'M PUTTING MYSELF THROUGH ENGINEERING SCHOOL.
I LOVE BUILDING, AND, YEAH, I CAN GET US SOME FAE-FIGHTING GEAR...
...ESPECIALLY SINCE GWEN AND I DON'T HAVE MAGIC SWORDS.
AH, YES, WELL, THAT'S ONLY BECAUSE YOUR QUEEN HAS YET TO BESTOW THEM.
EXPLAIN.
WHILE EXCALIBUR IS YOURS AND YOURS ALONE, YOU CAN SHARE THE, HM...
WELL, THE BURDEN OF PROTECTION WITH YOUR CHOSEN.
YOU MEAN I CAN GIVE THEM MAGICAL TATTOO SWORDS?
OOH, CAN IT BE AN AXE? I LOVE A BIG CHOPPER!
THIS IS COOL, BUT I'M STILL THINKING WE COULD USE MORE.
JUST CONCENTRATE, MY QUEEN. WILL IT TO HAPPEN.

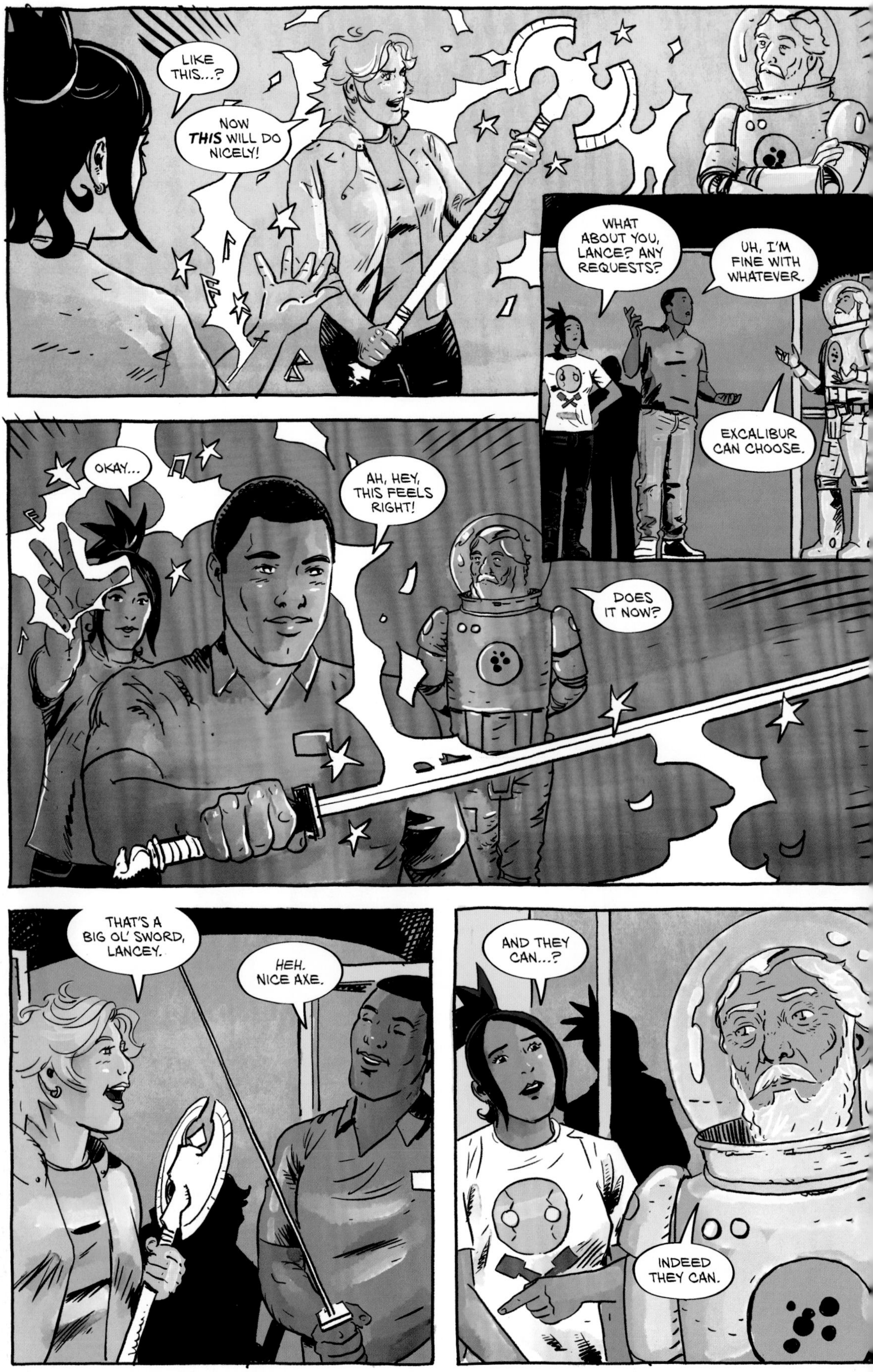
LIKE THIS...?
NOW THIS WILL DO NICELY!
WHAT ABOUT YOU, LANCE? ANY REQUESTS?
UH, I'M FINE WITH WHATEVER.
EXCALIBUR CAN CHOOSE.
OKAY...
AH, HEY, THIS FEELS RIGHT!
DOES IT NOW?
THAT'S A BIG OL' SWORD, LANCEY.
HEH. NICE AXE.
AND THEY CAN...?
INDEED THEY CAN.

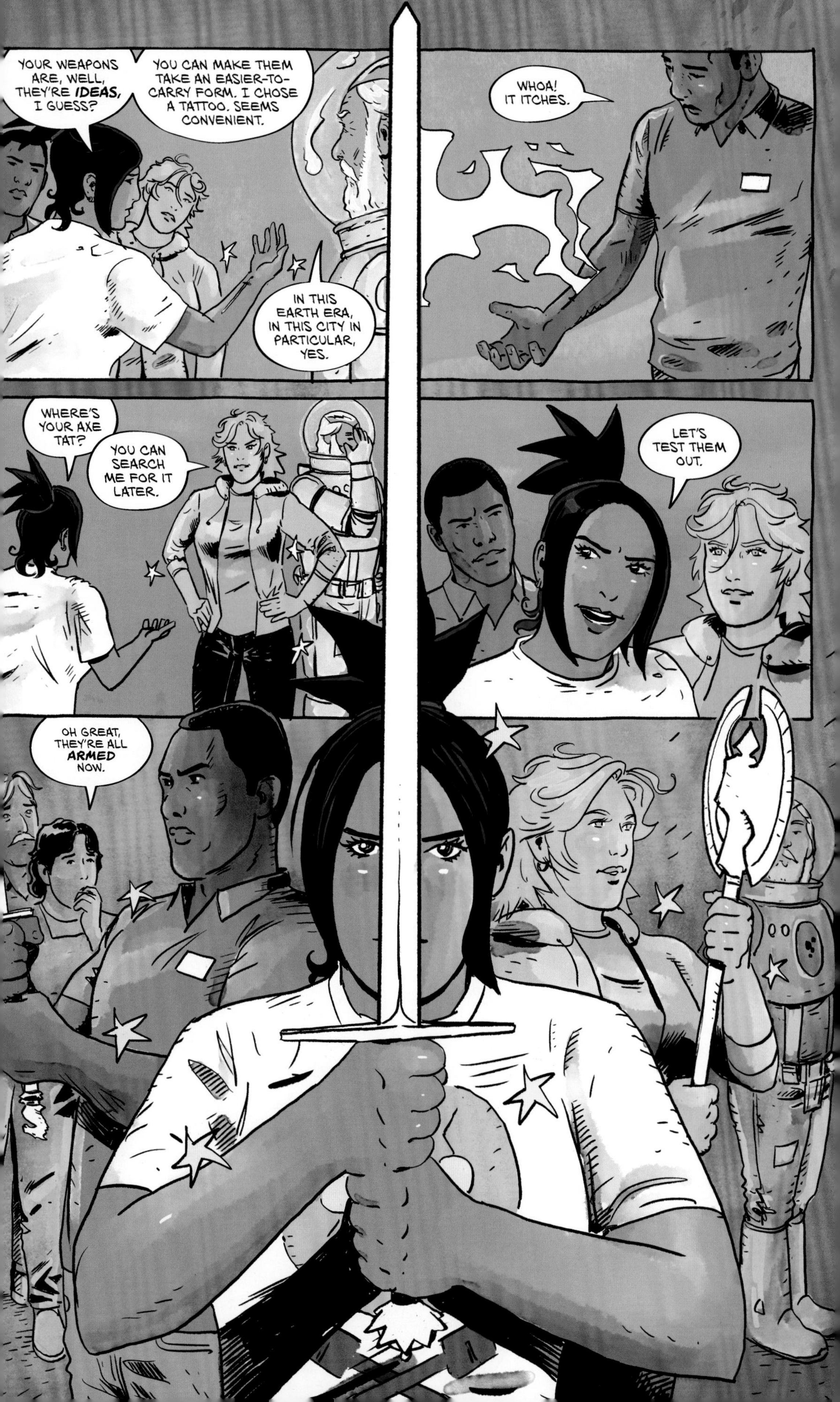

YOUR WEAPONS ARE, WELL, THEY'RE IDEAS, I GUESS?
YOU CAN MAKE THEM TAKE AN EASIER-TO-CARRY FORM. I CHOSE A TATTOO. SEEMS CONVENIENT.
IN THIS EARTH ERA, IN THIS CITY IN PARTICULAR, YES.
WHOA! IT ITCHES.
WHERE'S YOUR AXE TAT?
YOU CAN SEARCH ME FOR IT LATER.
LET'S TEST THEM OUT.
OH GREAT, THEY'RE ALL ARMED NOW.

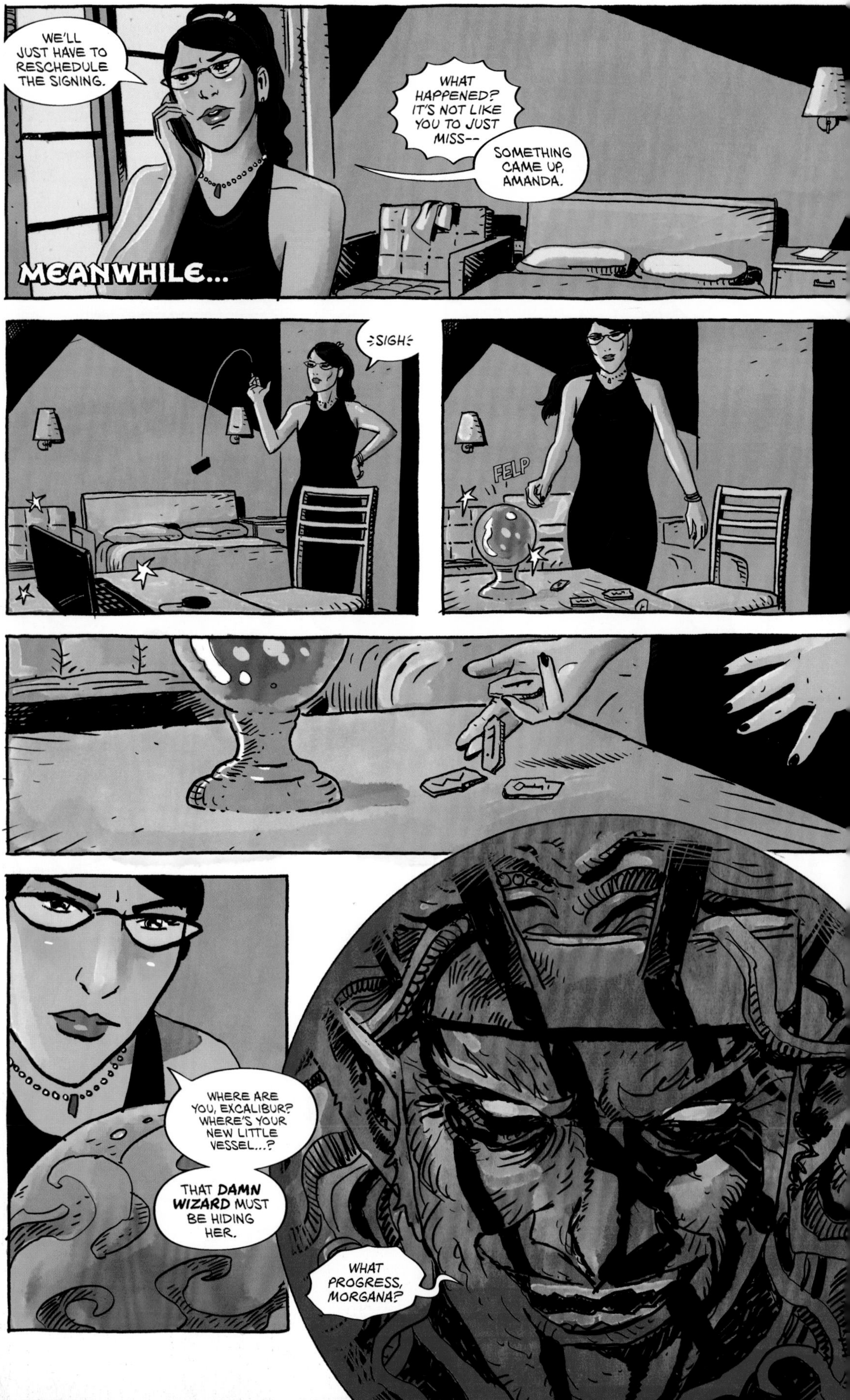
WE'LL JUST HAVE TO RESCHEDULE THE SIGNING.
WHAT HAPPENED? IT'S NOT LIKE YOU TO JUST MISS--
SOMETHING CAME UP, AMANDA.
MEANWHILE...
SIGH
FELP
WHERE ARE YOU, EXCALIBUR? WHERE'S YOUR NEW LITTLE VESSEL...?
THAT DAMN WIZARD MUST BE HIDING HER.
WHAT PROGRESS, MORGANA?

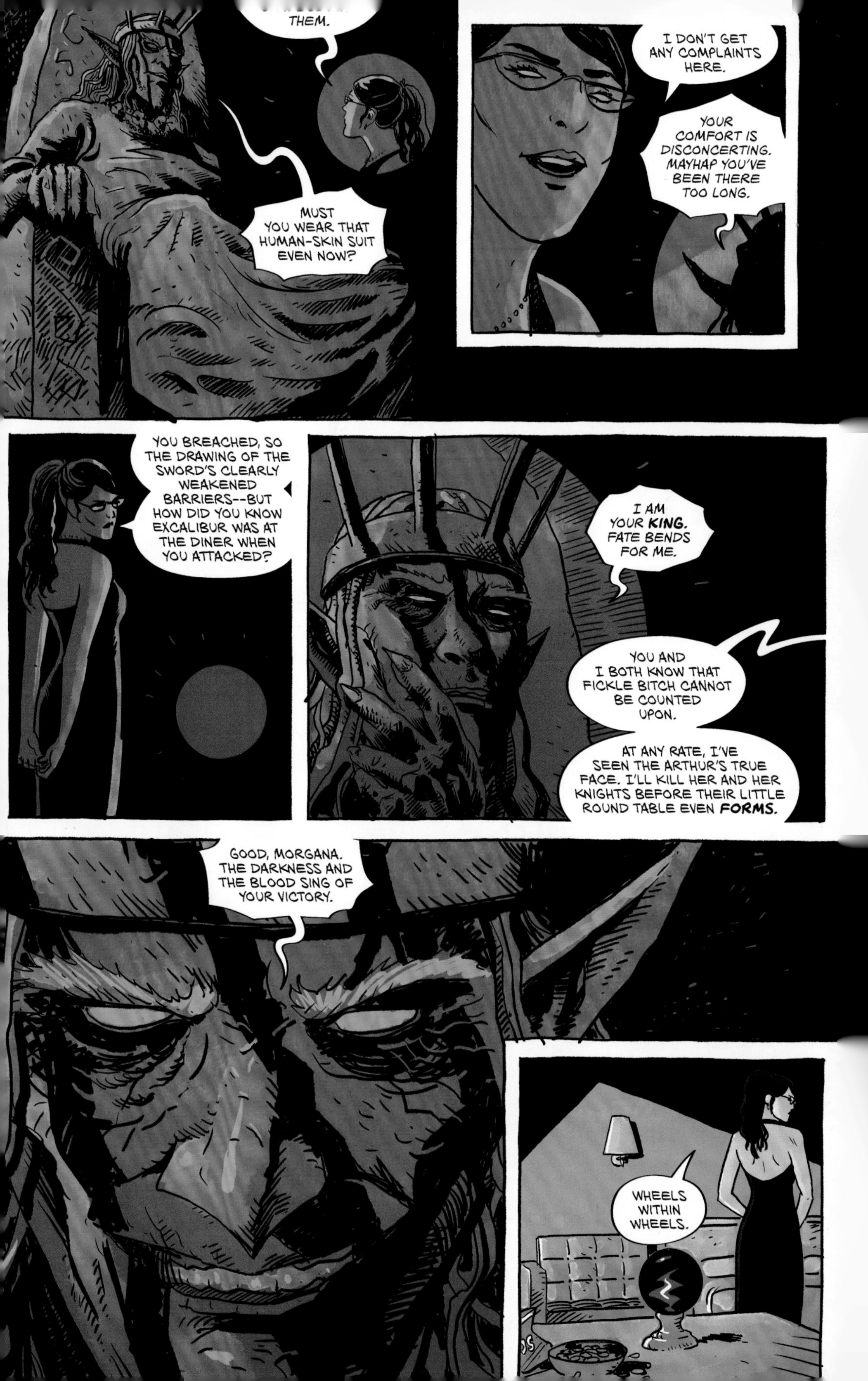
THEM.
MUST YOU WEAR THAT HUMAN-SKIN SUIT EVEN NOW?
I DON'T GET ANY COMPLAINTS HERE.
YOUR COMFORT IS DISCONCERTING. MAYHAP YOU'VE BEEN THERE TOO LONG.
YOU BREACHED, SO THE DRAWING OF THE SWORD'S CLEARLY WEAKENED BARRIERS--BUT HOW DID YOU KNOW EXCALIBUR WAS AT THE DINER WHEN YOU ATTACKED?
I AM YOUR KING. FATE BENDS FOR ME.
YOU AND I BOTH KNOW THAT FICKLE BITCH CANNOT BE COUNTED UPON.
AT ANY RATE, I'VE SEEN THE ARTHUR'S TRUE FACE. I'LL KILL HER AND HER KNIGHTS BEFORE THEIR LITTLE ROUND TABLE EVEN FORMS.
GOOD, MORGANA. THE DARKNESS AND THE BLOOD SING OF YOUR VICTORY.
WHEELS WITHIN WHEELS.

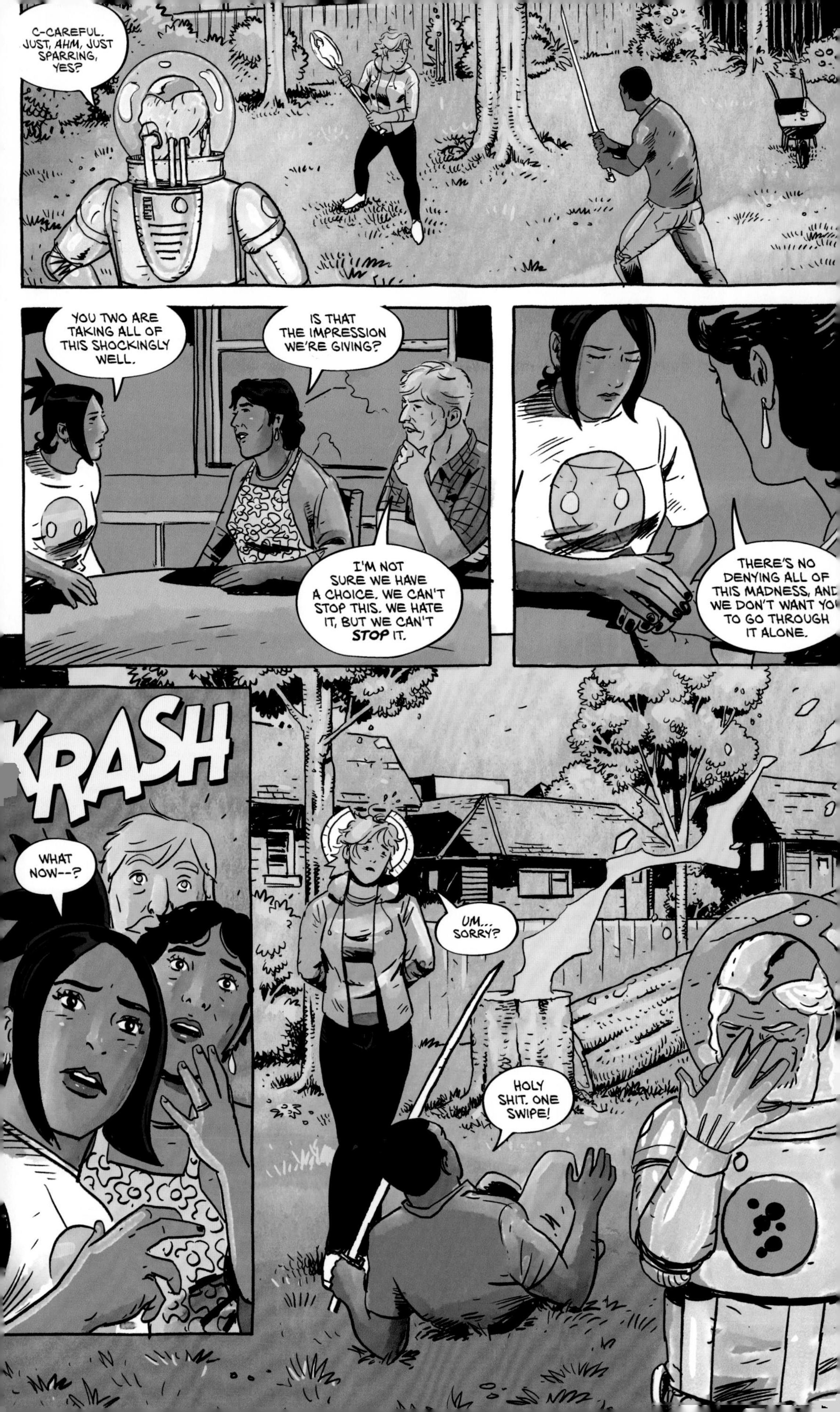
C-CAREFUL. JUST, AHM, JUST SPARRING, YES?
YOU TWO ARE TAKING ALL OF THIS SHOCKINGLY WELL.
IS THAT THE IMPRESSION WE'RE GIVING?
I'M NOT SURE WE HAVE A CHOICE. WE CAN'T STOP THIS. WE HATE IT, BUT WE CAN'T STOP IT.
THERE'S NO DENYING ALL OF THIS MADNESS, AND WE DON'T WANT YOU TO GO THROUGH IT ALONE.
KRASH
WHAT NOW--?
UM... SORRY?
HOLY SHIT. ONE SWIPE!

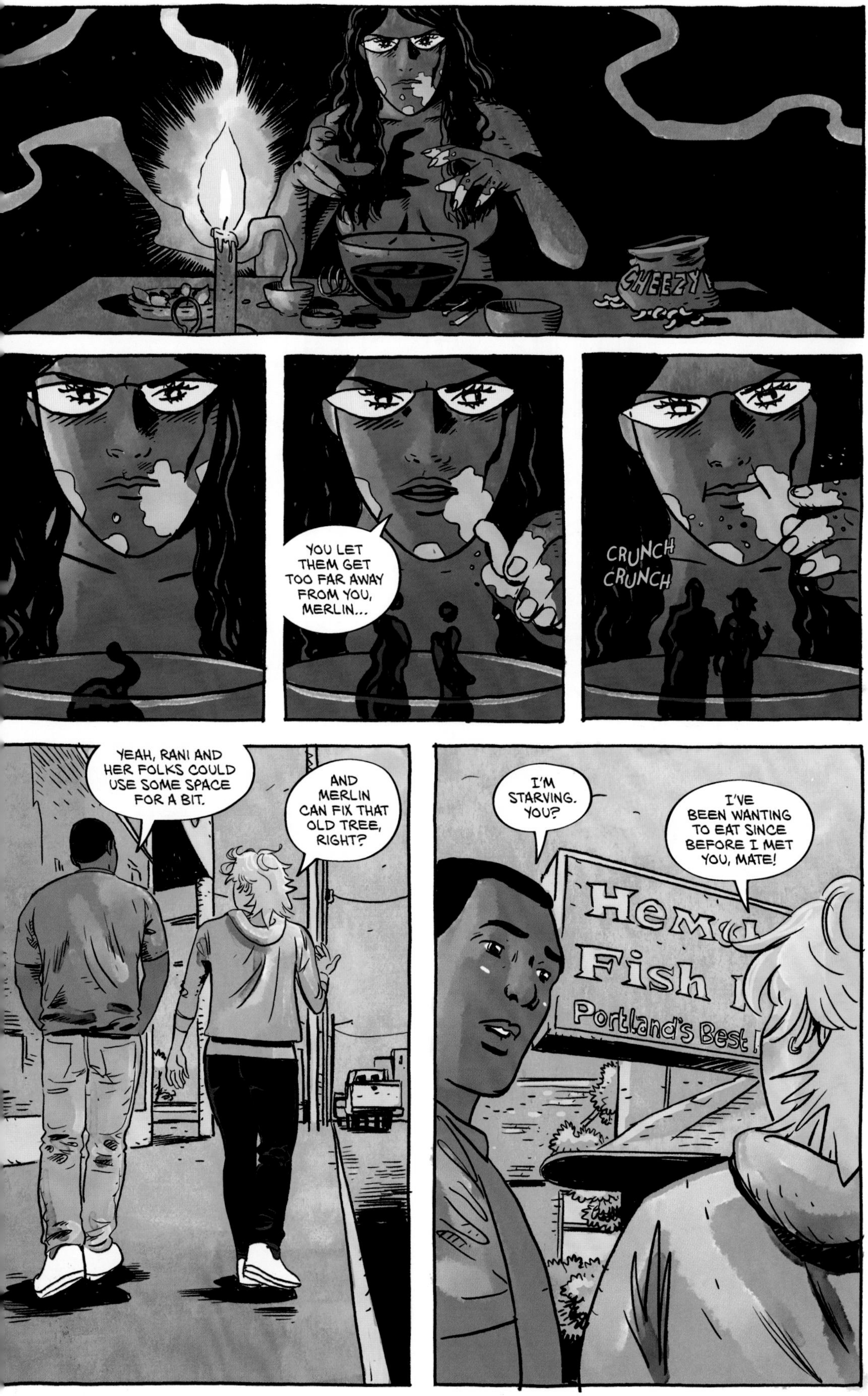
CHEEZY
YOU LET THEM GET TOO FAR AWAY FROM YOU, MERLIN...
CRUNCH CRUNCH
YEAH, RANI AND HER FOLKS COULD USE SOME SPACE FOR A BIT.
AND MERLIN CAN FIX THAT OLD TREE, RIGHT?
I'M STARVING. YOU?
I'VE BEEN WANTING TO EAT SINCE BEFORE I MET YOU, MATE!
Fish
Portland's Best

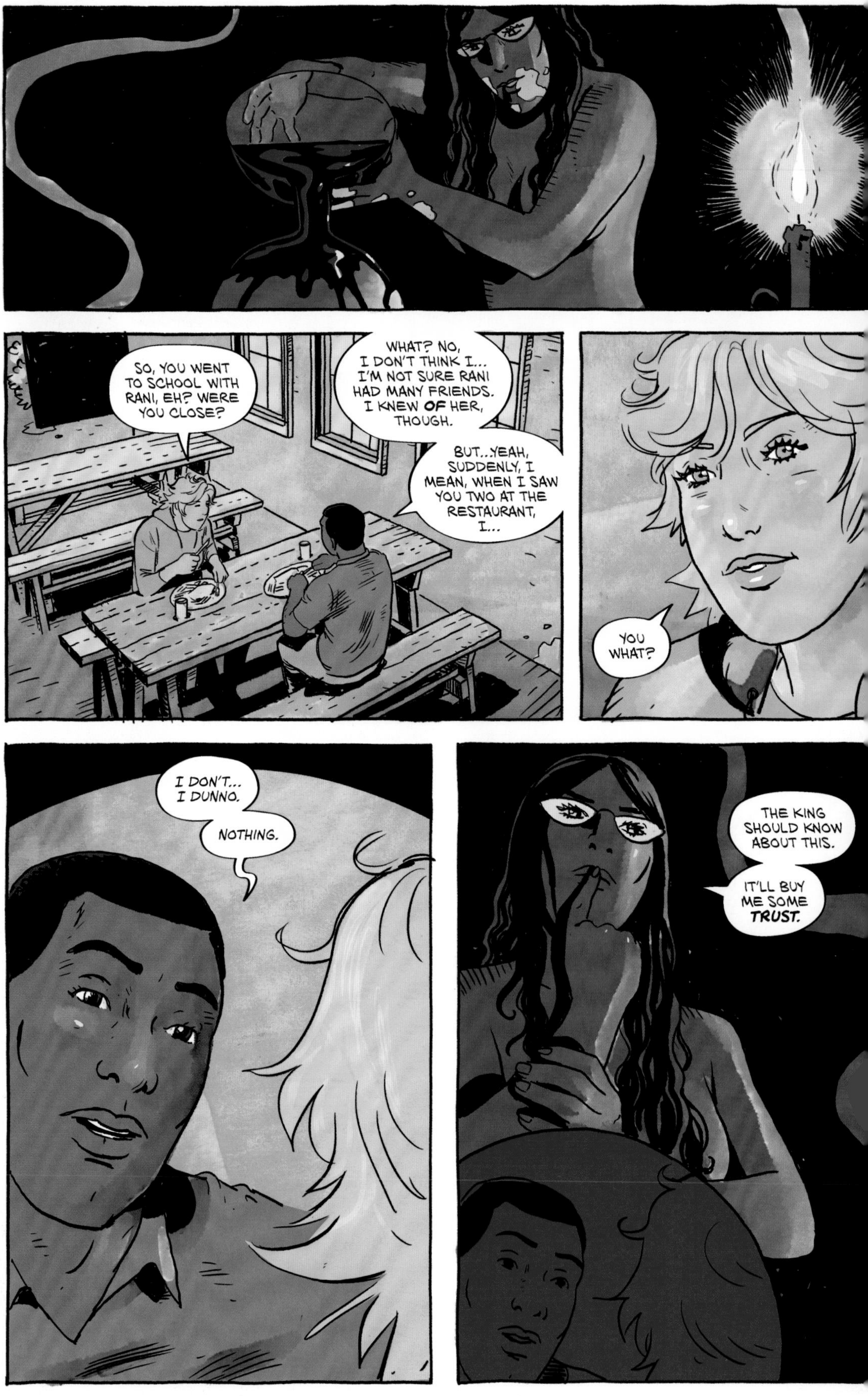

SO, YOU WENT TO SCHOOL WITH RANI, EH? WERE YOU CLOSE?
WHAT? NO, I DON'T THINK I... I'M NOT SURE RANI HAD MANY FRIENDS. I KNEW **OF** HER, THOUGH.
BUT...YEAH, SUDDENLY, I MEAN, WHEN I SAW YOU TWO AT THE RESTAURANT, I...
YOU WHAT?
I DON'T... I DUNNO.
NOTHING.
THE KING SHOULD KNOW ABOUT THIS.
IT'LL BUY ME SOME ***TRUST.***

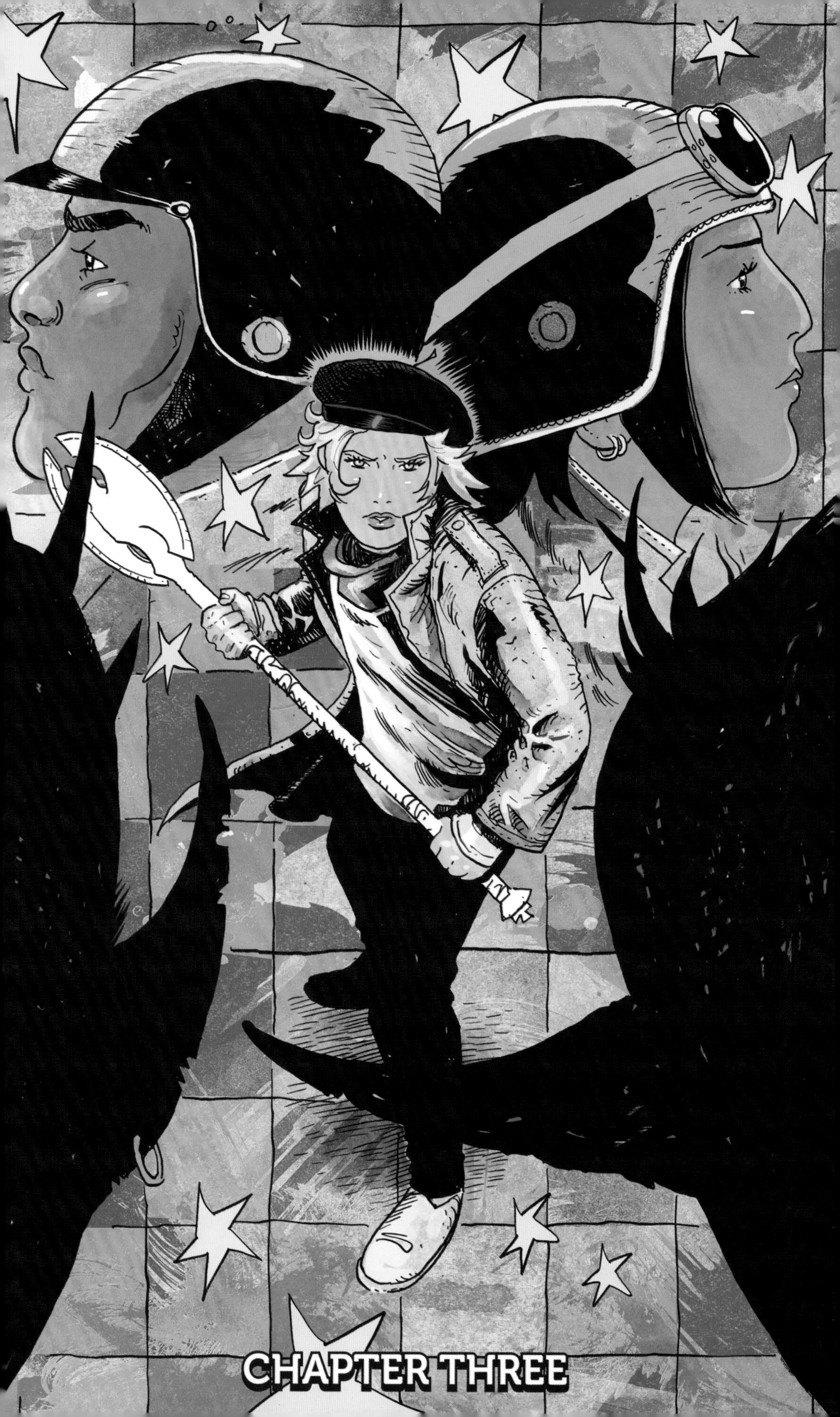
CHAPTER THREE

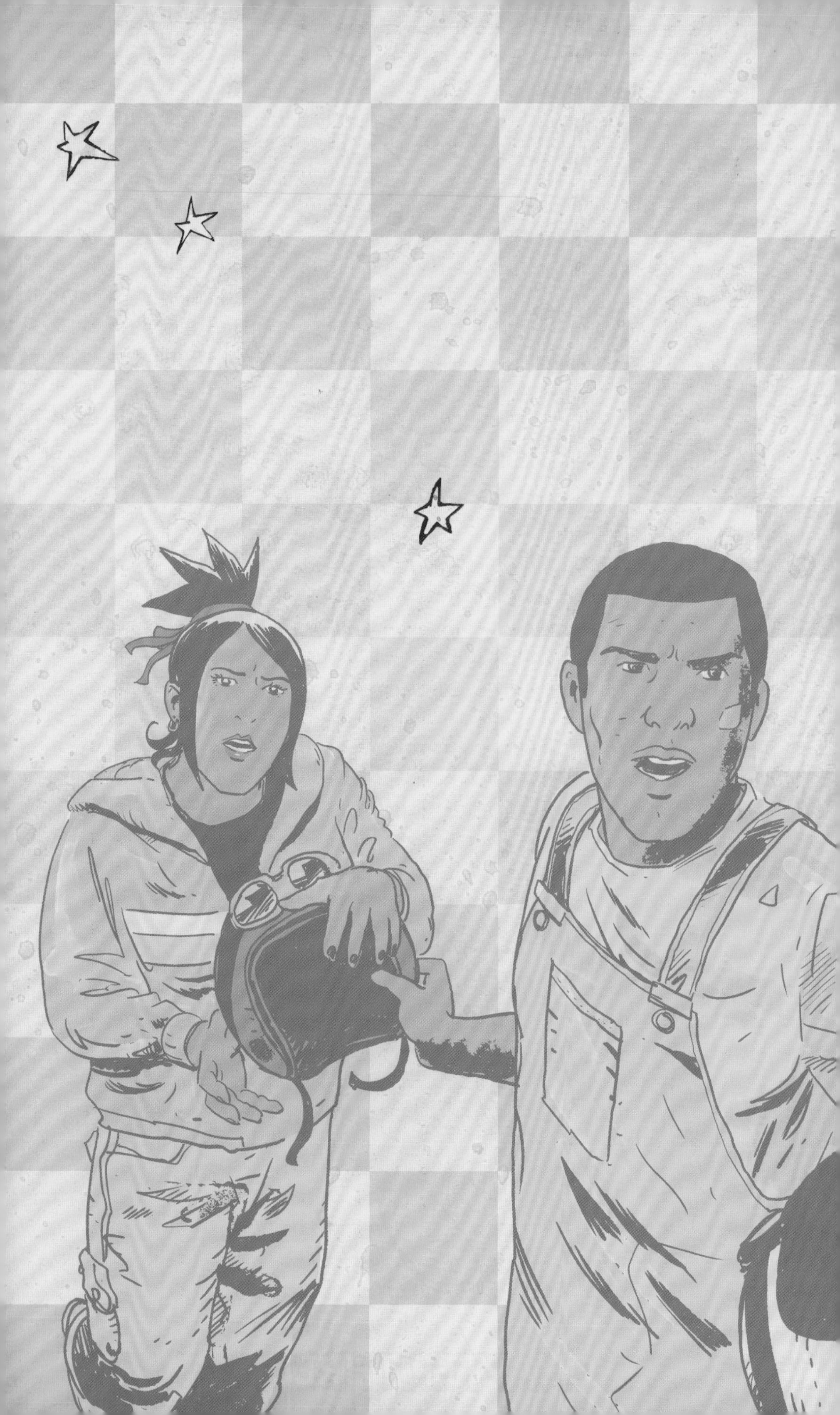

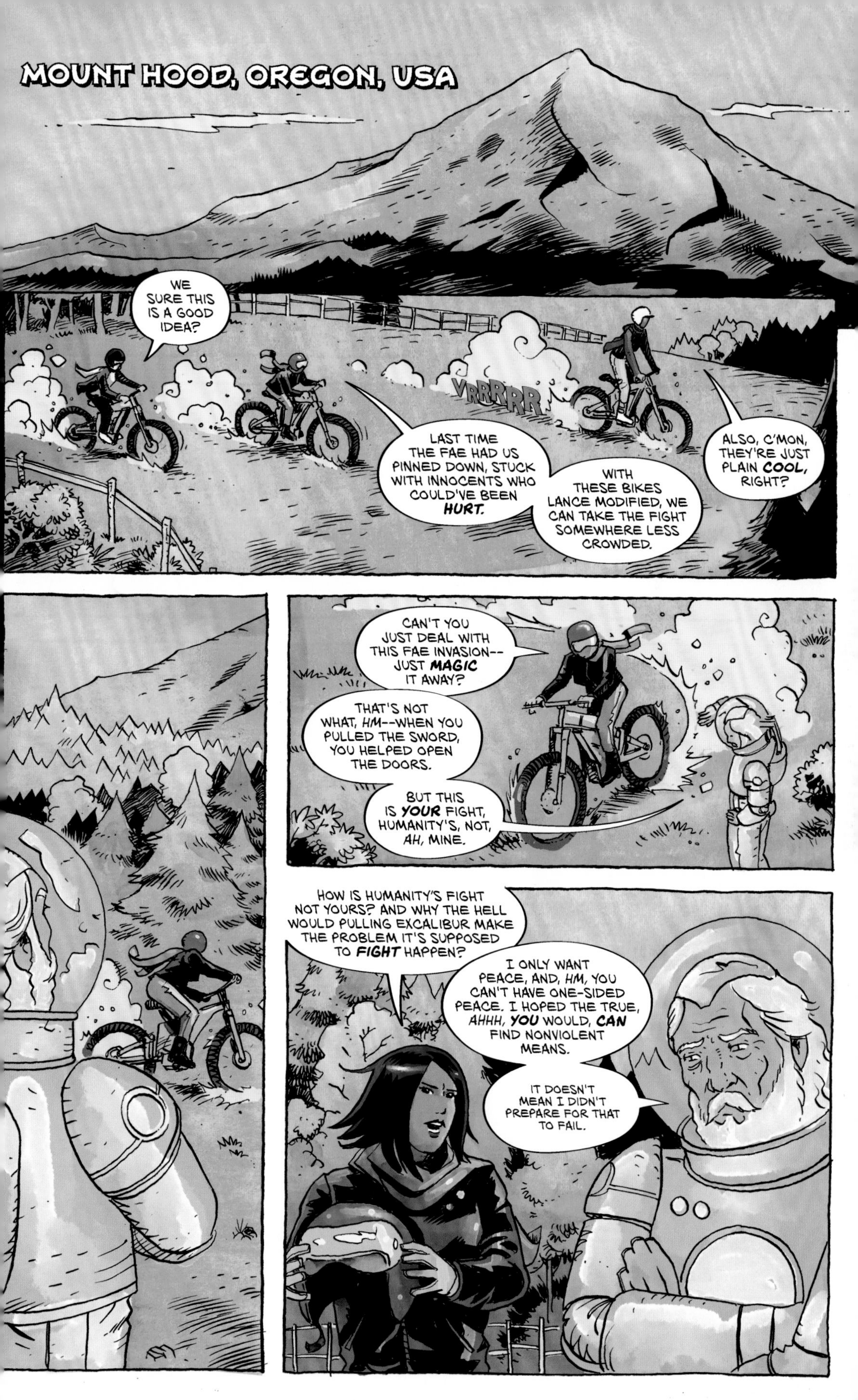
MOUNT HOOD, OREGON, USA
WE SURE THIS IS A GOOD IDEA?
VRRRRR
LAST TIME THE FAE HAD US PINNED DOWN, STUCK WITH INNOCENTS WHO COULD'VE BEEN HURT.
WITH THESE BIKES LANCE MODIFIED, WE CAN TAKE THE FIGHT SOMEWHERE LESS CROWDED.
ALSO, C'MON, THEY'RE JUST PLAIN COOL, RIGHT?
CAN'T YOU JUST DEAL WITH THIS FAE INVASION-- JUST MAGIC IT AWAY?
THAT'S NOT WHAT, HM--WHEN YOU PULLED THE SWORD, YOU HELPED OPEN THE DOORS.
BUT THIS IS YOUR FIGHT, HUMANITY'S, NOT, AH, MINE.
HOW IS HUMANITY'S FIGHT NOT YOURS? AND WHY THE HELL WOULD PULLING EXCALIBUR MAKE THE PROBLEM IT'S SUPPOSED TO FIGHT HAPPEN?
I ONLY WANT PEACE, AND, HM, YOU CAN'T HAVE ONE-SIDED PEACE. I HOPED THE TRUE, AHHH, YOU WOULD, CAN FIND NONVIOLENT MEANS.
IT DOESN'T MEAN I DIDN'T PREPARE FOR THAT TO FAIL.

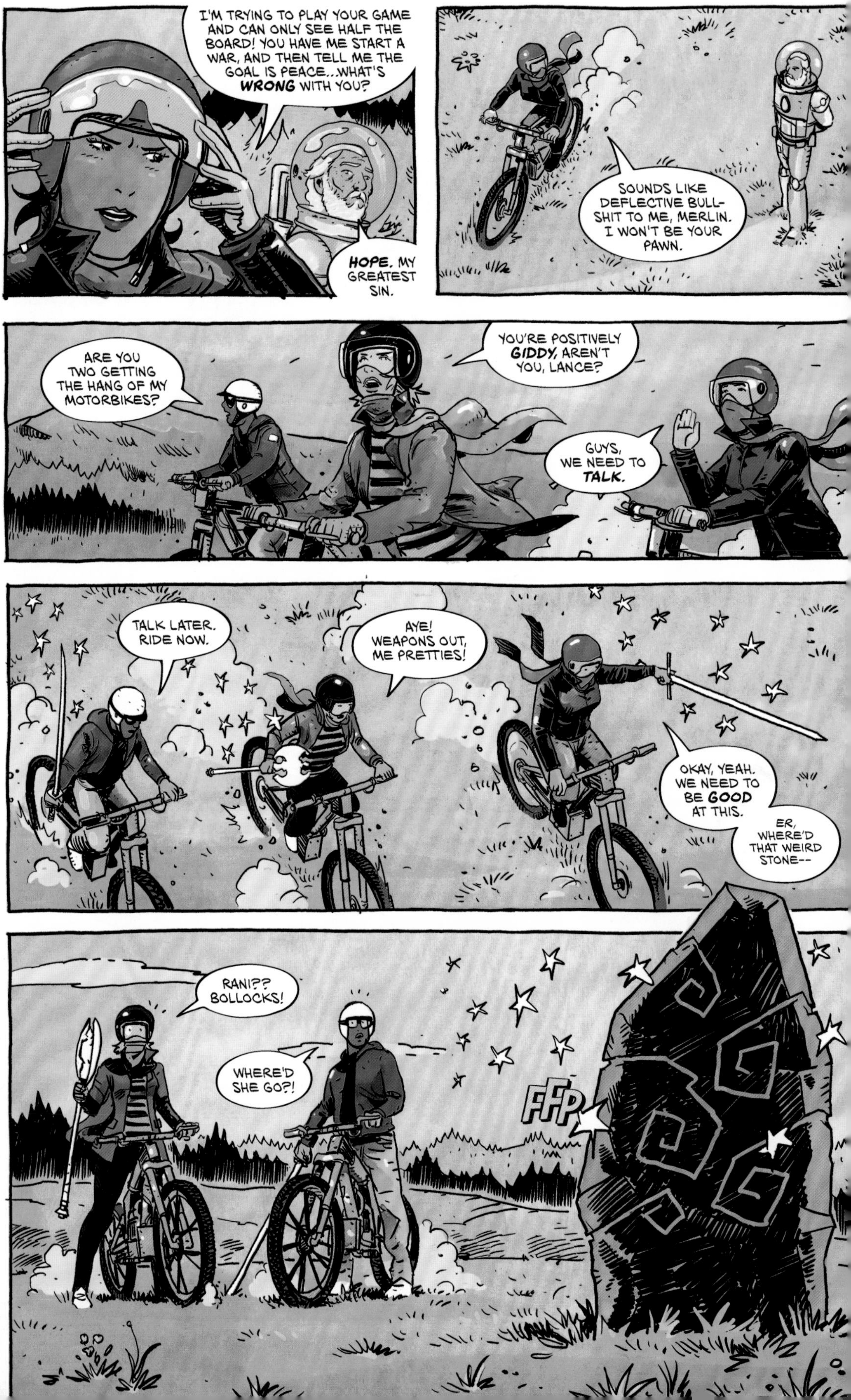
I'M TRYING TO PLAY YOUR GAME AND CAN ONLY SEE HALF THE BOARD! YOU HAVE ME START A WAR, AND THEN TELL ME THE GOAL IS PEACE...WHAT'S **WRONG** WITH YOU?
HOPE. MY GREATEST SIN.
SOUNDS LIKE DEFLECTIVE BULL-SHIT TO ME, MERLIN. I WON'T BE YOUR PAWN.
ARE YOU TWO GETTING THE HANG OF MY MOTORBIKES?
YOU'RE POSITIVELY **GIDDY,** AREN'T YOU, LANCE?
GUYS, WE NEED TO **TALK.**
TALK LATER. RIDE NOW.
AYE! WEAPONS OUT, ME PRETTIES!
OKAY, YEAH. WE NEED TO BE **GOOD** AT THIS.
ER, WHERE'D THAT WEIRD STONE--
RANI?? BOLLOCKS!
WHERE'D SHE GO?!
FFP

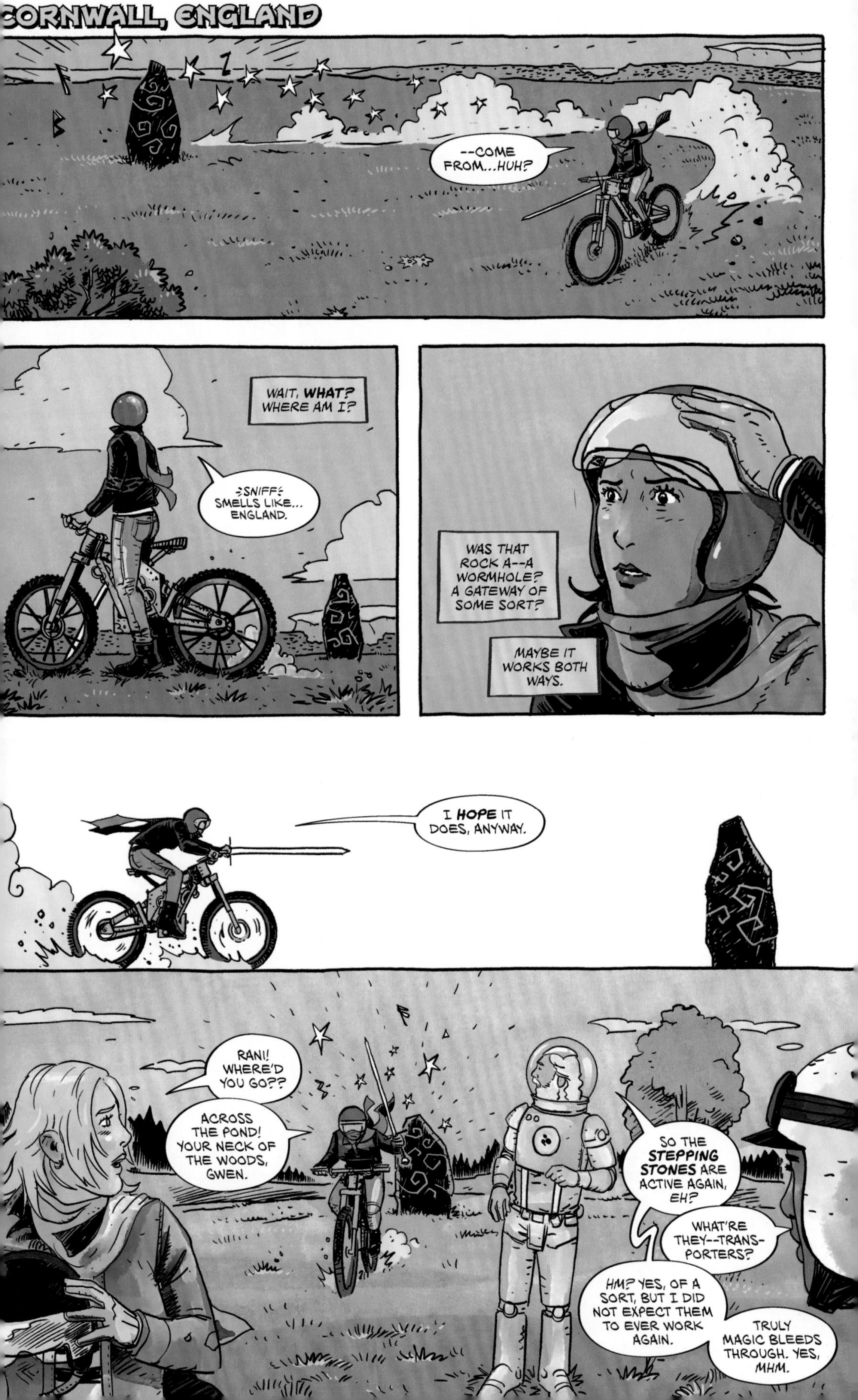
CORNWALL, ENGLAND
--COME FROM...HUH?
WAIT, WHAT? WHERE AM I?
SNIFF SMELLS LIKE... ENGLAND.
WAS THAT ROCK A--A WORMHOLE? A GATEWAY OF SOME SORT?
MAYBE IT WORKS BOTH WAYS.
I HOPE IT DOES, ANYWAY.
RANI! WHERE'D YOU GO??
ACROSS THE POND! YOUR NECK OF THE WOODS, GWEN.
SO THE STEPPING STONES ARE ACTIVE AGAIN, EH?
WHAT'RE THEY--TRANSPORTERS?
HM? YES, OF A SORT, BUT I DID NOT EXPECT THEM TO EVER WORK AGAIN.
TRULY MAGIC BLEEDS THROUGH. YES, MHM.

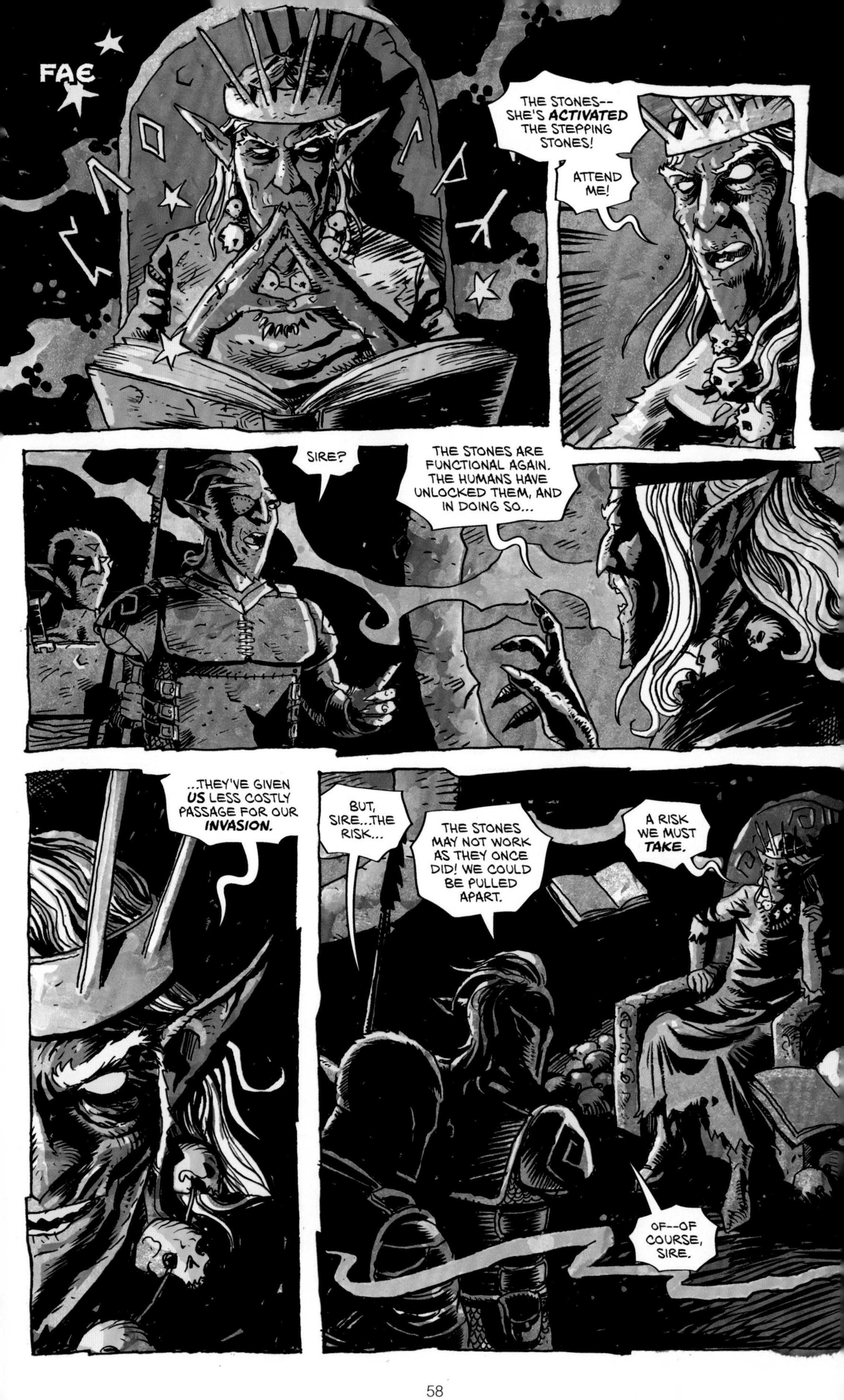
FAE
THE STONES-- SHE'S ACTIVATED THE STEPPING STONES!
ATTEND ME!
SIRE?
THE STONES ARE FUNCTIONAL AGAIN. THE HUMANS HAVE UNLOCKED THEM, AND IN DOING SO...
...THEY'VE GIVEN US LESS COSTLY PASSAGE FOR OUR INVASION.
BUT, SIRE...THE RISK...
THE STONES MAY NOT WORK AS THEY ONCE DID! WE COULD BE PULLED APART.
A RISK WE MUST TAKE.
OF--OF COURSE, SIRE.

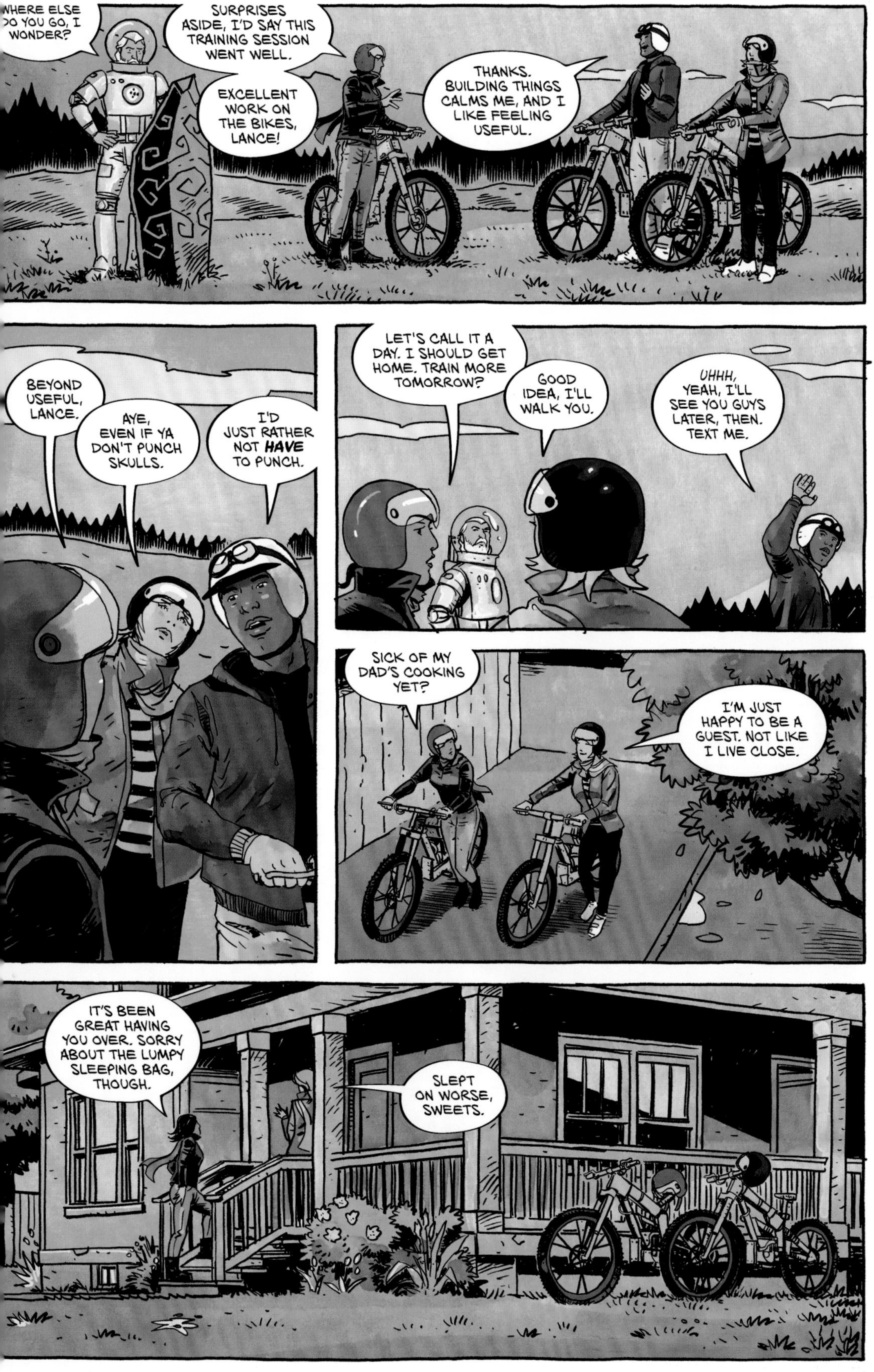
WHERE ELSE DO YOU GO, I WONDER?
SURPRISES ASIDE, I'D SAY THIS TRAINING SESSION WENT WELL.
EXCELLENT WORK ON THE BIKES, LANCE!
THANKS. BUILDING THINGS CALMS ME, AND I LIKE FEELING USEFUL.
BEYOND USEFUL, LANCE.
AYE, EVEN IF YA DON'T PUNCH SKULLS.
I'D JUST RATHER NOT HAVE TO PUNCH.
LET'S CALL IT A DAY. I SHOULD GET HOME. TRAIN MORE TOMORROW?
GOOD IDEA, I'LL WALK YOU.
UHHH, YEAH, I'LL SEE YOU GUYS LATER, THEN. TEXT ME.
SICK OF MY DAD'S COOKING YET?
I'M JUST HAPPY TO BE A GUEST. NOT LIKE I LIVE CLOSE.
IT'S BEEN GREAT HAVING YOU OVER. SORRY ABOUT THE LUMPY SLEEPING BAG, THOUGH.
SLEPT ON WORSE, SWEETS.

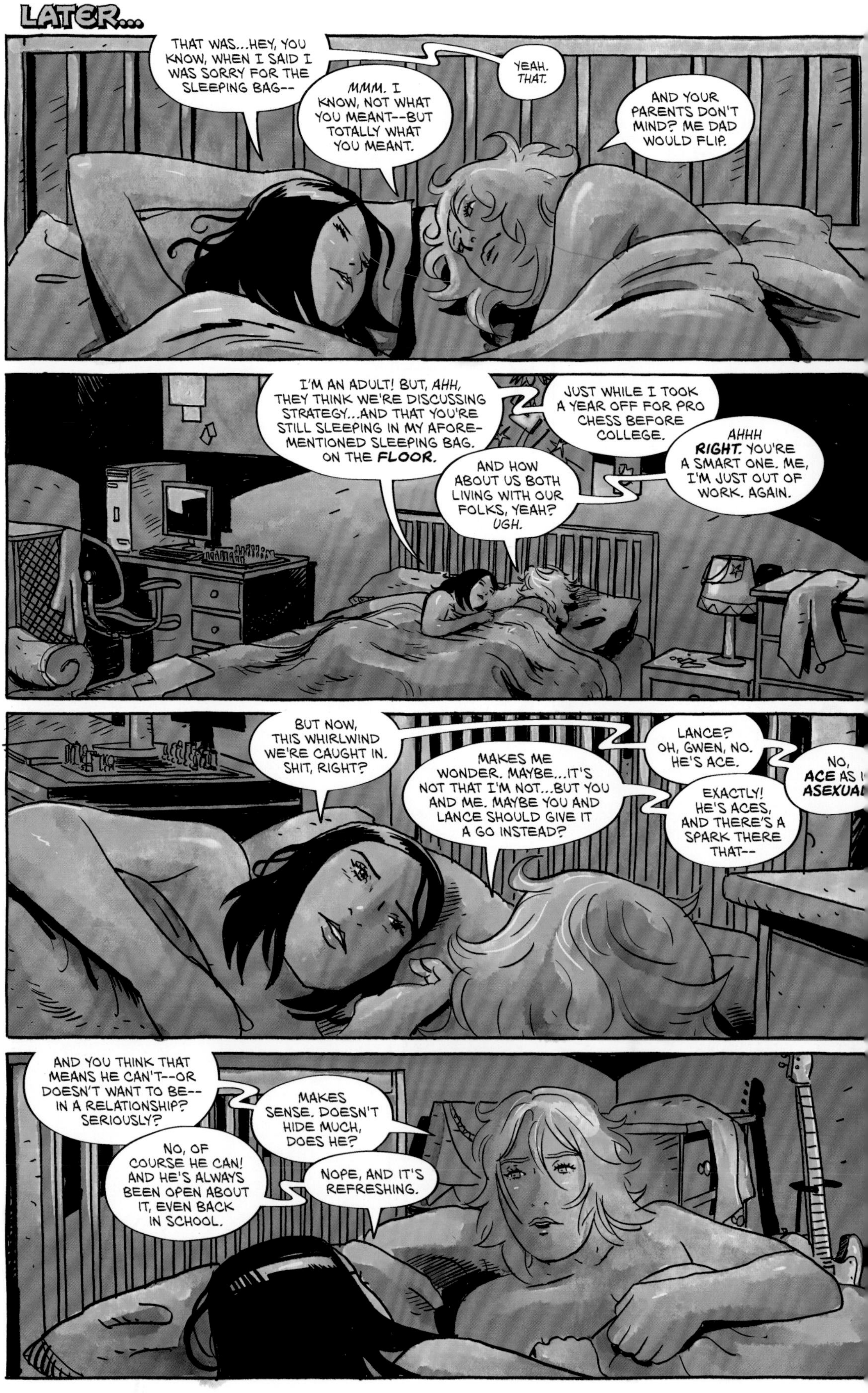
LATER...
THAT WAS...HEY, YOU KNOW, WHEN I SAID I WAS SORRY FOR THE SLEEPING BAG--
MMM. I KNOW, NOT WHAT YOU MEANT--BUT TOTALLY WHAT YOU MEANT.
YEAH. THAT.
AND YOUR PARENTS DON'T MIND? ME DAD WOULD FLIP.
I'M AN ADULT! BUT, AHH, THEY THINK WE'RE DISCUSSING STRATEGY...AND THAT YOU'RE STILL SLEEPING IN MY AFORE-MENTIONED SLEEPING BAG. ON THE FLOOR.
JUST WHILE I TOOK A YEAR OFF FOR PRO CHESS BEFORE COLLEGE.
AND HOW ABOUT US BOTH LIVING WITH OUR FOLKS, YEAH? UGH.
AHHH RIGHT. YOU'RE A SMART ONE. ME, I'M JUST OUT OF WORK. AGAIN.
BUT NOW, THIS WHIRLWIND WE'RE CAUGHT IN. SHIT, RIGHT?
MAKES ME WONDER. MAYBE...IT'S NOT THAT I'M NOT...BUT YOU AND ME. MAYBE YOU AND LANCE SHOULD GIVE IT A GO INSTEAD?
LANCE? OH, GWEN, NO. HE'S ACE.
EXACTLY! HE'S ACES, AND THERE'S A SPARK THERE THAT--
NO, ACE AS I
ASEXUA
AND YOU THINK THAT MEANS HE CAN'T--OR DOESN'T WANT TO BE--IN A RELATIONSHIP? SERIOUSLY?
MAKES SENSE. DOESN'T HIDE MUCH, DOES HE?
NO, OF COURSE HE CAN! AND HE'S ALWAYS BEEN OPEN ABOUT IT, EVEN BACK IN SCHOOL.
NOPE, AND IT'S REFRESHING.

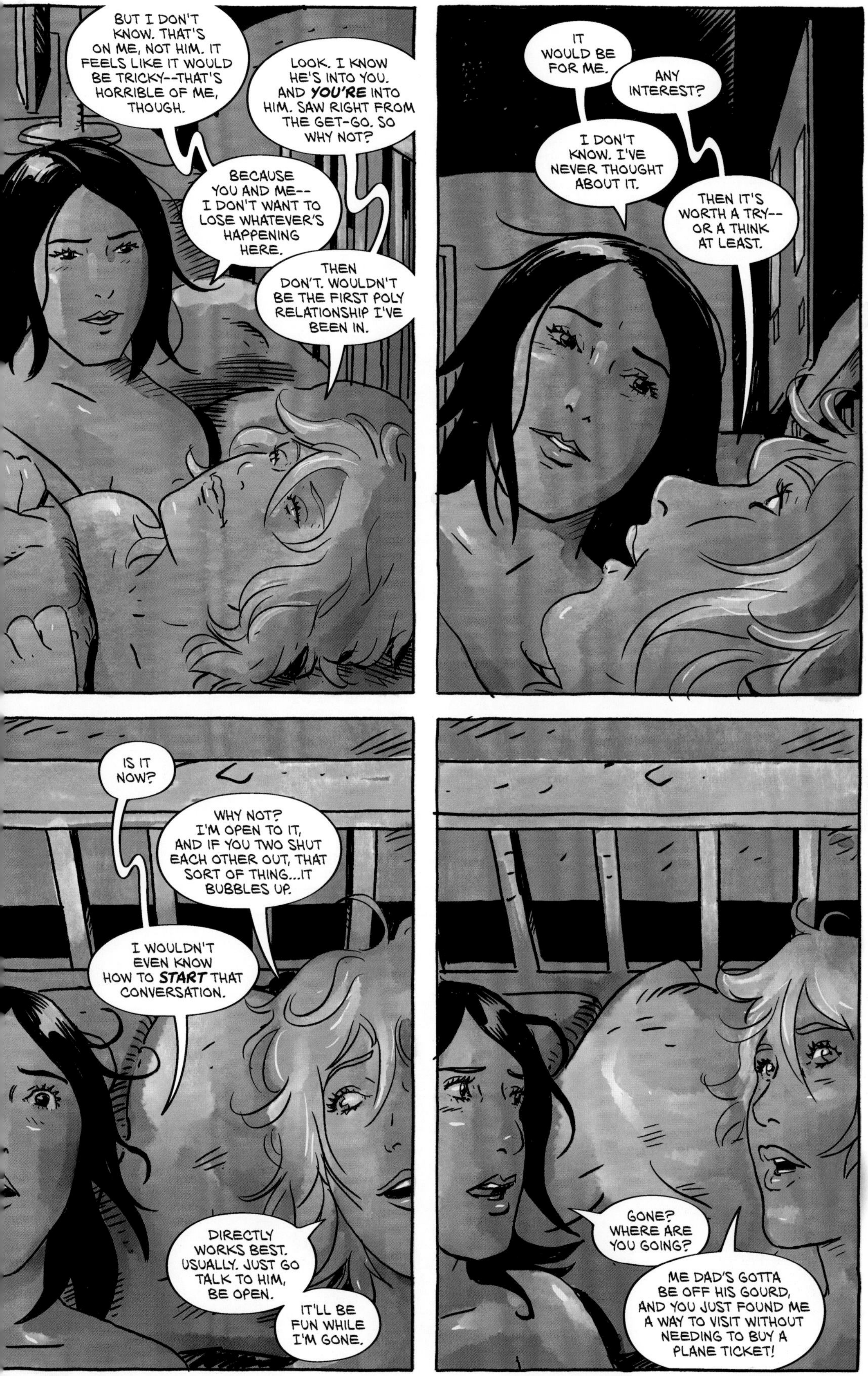
BUT I DON'T KNOW. THAT'S ON ME, NOT HIM. IT FEELS LIKE IT WOULD BE TRICKY--THAT'S HORRIBLE OF ME, THOUGH.
LOOK. I KNOW HE'S INTO YOU. AND YOU'RE INTO HIM. SAW RIGHT FROM THE GET-GO. SO WHY NOT?
BECAUSE YOU AND ME-- I DON'T WANT TO LOSE WHATEVER'S HAPPENING HERE.
THEN DON'T. WOULDN'T BE THE FIRST POLY RELATIONSHIP I'VE BEEN IN.
IT WOULD BE FOR ME.
ANY INTEREST?
I DON'T KNOW. I'VE NEVER THOUGHT ABOUT IT.
THEN IT'S WORTH A TRY-- OR A THINK AT LEAST.
IS IT NOW?
WHY NOT? I'M OPEN TO IT, AND IF YOU TWO SHUT EACH OTHER OUT, THAT SORT OF THING...IT BUBBLES UP.
I WOULDN'T EVEN KNOW HOW TO START THAT CONVERSATION.
DIRECTLY WORKS BEST. USUALLY. JUST GO TALK TO HIM, BE OPEN.
IT'LL BE FUN WHILE I'M GONE.
GONE? WHERE ARE YOU GOING?
ME DAD'S GOTTA BE OFF HIS GOURD, AND YOU JUST FOUND ME A WAY TO VISIT WITHOUT NEEDING TO BUY A PLANE TICKET!

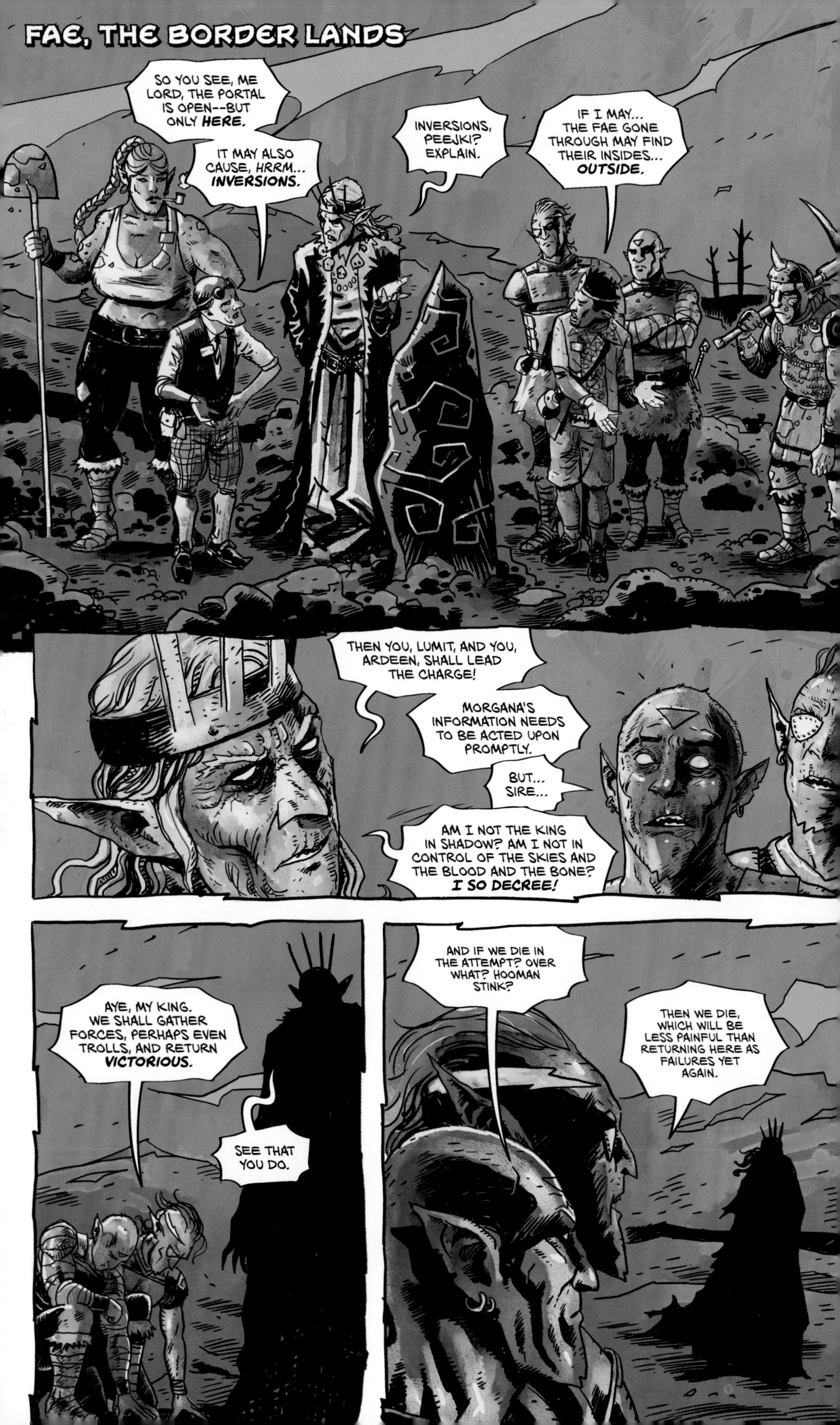
FAE, THE BORDER LANDS
SO YOU SEE, ME LORD, THE PORTAL IS OPEN--BUT ONLY HERE.
IT MAY ALSO CAUSE, HRRM... INVERSIONS.
INVERSIONS, PEEJKI? EXPLAIN.
IF I MAY... THE FAE GONE THROUGH MAY FIND THEIR INSIDES... OUTSIDE.
THEN YOU, LUMIT, AND YOU, ARDEEN, SHALL LEAD THE CHARGE!
MORGANA'S INFORMATION NEEDS TO BE ACTED UPON PROMPTLY.
BUT... SIRE...
AM I NOT THE KING IN SHADOW? AM I NOT IN CONTROL OF THE SKIES AND THE BLOOD AND THE BONE? I SO DECREE!
AYE, MY KING. WE SHALL GATHER FORCES, PERHAPS EVEN TROLLS, AND RETURN VICTORIOUS.
SEE THAT YOU DO.
AND IF WE DIE IN THE ATTEMPT? OVER WHAT? HOOMAN STINK?
THEN WE DIE, WHICH WILL BE LESS PAINFUL THAN RETURNING HERE AS FAILURES YET AGAIN.

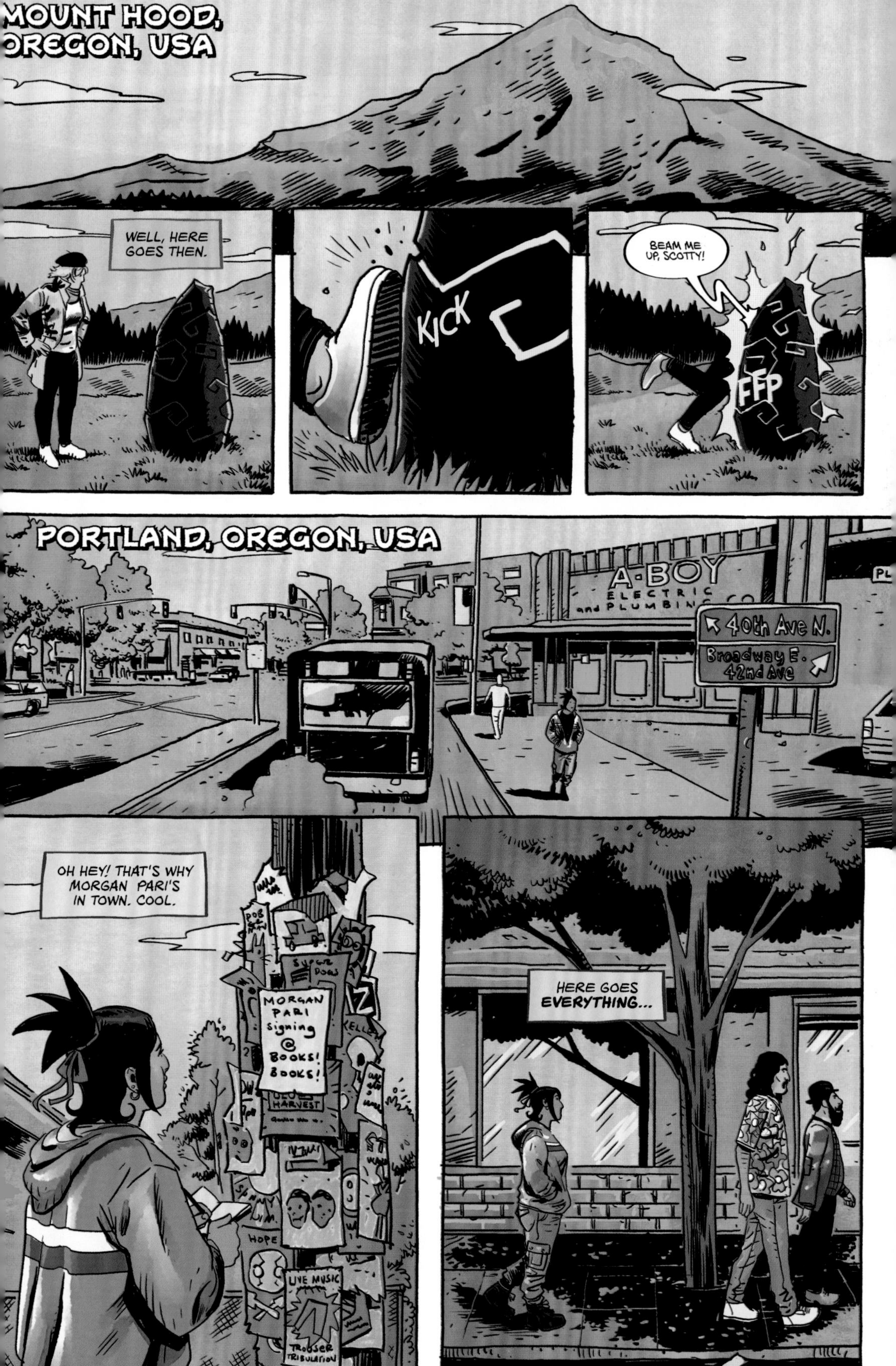
MOUNT HOOD, OREGON, USA
WELL, HERE GOES THEN.
KICK
BEAM ME UP, SCOTTY!
FFP
PORTLAND, OREGON, USA
A-BOY ELECTRIC and PLUMBING
40th Ave N.
Broadway E. 42nd Ave
OH HEY! THAT'S WHY MORGAN PARI'S IN TOWN. COOL.
MORGAN PARI signing @ BOOKS! BOOKS!
HARVEST
HOPE
LIVE MUSIC
TROUSER TRIBULATION
HERE GOES EVERYTHING...

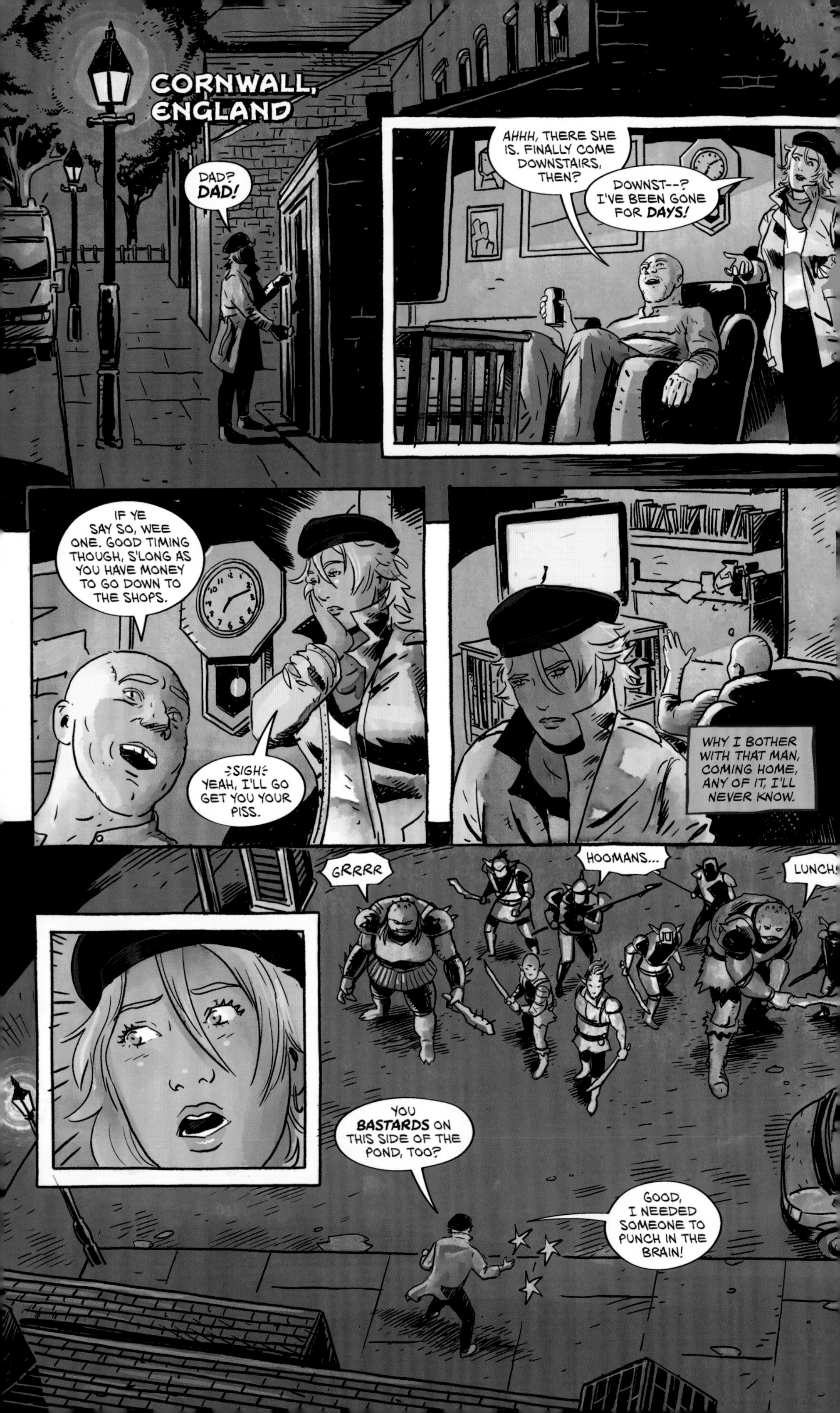
CORNWALL, ENGLAND
DAD? DAD!
AHHH, THERE SHE IS. FINALLY COME DOWNSTAIRS, THEN?
DOWNST--? I'VE BEEN GONE FOR DAYS!
IF YE SAY SO, WEE ONE. GOOD TIMING THOUGH, S'LONG AS YOU HAVE MONEY TO GO DOWN TO THE SHOPS.
SIGH YEAH, I'LL GO GET YOU YOUR PISS.
WHY I BOTHER WITH THAT MAN, COMING HOME, ANY OF IT, I'LL NEVER KNOW.
GRRRR
HOOMANS...
LUNCH!
YOU BASTARDS ON THIS SIDE OF THE POND, TOO?
GOOD, I NEEDED SOMEONE TO PUNCH IN THE BRAIN!

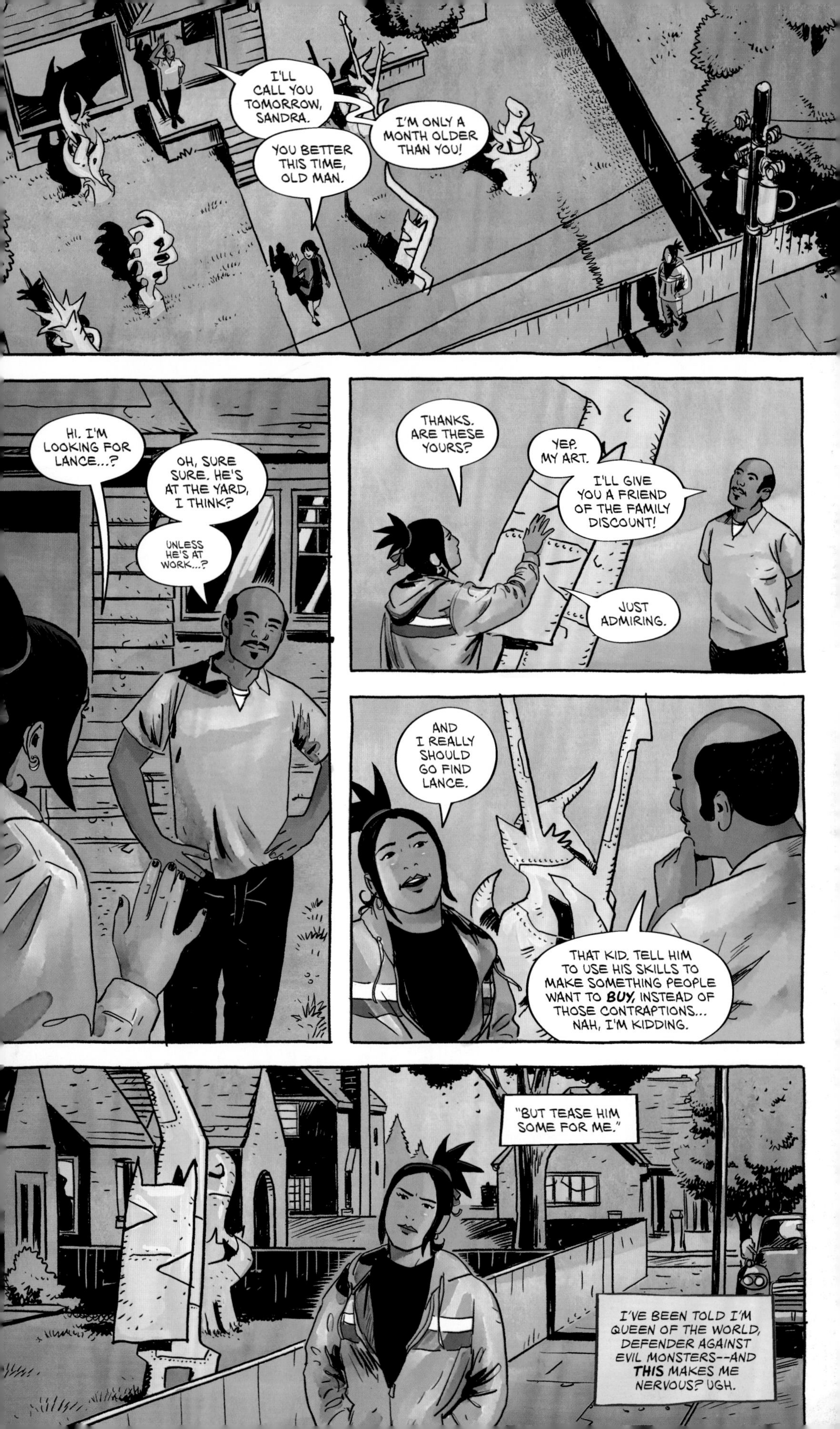
I'LL CALL YOU TOMORROW, SANDRA.
YOU BETTER THIS TIME, OLD MAN.
I'M ONLY A MONTH OLDER THAN YOU!
HI. I'M LOOKING FOR LANCE...?
OH, SURE SURE. HE'S AT THE YARD, I THINK?
UNLESS HE'S AT WORK...?
THANKS. ARE THESE YOURS?
YEP. MY ART.
I'LL GIVE YOU A FRIEND OF THE FAMILY DISCOUNT!
JUST ADMIRING.
AND I REALLY SHOULD GO FIND LANCE.
THAT KID. TELL HIM TO USE HIS SKILLS TO MAKE SOMETHING PEOPLE WANT TO **BUY,** INSTEAD OF THOSE CONTRAPTIONS... NAH, I'M KIDDING.
"BUT TEASE HIM SOME FOR ME."
I'VE BEEN TOLD I'M QUEEN OF THE WORLD, DEFENDER AGAINST EVIL MONSTERS--AND **THIS** MAKES ME NERVOUS? UGH.

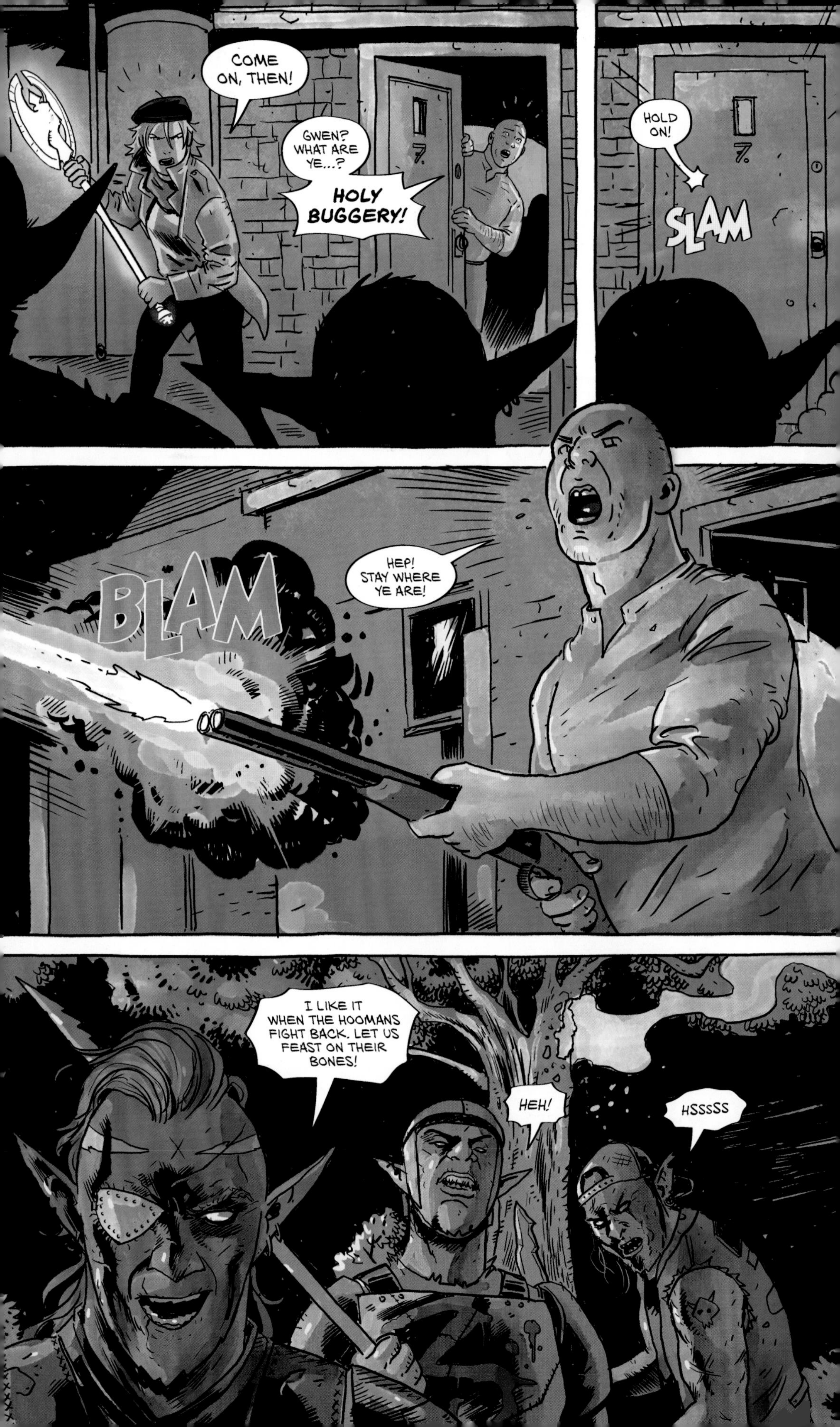
COME ON, THEN!
GWEN? WHAT ARE YE...?
HOLY BUGGERY!
HOLD ON!
SLAM
BLAM
HEP! STAY WHERE YE ARE!
I LIKE IT WHEN THE HOOMANS FIGHT BACK. LET US FEAST ON THEIR BONES!
HEH!
HSSSSS

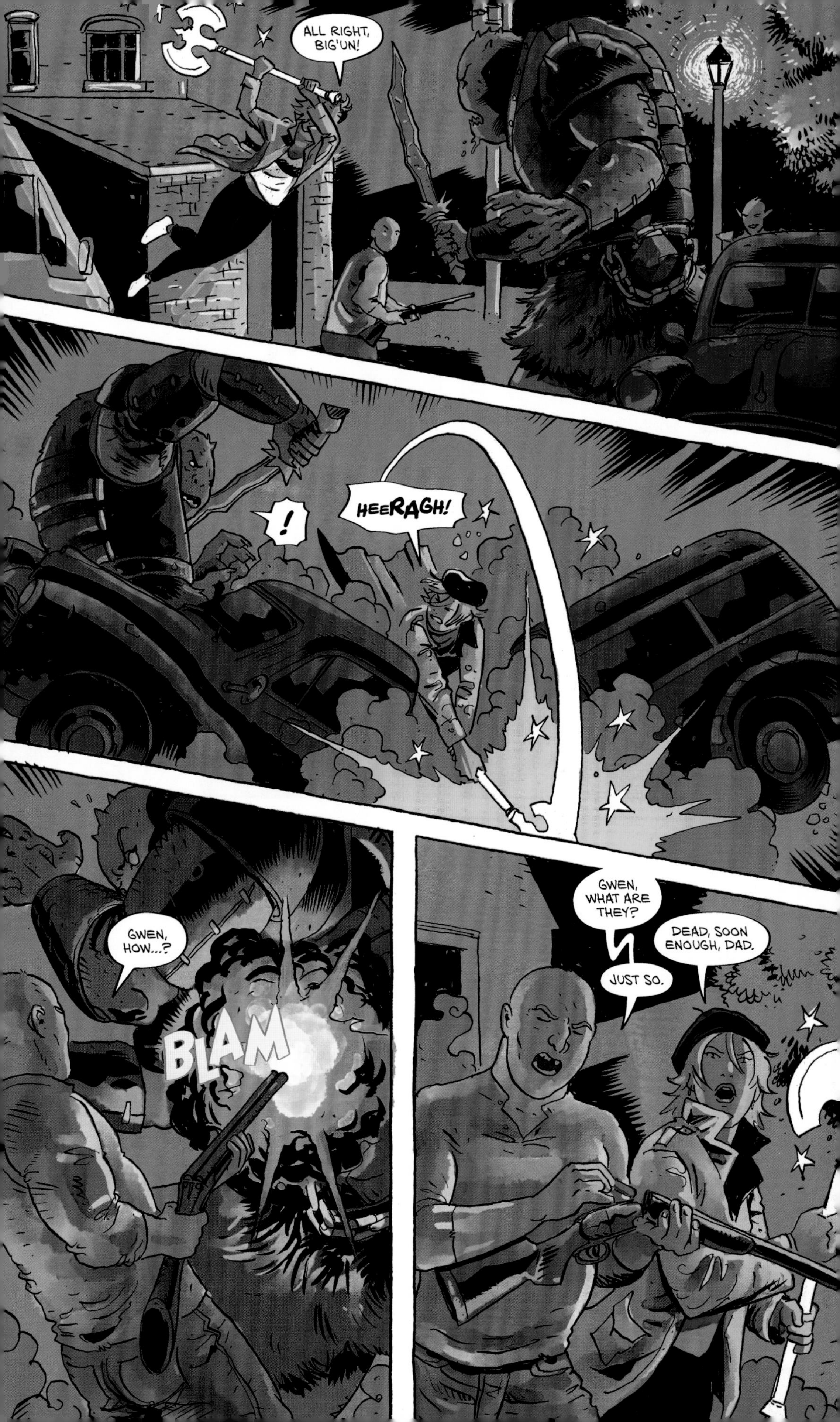

ALL RIGHT, BIG'UN!
!
HEERAGH!
GWEN, HOW...?
BLAM
GWEN, WHAT ARE THEY?
JUST SO.
DEAD, SOON ENOUGH, DAD.

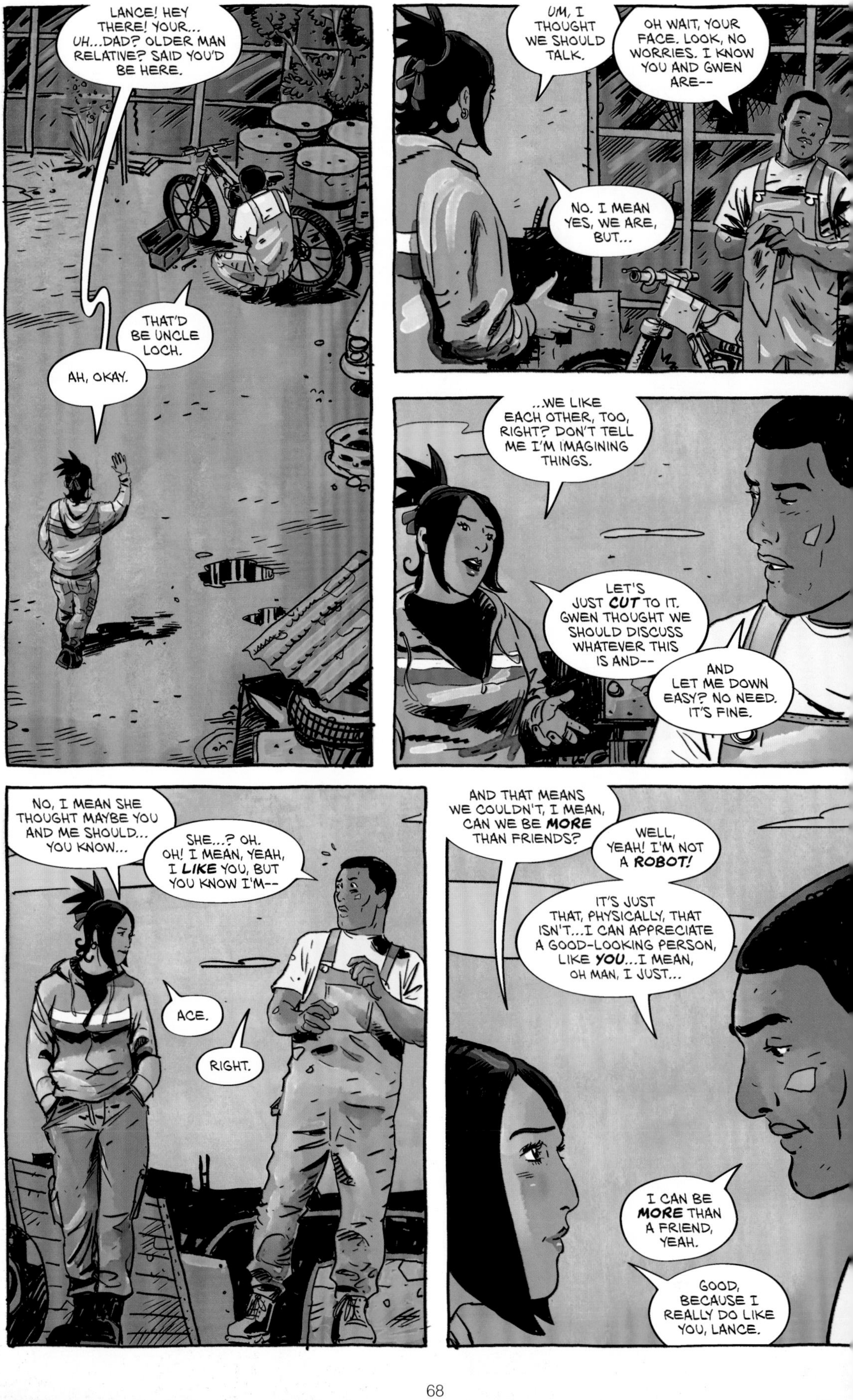
LANCE! HEY THERE! YOUR... UH...DAD? OLDER MAN RELATIVE? SAID YOU'D BE HERE.
THAT'D BE UNCLE LOCH.
AH, OKAY.
UM, I THOUGHT WE SHOULD TALK.
OH WAIT, YOUR FACE. LOOK, NO WORRIES. I KNOW YOU AND GWEN ARE--
NO. I MEAN YES, WE ARE, BUT...
...WE LIKE EACH OTHER, TOO, RIGHT? DON'T TELL ME I'M IMAGINING THINGS.
LET'S JUST CUT TO IT. GWEN THOUGHT WE SHOULD DISCUSS WHATEVER THIS IS AND--
AND LET ME DOWN EASY? NO NEED. IT'S FINE.
NO, I MEAN SHE THOUGHT MAYBE YOU AND ME SHOULD... YOU KNOW...
SHE...? OH. OH! I MEAN, YEAH, I LIKE YOU, BUT YOU KNOW I'M--
ACE.
RIGHT.
AND THAT MEANS WE COULDN'T, I MEAN, CAN WE BE MORE THAN FRIENDS?
WELL, YEAH! I'M NOT A ROBOT!
IT'S JUST THAT, PHYSICALLY, THAT ISN'T...I CAN APPRECIATE A GOOD-LOOKING PERSON, LIKE YOU...I MEAN, OH MAN, I JUST...
I CAN BE MORE THAN A FRIEND, YEAH.
GOOD, BECAUSE I REALLY DO LIKE YOU, LANCE.

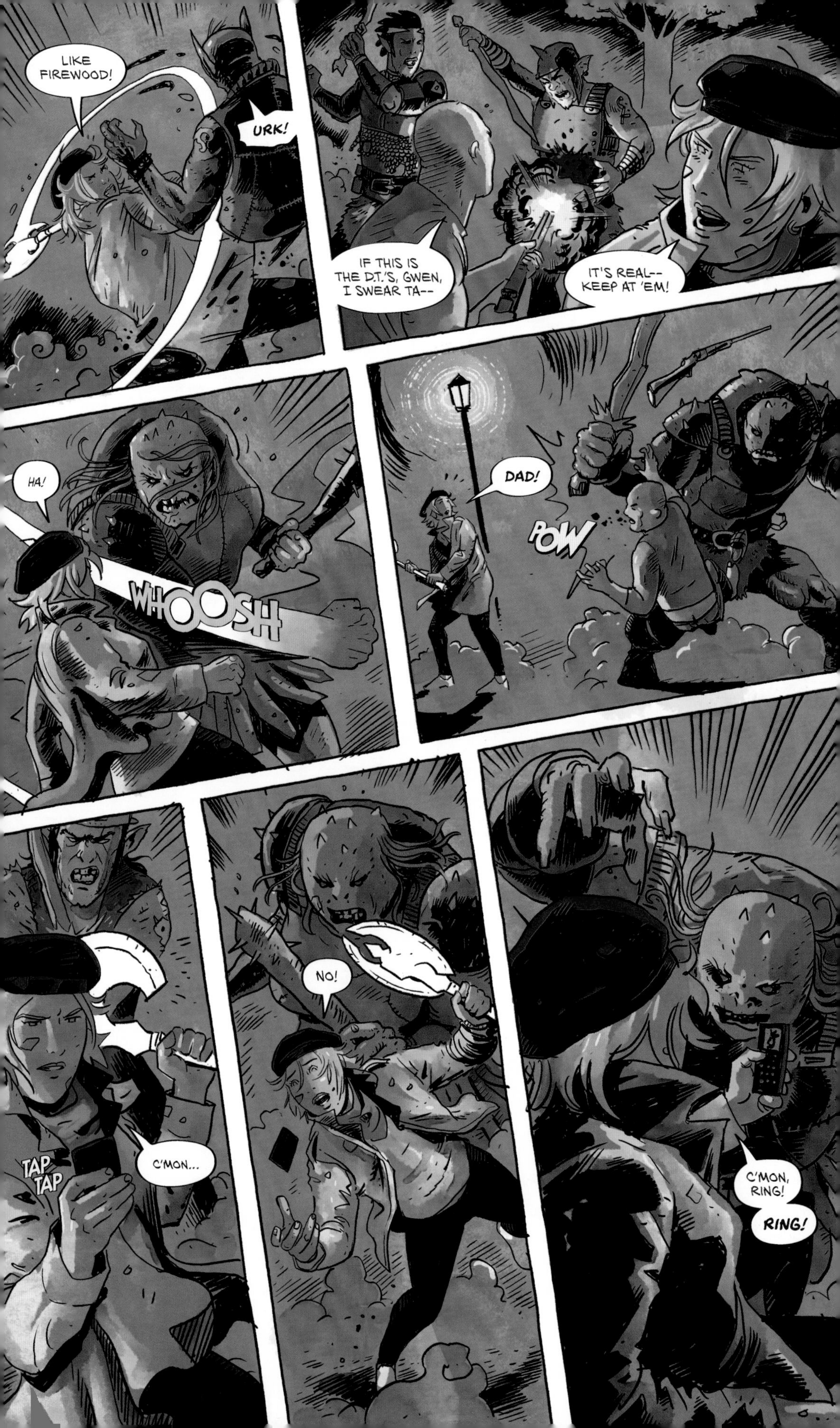
LIKE FIREWOOD!
URK!
IF THIS IS THE D.T.'S, GWEN, I SWEAR TA--
IT'S REAL-- KEEP AT 'EM!
HA!
WHOOSH
DAD!
POW
TAP TAP
C'MON...
NO!
C'MON, RING!
RING!

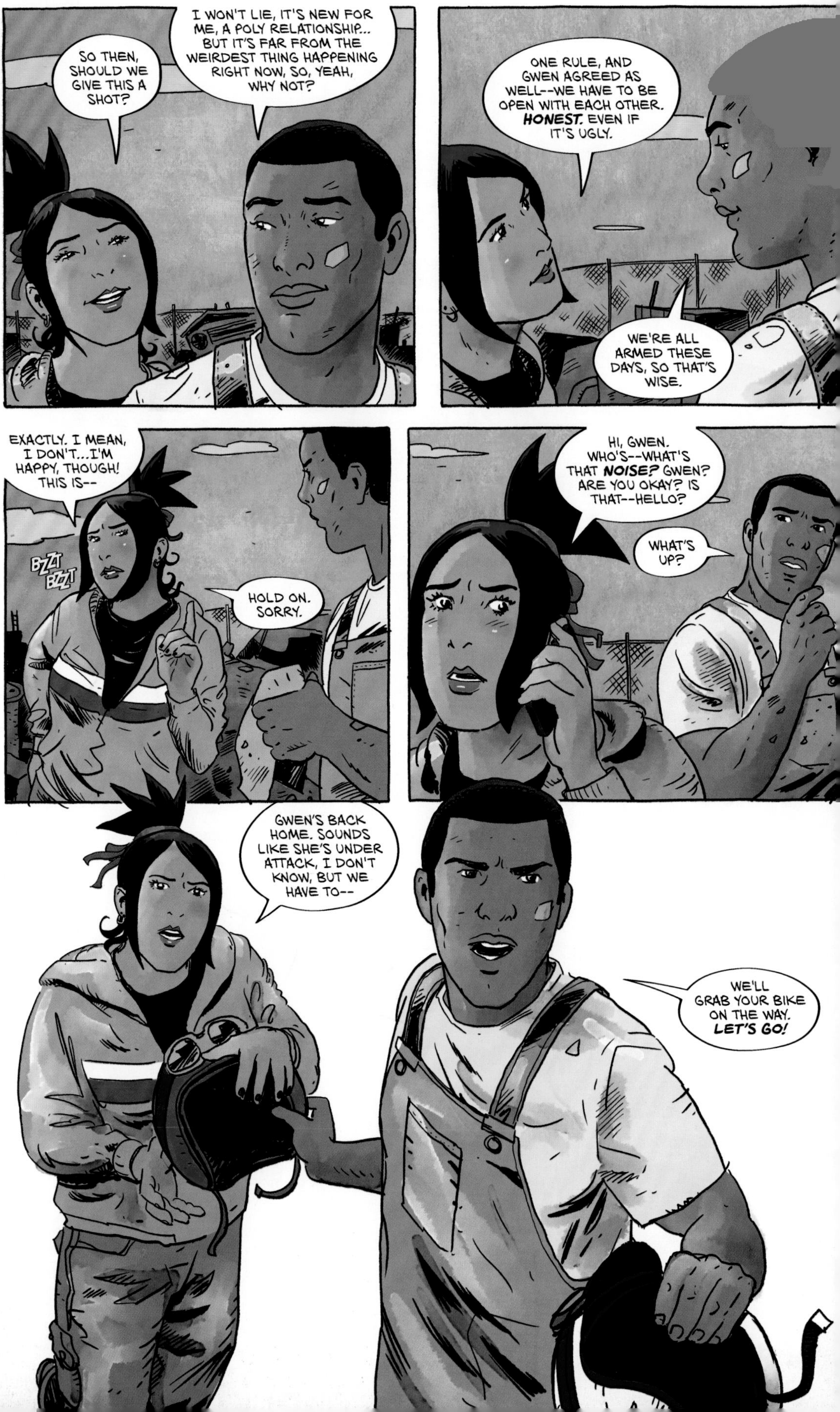

SO THEN, SHOULD WE GIVE THIS A SHOT?
I WON'T LIE, IT'S NEW FOR ME, A POLY RELATIONSHIP... BUT IT'S FAR FROM THE WEIRDEST THING HAPPENING RIGHT NOW, SO, YEAH, WHY NOT?
ONE RULE, AND GWEN AGREED AS WELL--WE HAVE TO BE OPEN WITH EACH OTHER. **HONEST.** EVEN IF IT'S UGLY.
WE'RE ALL ARMED THESE DAYS, SO THAT'S WISE.
EXACTLY. I MEAN, I DON'T...I'M HAPPY, THOUGH! THIS IS--
BZZT BZZT
HOLD ON. SORRY.
HI, GWEN. WHO'S--WHAT'S THAT **NOISE?** GWEN? ARE YOU OKAY? IS THAT--HELLO?
WHAT'S UP?
GWEN'S BACK HOME. SOUNDS LIKE SHE'S UNDER ATTACK, I DON'T KNOW, BUT WE HAVE TO--
WE'LL GRAB YOUR BIKE ON THE WAY. ***LET'S GO!***

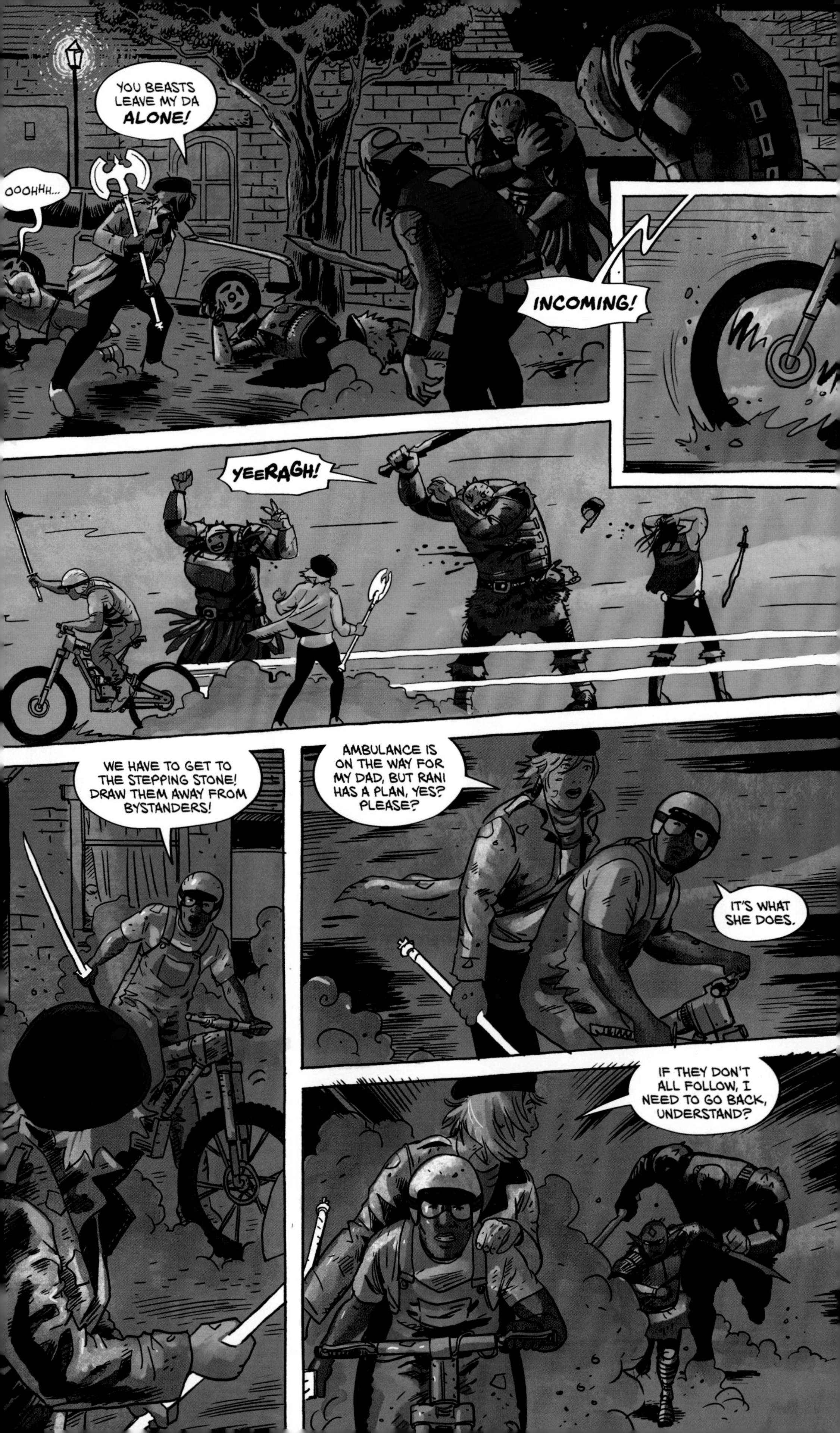
YOU BEASTS LEAVE MY DA ALONE!
OOOHHH...
INCOMING!
YEERAGH!
WE HAVE TO GET TO THE STEPPING STONE! DRAW THEM AWAY FROM BYSTANDERS!
AMBULANCE IS ON THE WAY FOR MY DAD, BUT RANI HAS A PLAN, YES? PLEASE?
IT'S WHAT SHE DOES.
IF THEY DON'T ALL FOLLOW, I NEED TO GO BACK, UNDERSTAND?

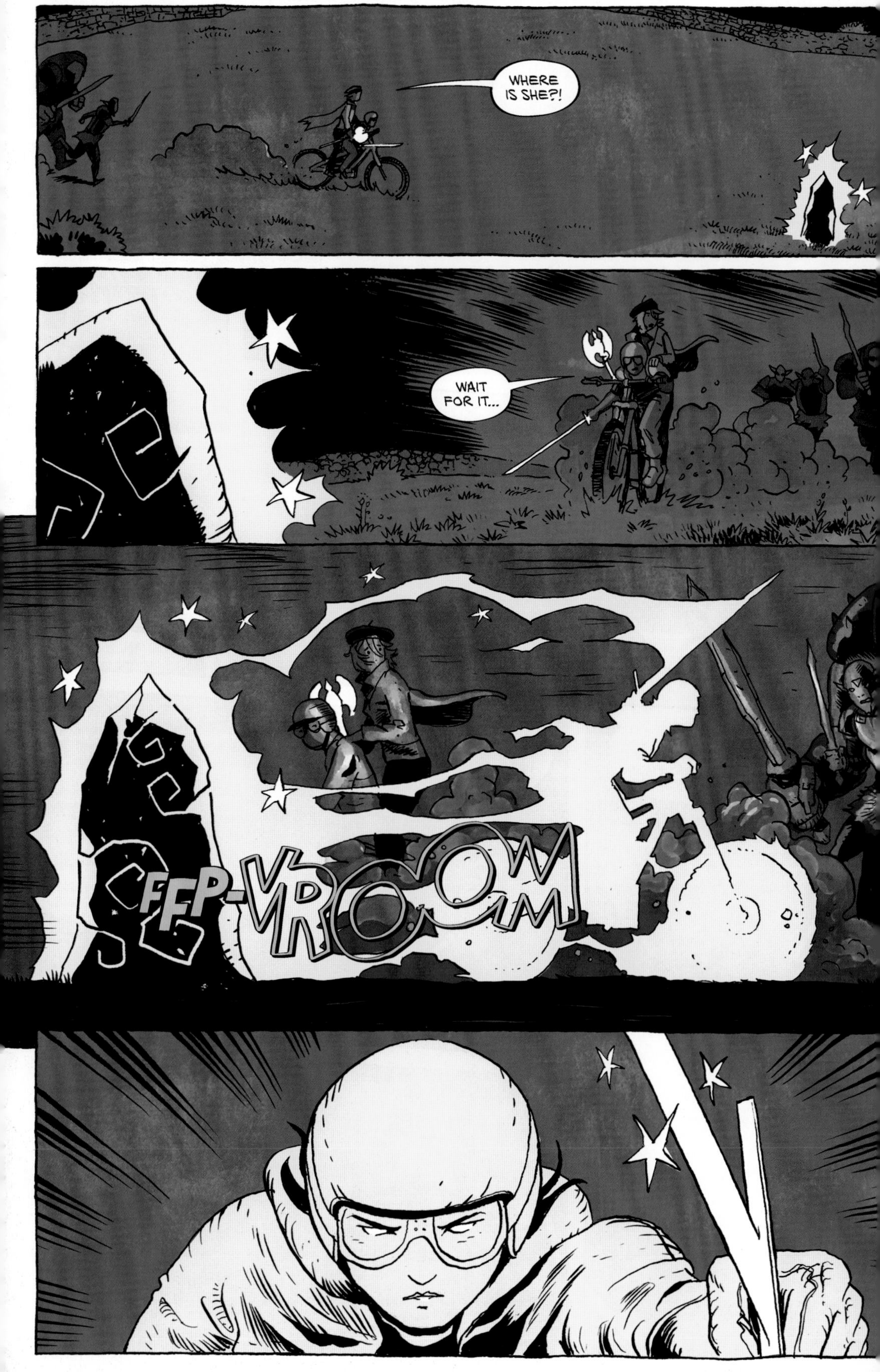
WHERE IS SHE?!
WAIT FOR IT...
FFP-VROOM

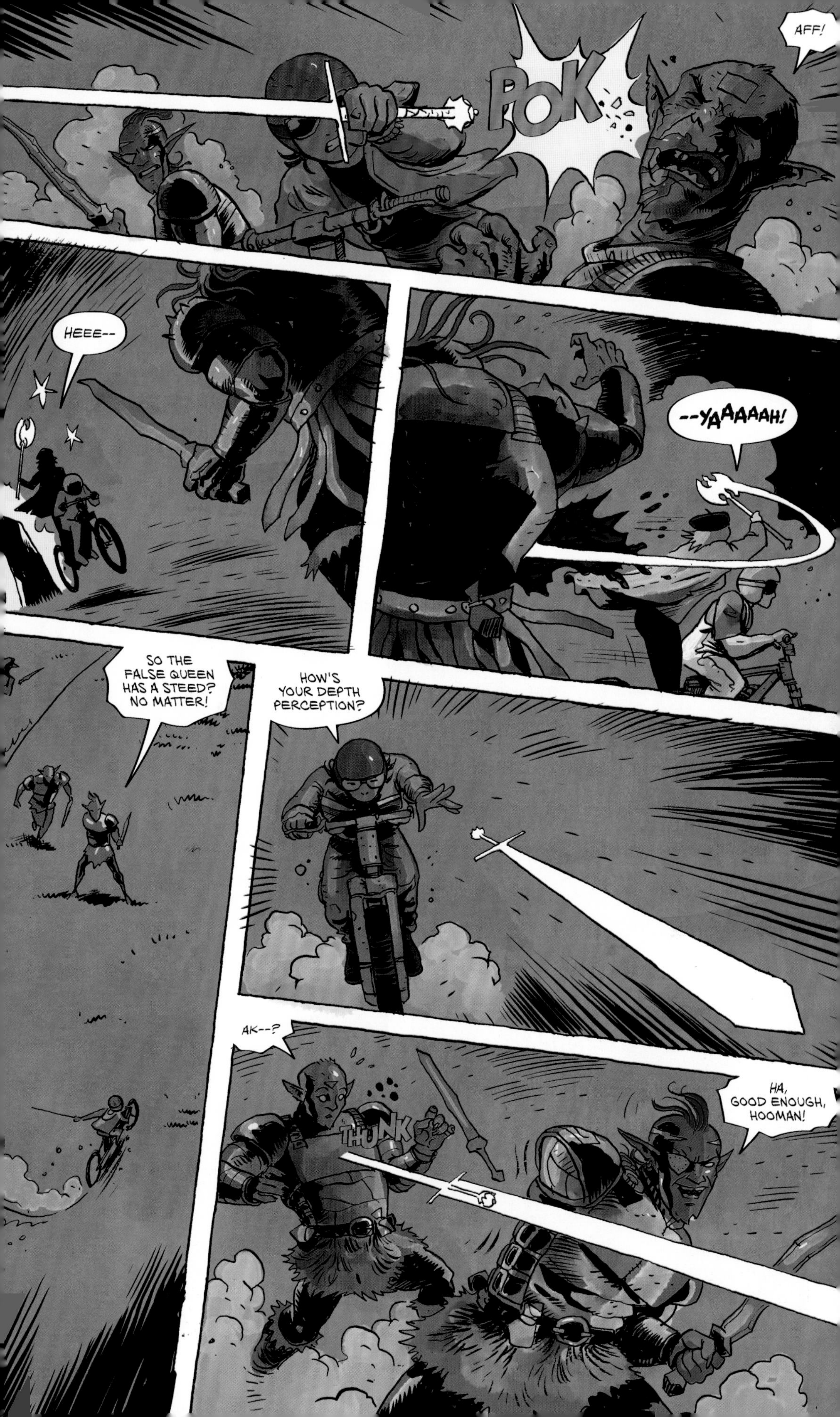
POK
AFF!
HEEE--
--YAAAAAH!
SO THE FALSE QUEEN HAS A STEED? NO MATTER!
HOW'S YOUR DEPTH PERCEPTION?
AK--?
THUNK
HA, GOOD ENOUGH, HOOMAN!

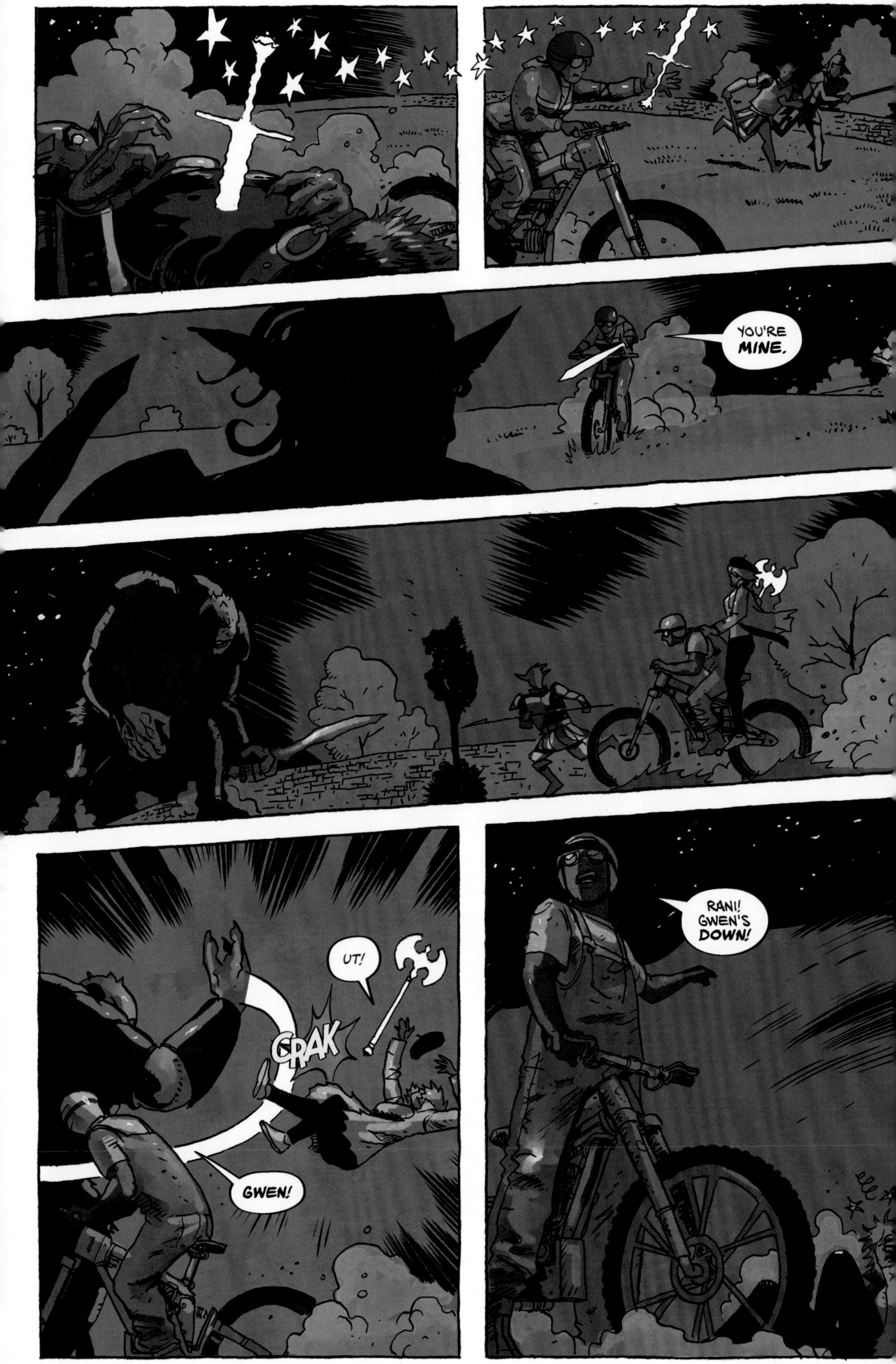
YOU'RE MINE.
UT!
CRAK
GWEN!
RANI! GWEN'S DOWN!

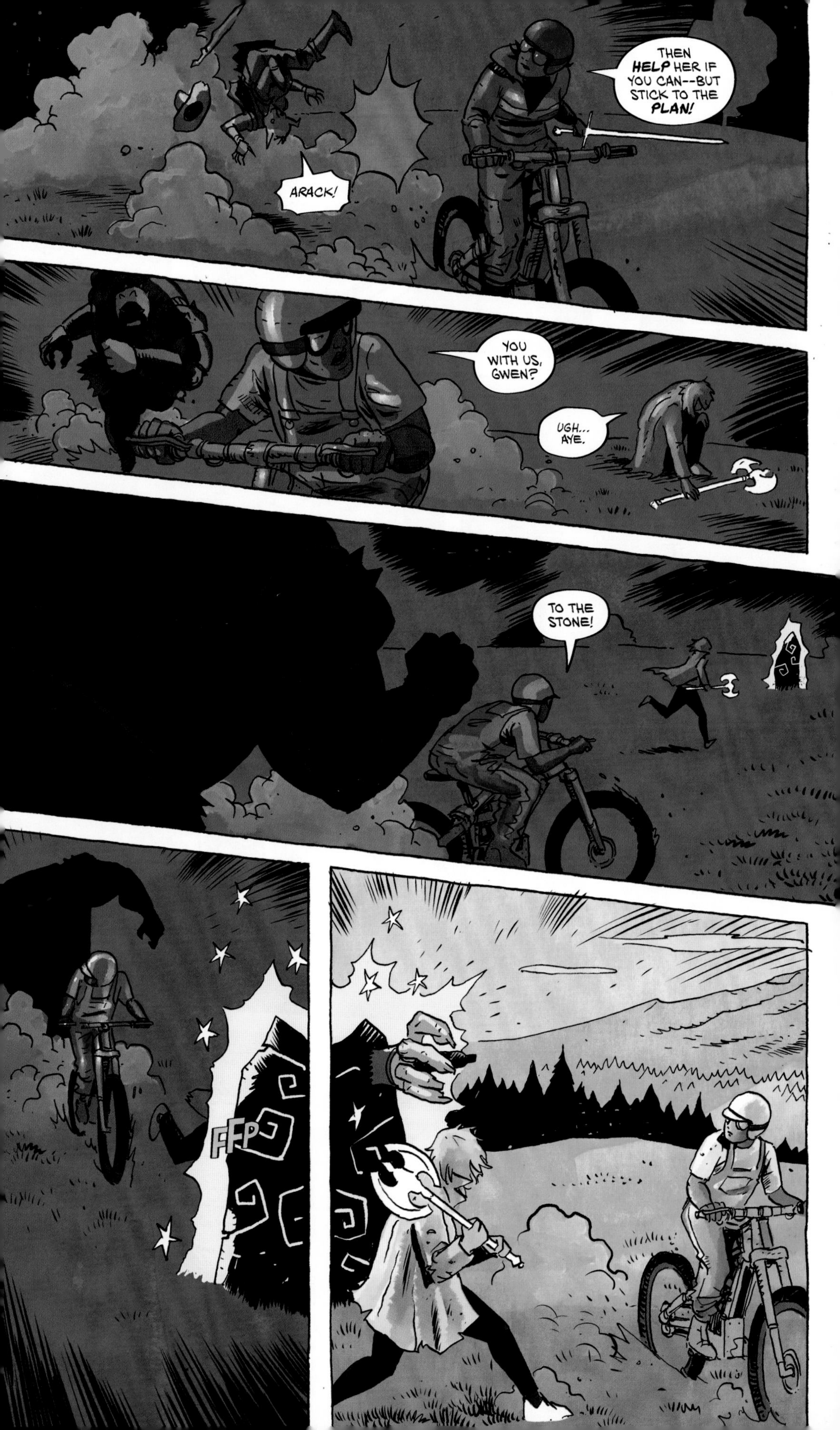
THEN HELP HER IF YOU CAN--BUT STICK TO THE PLAN!
ARACK!
YOU WITH US, GWEN?
UGH... AYE.
TO THE STONE!
FFP

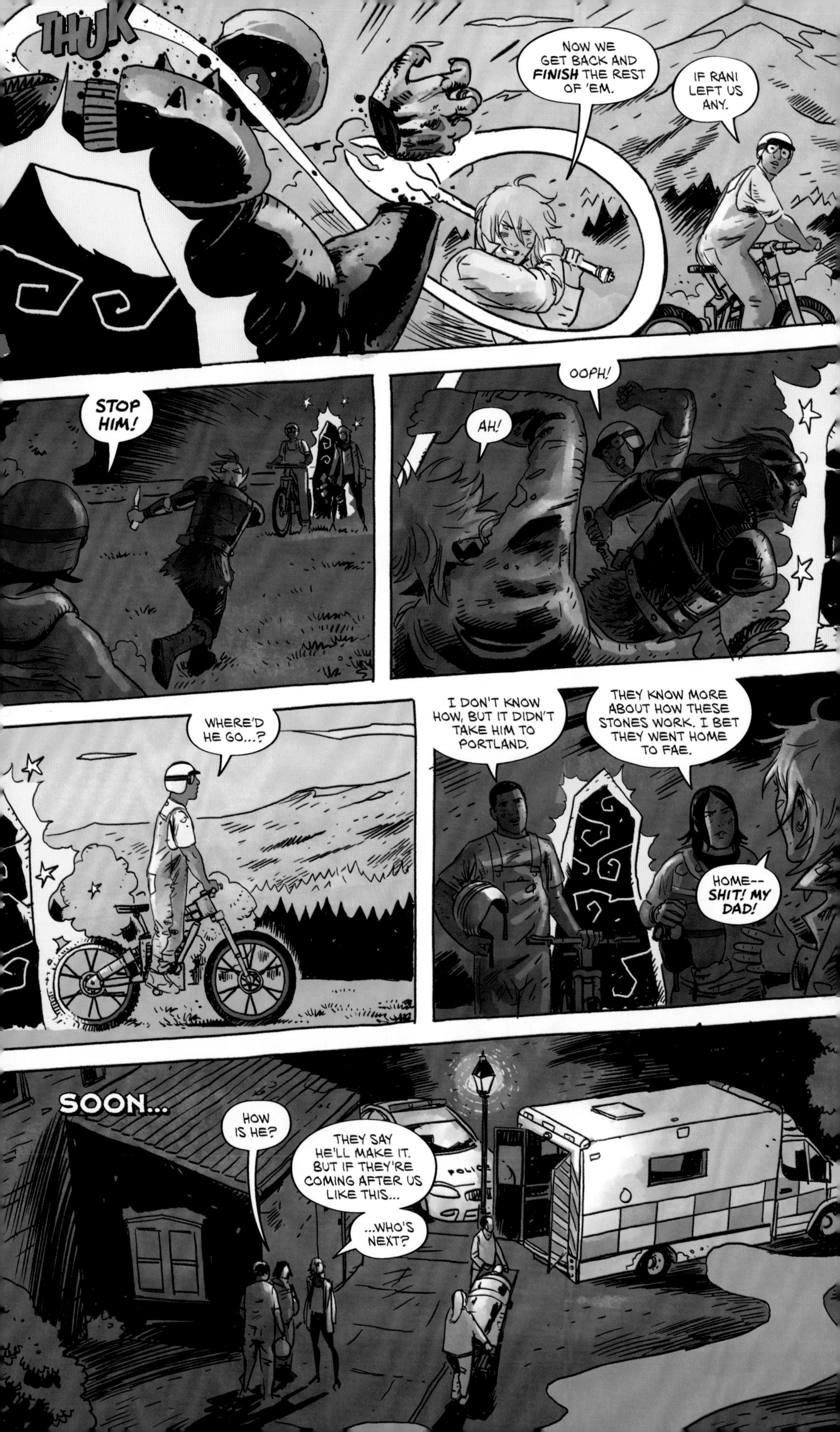
THUK
NOW WE GET BACK AND FINISH THE REST OF 'EM.
IF RANI LEFT US ANY.
STOP HIM!
OOPH!
AH!
WHERE'D HE GO...?
I DON'T KNOW HOW, BUT IT DIDN'T TAKE HIM TO PORTLAND.
THEY KNOW MORE ABOUT HOW THESE STONES WORK. I BET THEY WENT HOME TO FAE.
HOME-- SHIT! MY DAD!
SOON...
HOW IS HE?
THEY SAY HE'LL MAKE IT. BUT IF THEY'RE COMING AFTER US LIKE THIS...
...WHO'S NEXT?
POLICE

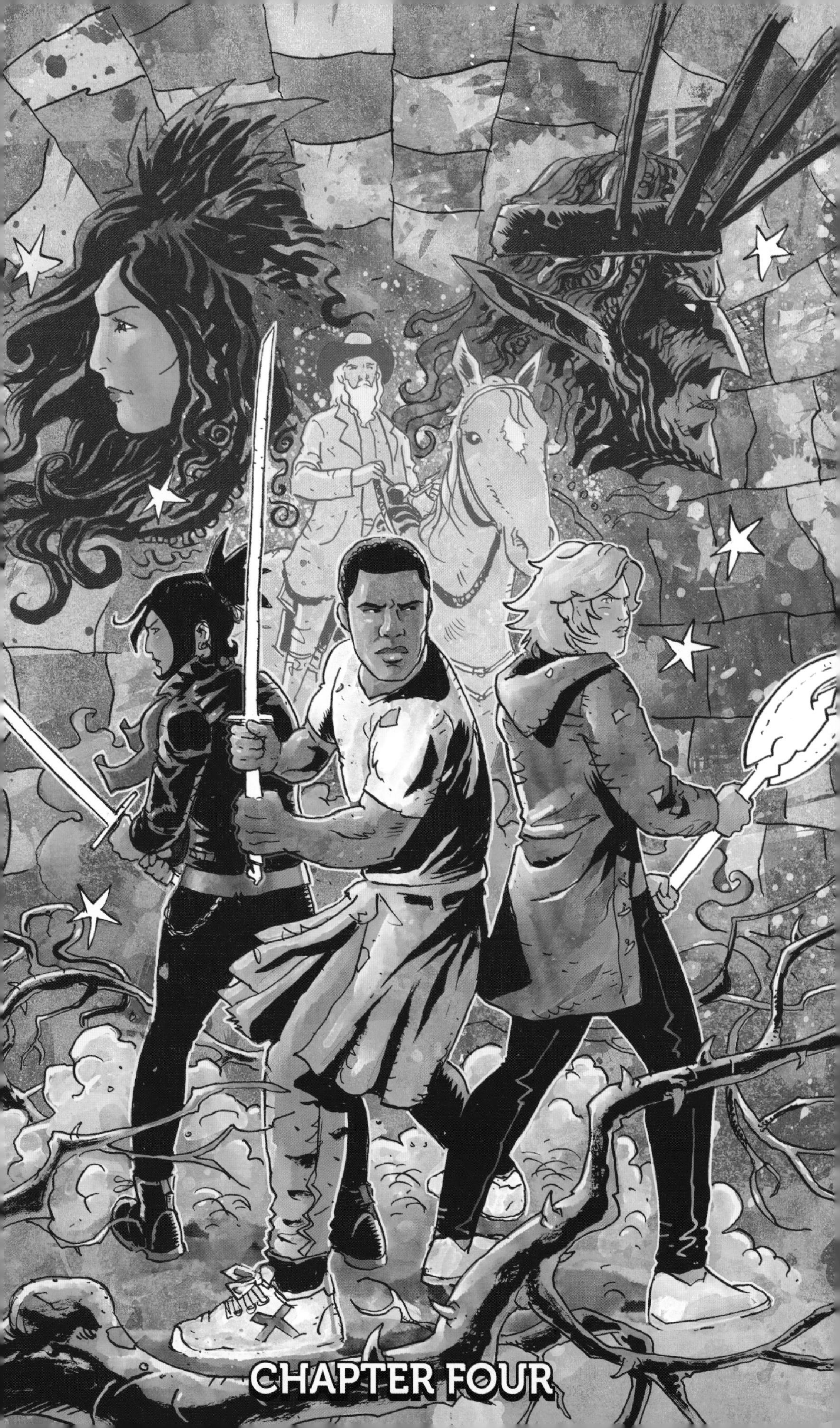

CHAPTER FOUR

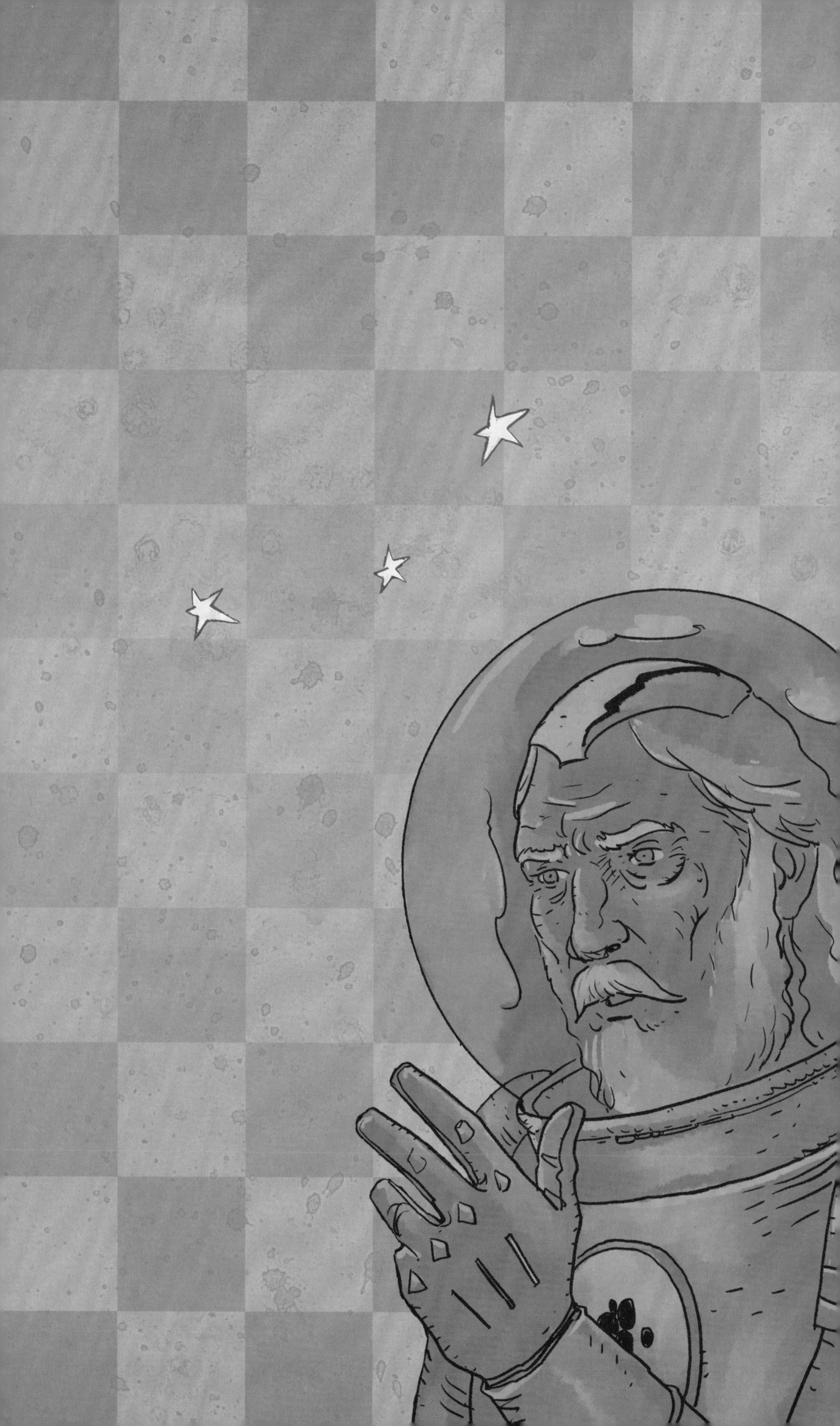

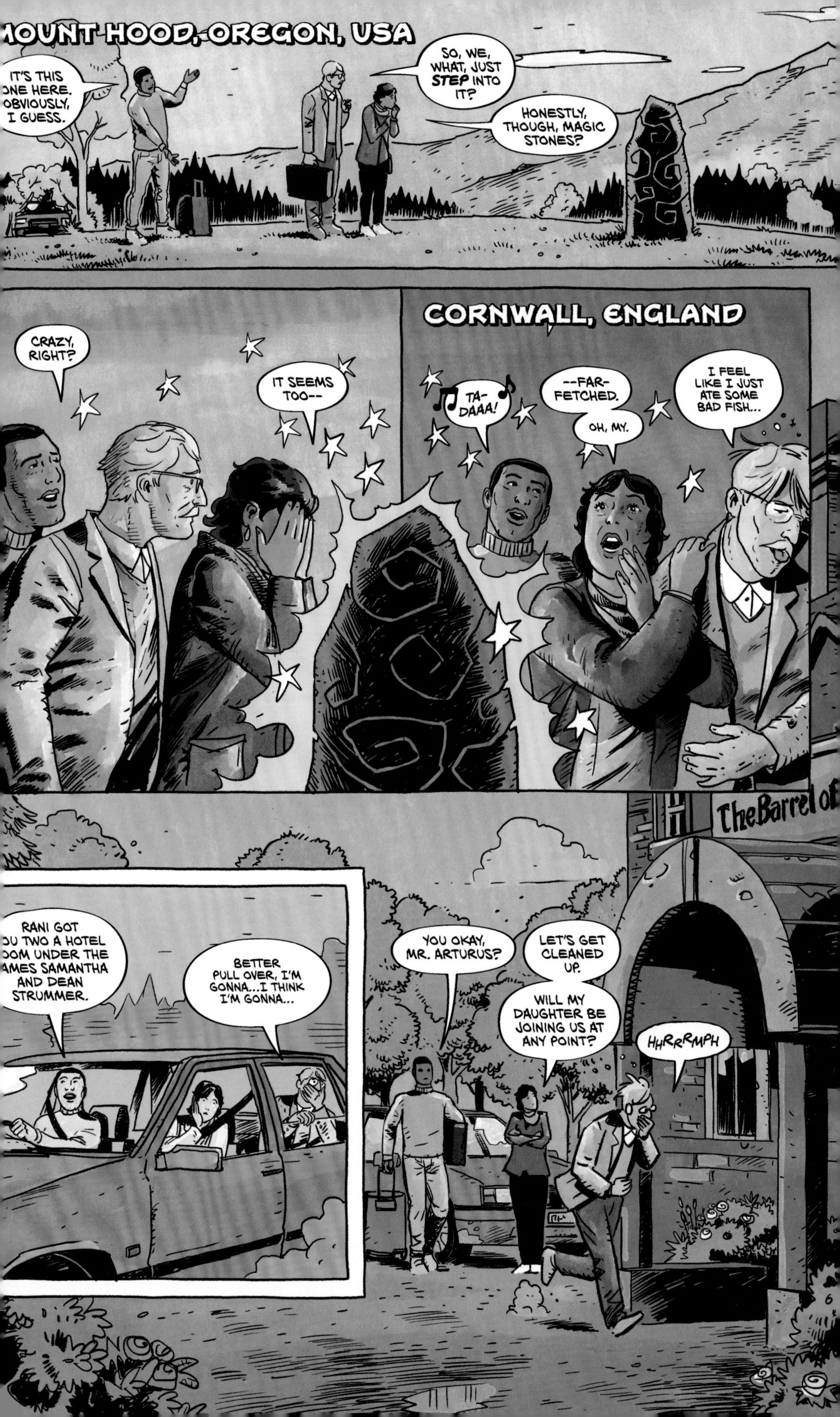
MOUNT HOOD, OREGON, USA
IT'S THIS ONE HERE. OBVIOUSLY, I GUESS.
SO, WE, WHAT, JUST STEP INTO IT?
HONESTLY, THOUGH, MAGIC STONES?
CRAZY, RIGHT?
IT SEEMS TOO--
CORNWALL, ENGLAND
TA-DAAA!
--FAR-FETCHED.
OH, MY.
I FEEL LIKE I JUST ATE SOME BAD FISH...
TheBarrel of
RANI GOT OU TWO A HOTEL OOM UNDER THE AMES SAMANTHA AND DEAN STRUMMER.
BETTER PULL OVER, I'M GONNA...I THINK I'M GONNA...
YOU OKAY, MR. ARTURUS?
LET'S GET CLEANED UP.
WILL MY DAUGHTER BE JOINING US AT ANY POINT?
HHRRRMPH

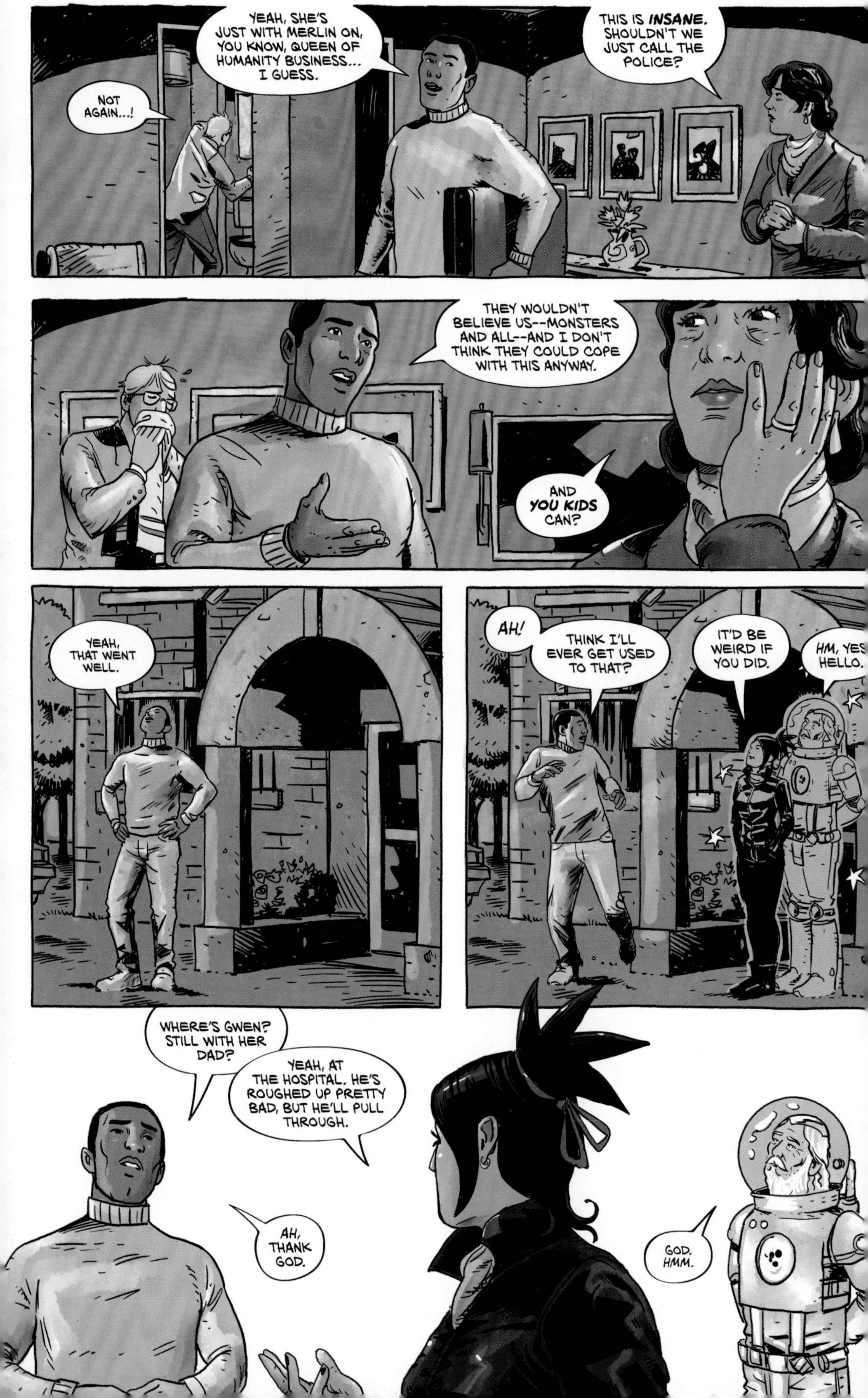

NOT AGAIN...!
YEAH, SHE'S JUST WITH MERLIN ON, YOU KNOW, QUEEN OF HUMANITY BUSINESS... I GUESS.
THIS IS INSANE. SHOULDN'T WE JUST CALL THE POLICE?
THEY WOULDN'T BELIEVE US--MONSTERS AND ALL--AND I DON'T THINK THEY COULD COPE WITH THIS ANYWAY.
AND YOU KIDS CAN?
YEAH, THAT WENT WELL.
AH!
THINK I'LL EVER GET USED TO THAT?
IT'D BE WEIRD IF YOU DID.
HM, YES HELLO.
WHERE'S GWEN? STILL WITH HER DAD?
YEAH, AT THE HOSPITAL. HE'S ROUGHED UP PRETTY BAD, BUT HE'LL PULL THROUGH.
AH, THANK GOD.
GOD. HMM.

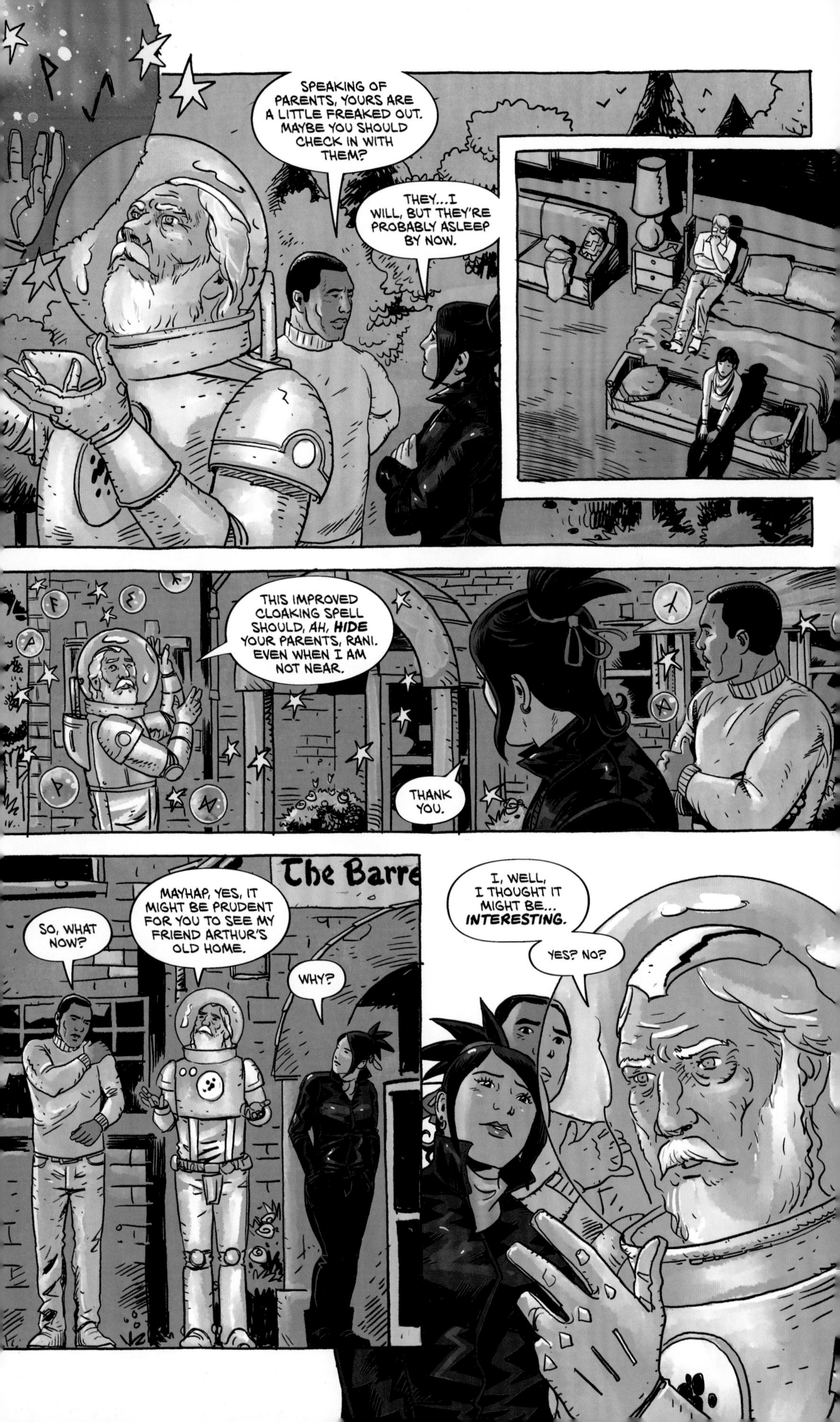
SPEAKING OF PARENTS, YOURS ARE A LITTLE FREAKED OUT. MAYBE YOU SHOULD CHECK IN WITH THEM?
THEY...I WILL, BUT THEY'RE PROBABLY ASLEEP BY NOW.
THIS IMPROVED CLOAKING SPELL SHOULD, *AH,* **HIDE** YOUR PARENTS, RANI. EVEN WHEN I AM NOT NEAR.
THANK YOU.
The Barre
SO, WHAT NOW?
MAYHAP, YES, IT MIGHT BE PRUDENT FOR YOU TO SEE MY FRIEND ARTHUR'S OLD HOME.
WHY?
I, WELL, I THOUGHT IT MIGHT BE... ***INTERESTING.***
YES? NO?

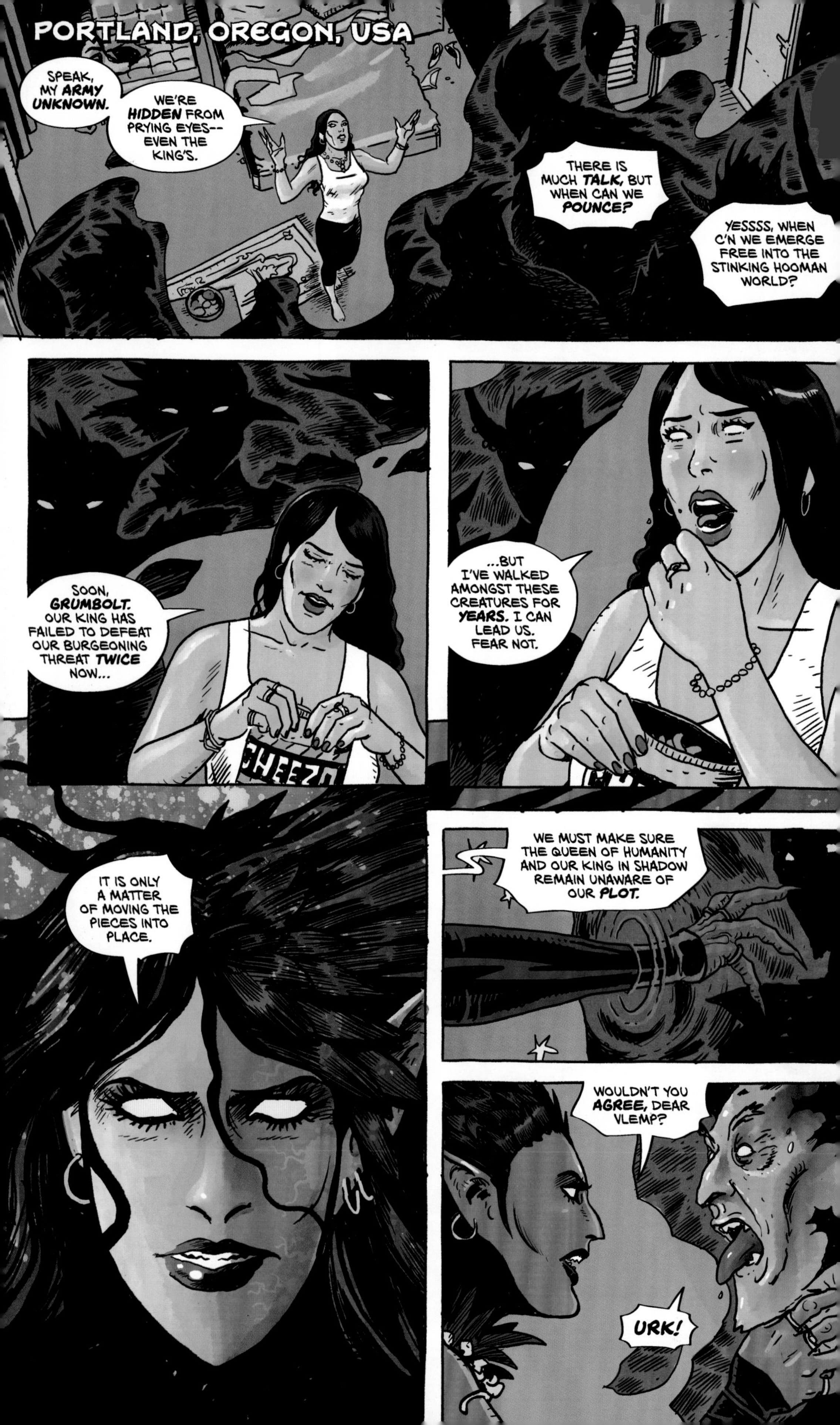

PORTLAND, OREGON, USA
SPEAK, MY ARMY UNKNOWN.
WE'RE HIDDEN FROM PRYING EYES-- EVEN THE KING'S.
THERE IS MUCH TALK, BUT WHEN CAN WE POUNCE?
YESSSS, WHEN C'N WE EMERGE FREE INTO THE STINKING HOOMAN WORLD?
SOON, GRUMBOLT. OUR KING HAS FAILED TO DEFEAT OUR BURGEONING THREAT TWICE NOW...
...BUT I'VE WALKED AMONGST THESE CREATURES FOR YEARS. I CAN LEAD US. FEAR NOT.
IT IS ONLY A MATTER OF MOVING THE PIECES INTO PLACE.
WE MUST MAKE SURE THE QUEEN OF HUMANITY AND OUR KING IN SHADOW REMAIN UNAWARE OF OUR PLOT.
WOULDN'T YOU AGREE, DEAR VLEMP?
URK!

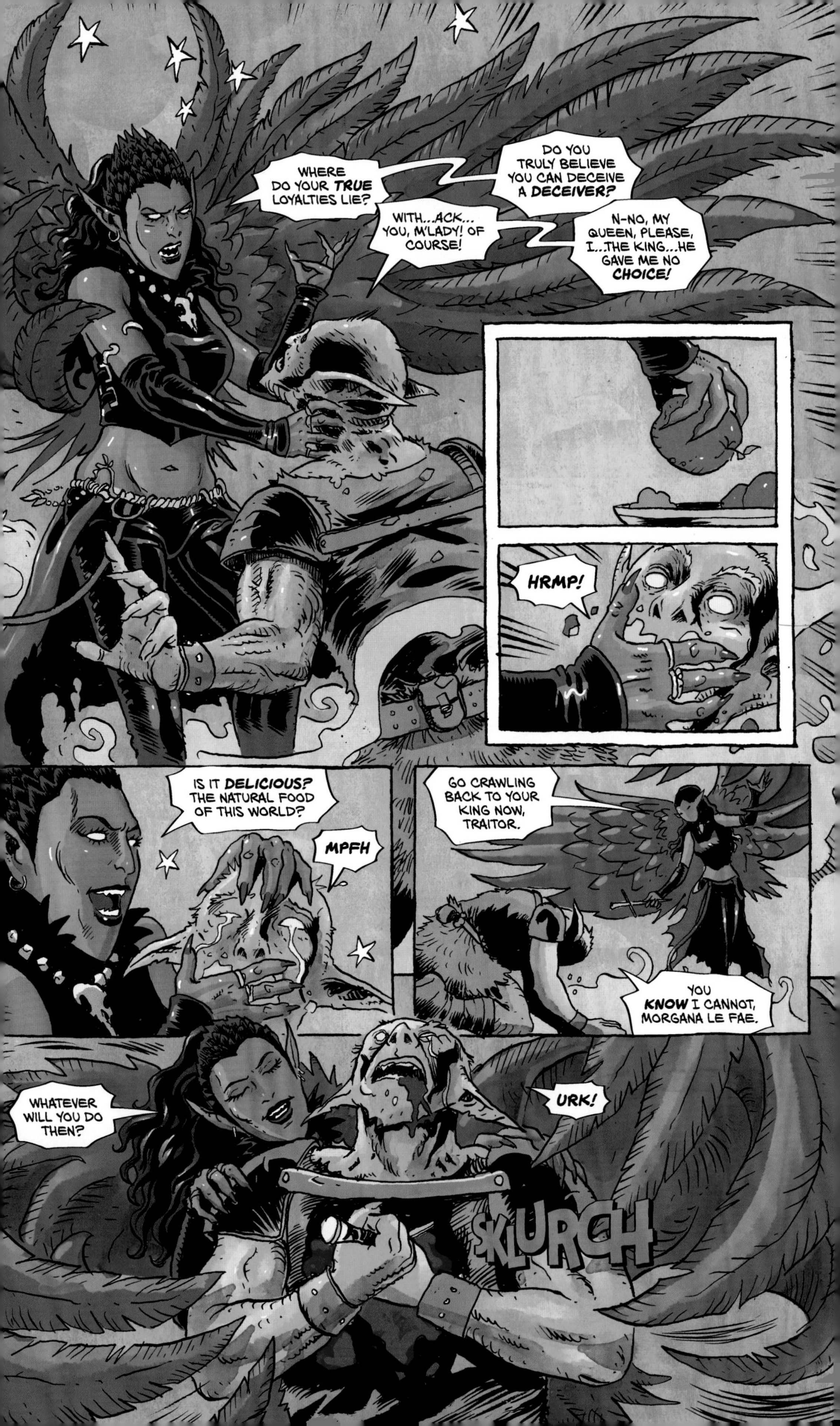

WHERE DO YOUR TRUE LOYALTIES LIE?
WITH...ACK... YOU, M'LADY! OF COURSE!
DO YOU TRULY BELIEVE YOU CAN DECEIVE A DECEIVER?
N-NO, MY QUEEN, PLEASE, I...THE KING...HE GAVE ME NO CHOICE!
HRMP!
IS IT DELICIOUS? THE NATURAL FOOD OF THIS WORLD?
MPFH
GO CRAWLING BACK TO YOUR KING NOW, TRAITOR.
YOU KNOW I CANNOT, MORGANA LE FAE.
WHATEVER WILL YOU DO THEN?
URK!
SKLURCH

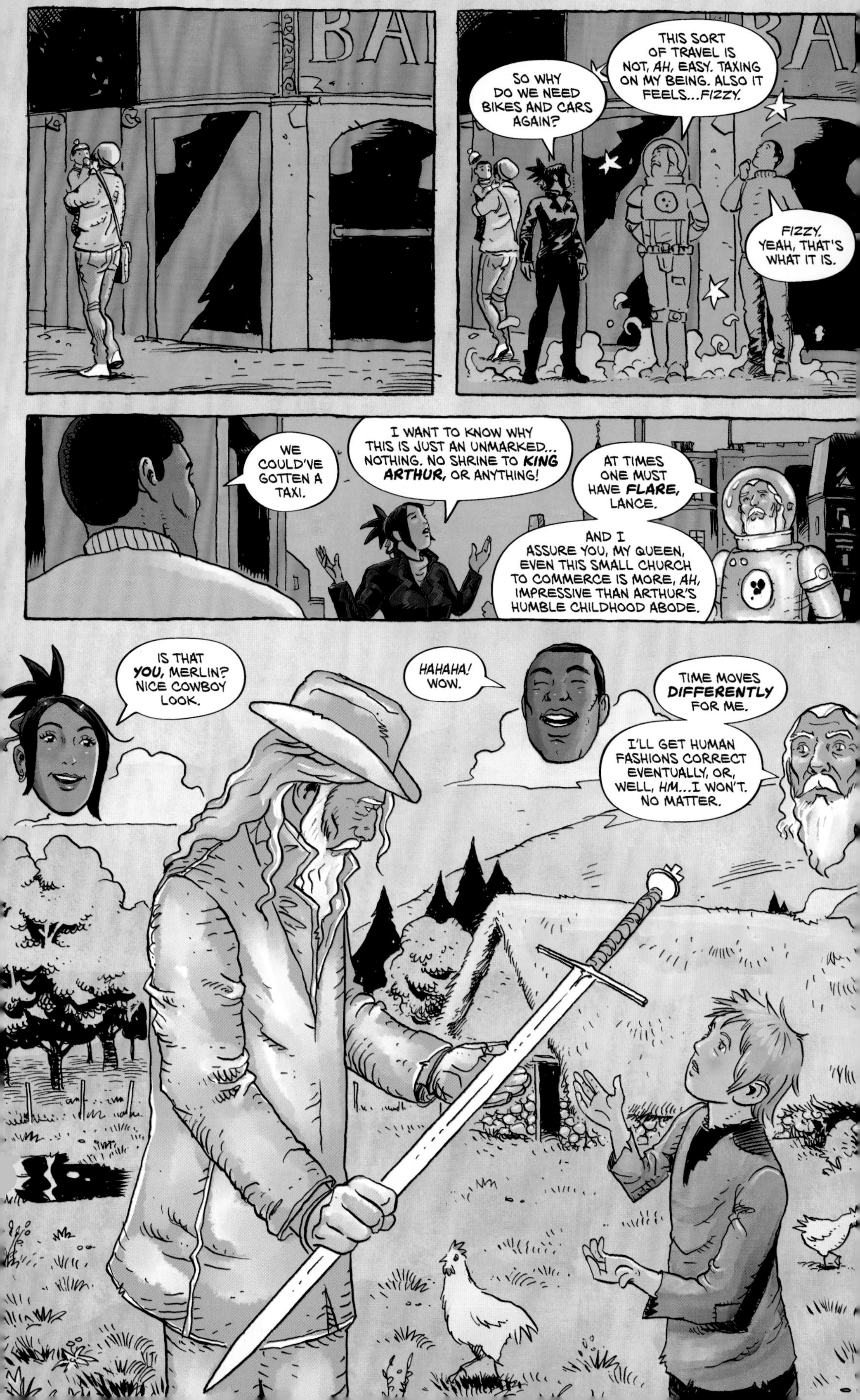
SO WHY DO WE NEED BIKES AND CARS AGAIN?
THIS SORT OF TRAVEL IS NOT, *AH,* EASY. TAXING ON MY BEING. ALSO IT FEELS... *FIZZY.*
FIZZY. YEAH, THAT'S WHAT IT IS.
WE COULD'VE GOTTEN A TAXI.
I WANT TO KNOW WHY THIS IS JUST AN UNMARKED... NOTHING. NO SHRINE TO **KING ARTHUR,** OR ANYTHING!
AT TIMES ONE MUST HAVE **FLARE,** LANCE.
AND I ASSURE YOU, MY QUEEN, EVEN THIS SMALL CHURCH TO COMMERCE IS MORE, AH, IMPRESSIVE THAN ARTHUR'S HUMBLE CHILDHOOD ABODE.
IS THAT ***YOU,*** MERLIN? NICE COWBOY LOOK.
HAHAHA! WOW.
TIME MOVES ***DIFFERENTLY*** FOR ME.
I'LL GET HUMAN FASHIONS CORRECT EVENTUALLY, OR, WELL, *HM*... I WON'T. NO MATTER.

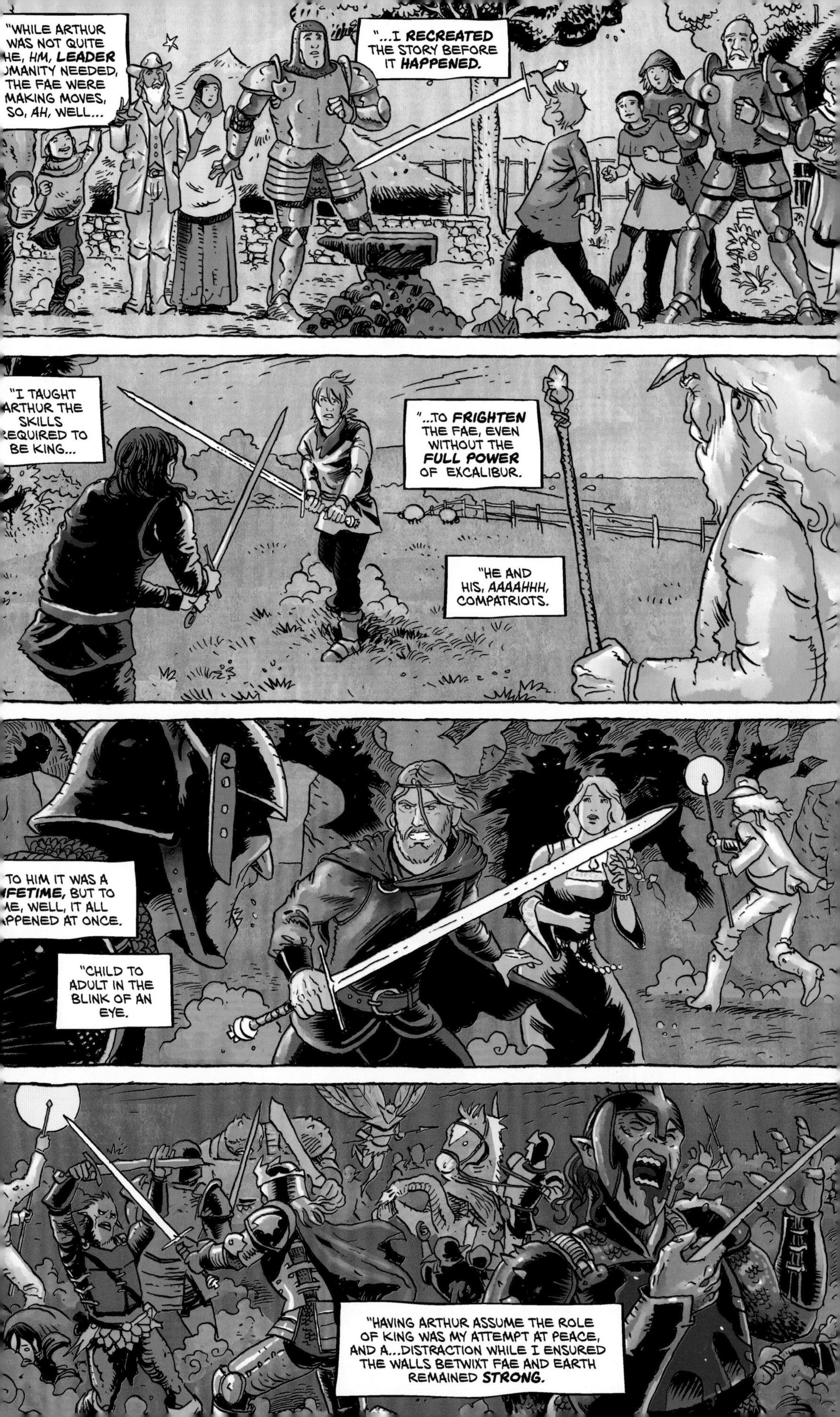
"WHILE ARTHUR WAS NOT QUITE HE, HM, LEADER UMANITY NEEDED, THE FAE WERE MAKING MOVES, SO, AH, WELL...
"...I RECREATED THE STORY BEFORE IT HAPPENED.
"I TAUGHT ARTHUR THE SKILLS EQUIRED TO BE KING...
"...TO FRIGHTEN THE FAE, EVEN WITHOUT THE FULL POWER OF EXCALIBUR.
"HE AND HIS, AAAAHHH, COMPATRIOTS.
TO HIM IT WAS A IFETIME, BUT TO E, WELL, IT ALL PPENED AT ONCE.
"CHILD TO ADULT IN THE BLINK OF AN EYE.
"HAVING ARTHUR ASSUME THE ROLE OF KING WAS MY ATTEMPT AT PEACE, AND A...DISTRACTION WHILE I ENSURED THE WALLS BETWIXT FAE AND EARTH REMAINED STRONG.

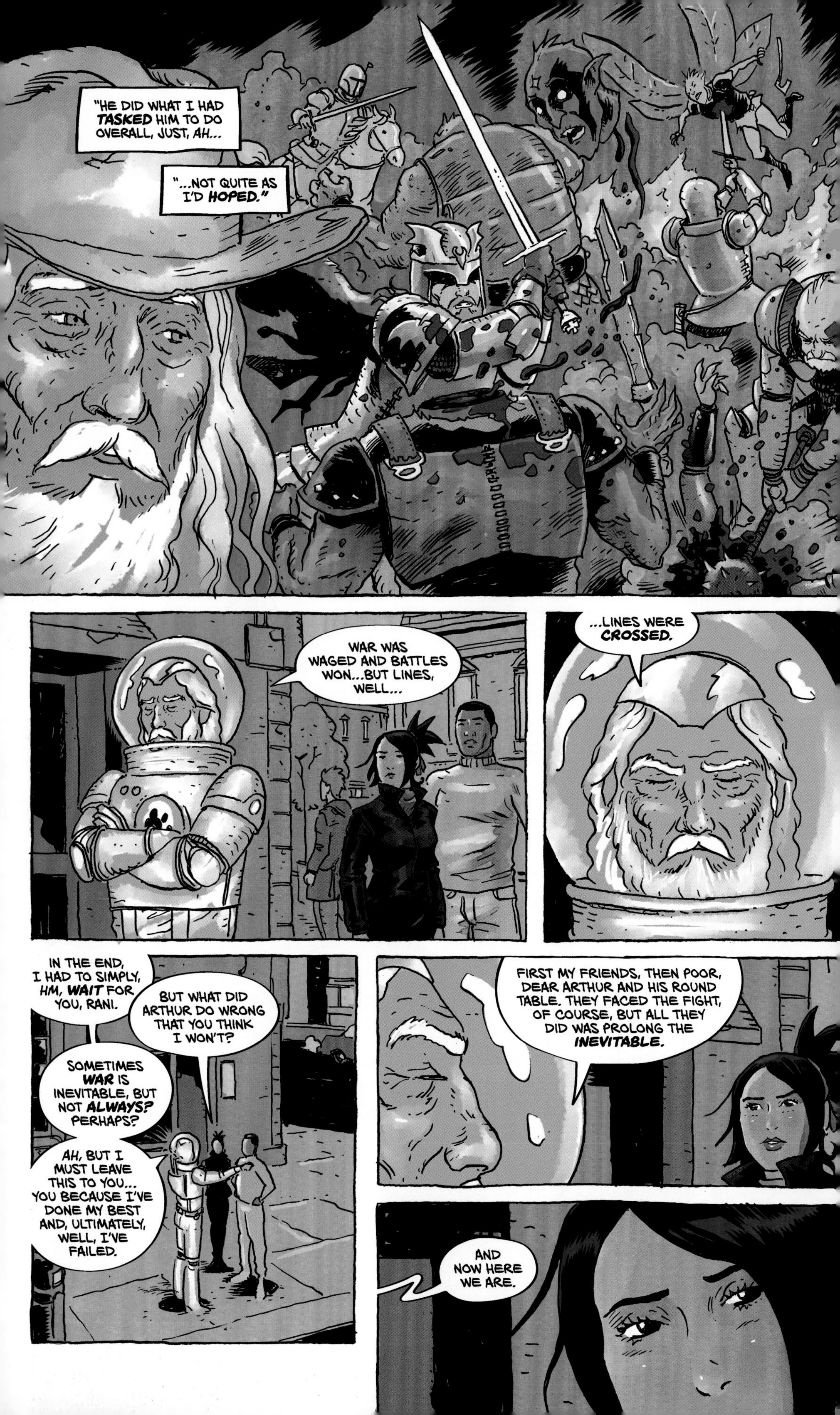
"HE DID WHAT I HAD TASKED HIM TO DO OVERALL, JUST, AH...
"...NOT QUITE AS I'D HOPED."
WAR WAS WAGED AND BATTLES WON...BUT LINES, WELL...
...LINES WERE CROSSED.
IN THE END, I HAD TO SIMPLY, HM, WAIT FOR YOU, RANI.
BUT WHAT DID ARTHUR DO WRONG THAT YOU THINK I WON'T?
SOMETIMES WAR IS INEVITABLE, BUT NOT ALWAYS? PERHAPS?
AH, BUT I MUST LEAVE THIS TO YOU... YOU BECAUSE I'VE DONE MY BEST AND, ULTIMATELY, WELL, I'VE FAILED.
FIRST MY FRIENDS, THEN POOR, DEAR ARTHUR AND HIS ROUND TABLE. THEY FACED THE FIGHT, OF COURSE, BUT ALL THEY DID WAS PROLONG THE INEVITABLE.
AND NOW HERE WE ARE.

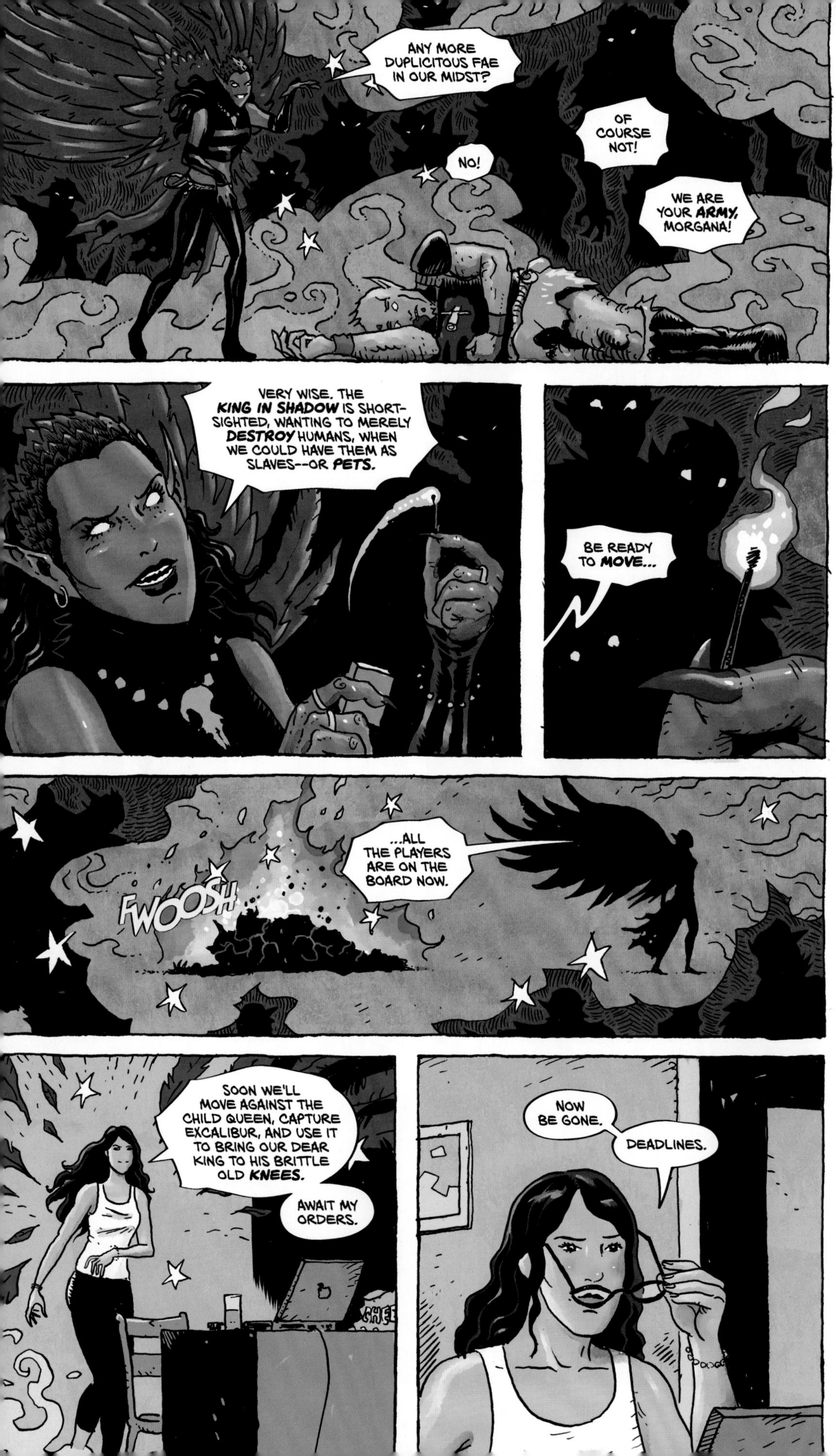
ANY MORE DUPLICITOUS FAE IN OUR MIDST?
NO!
OF COURSE NOT!
WE ARE YOUR ARMY, MORGANA!
VERY WISE. THE KING IN SHADOW IS SHORT-SIGHTED, WANTING TO MERELY DESTROY HUMANS, WHEN WE COULD HAVE THEM AS SLAVES--OR PETS.
BE READY TO MOVE...
...ALL THE PLAYERS ARE ON THE BOARD NOW.
FWOOSH
SOON WE'LL MOVE AGAINST THE CHILD QUEEN, CAPTURE EXCALIBUR, AND USE IT TO BRING OUR DEAR KING TO HIS BRITTLE OLD KNEES.
AWAIT MY ORDERS.
NOW BE GONE.
DEADLINES.

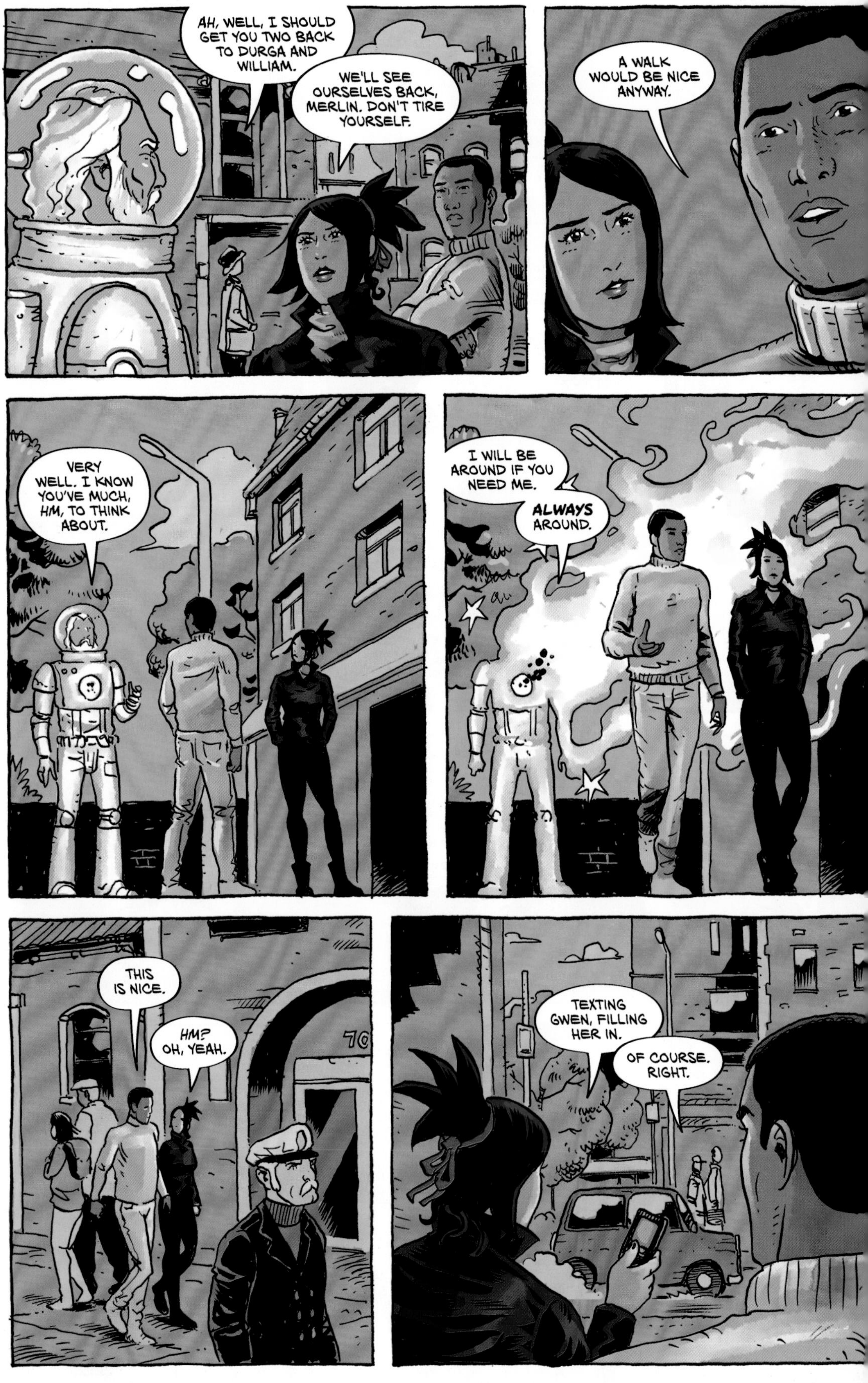

AH, WELL, I SHOULD GET YOU TWO BACK TO DURGA AND WILLIAM.
WE'LL SEE OURSELVES BACK, MERLIN. DON'T TIRE YOURSELF.
A WALK WOULD BE NICE ANYWAY.
VERY WELL. I KNOW YOU'VE MUCH, HM, TO THINK ABOUT.
I WILL BE AROUND IF YOU NEED ME.
ALWAYS AROUND.
THIS IS NICE.
HM? OH, YEAH.
70
TEXTING GWEN, FILLING HER IN.
OF COURSE. RIGHT.

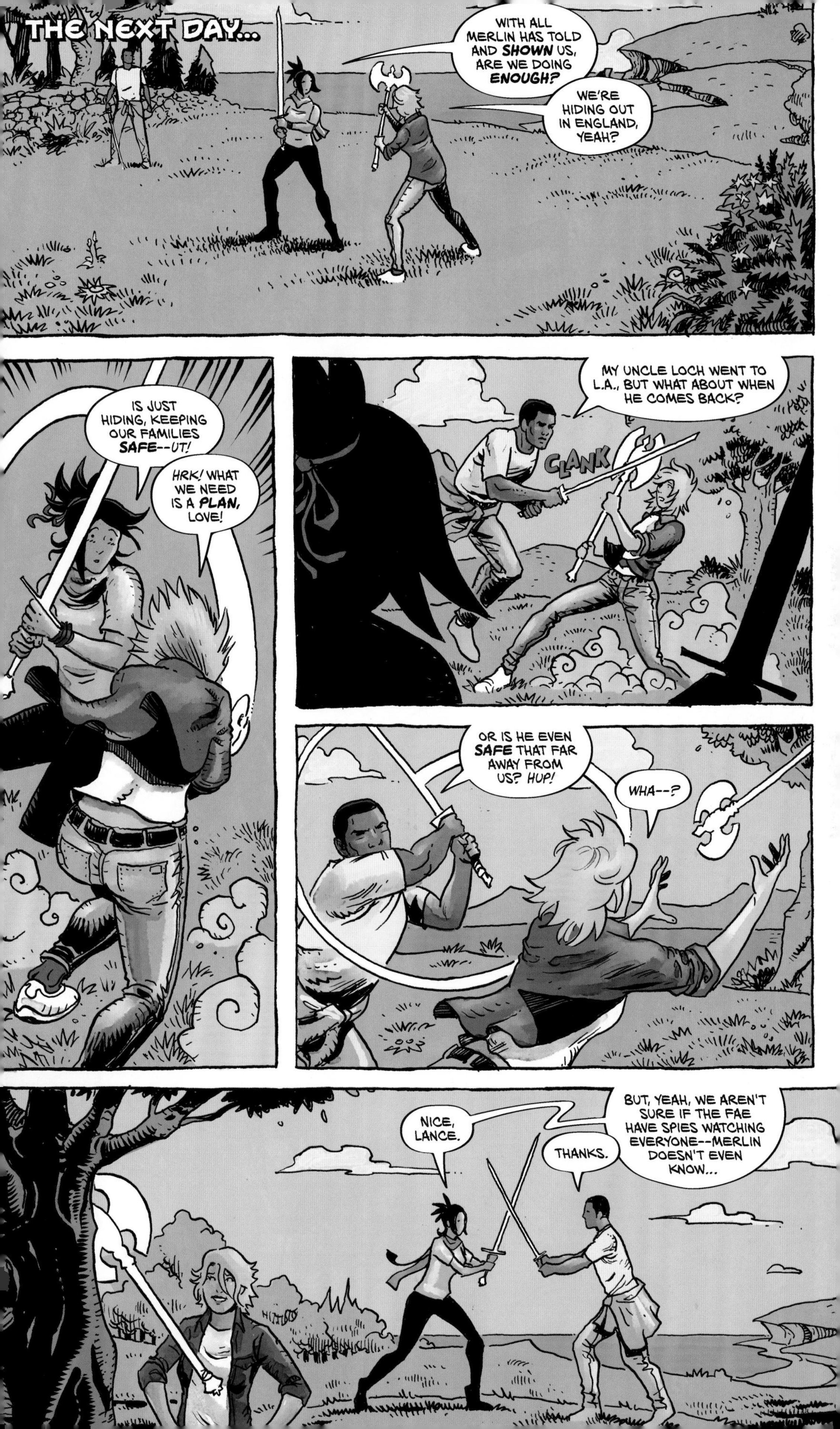
THE NEXT DAY...
WITH ALL MERLIN HAS TOLD AND SHOWN US, ARE WE DOING ENOUGH?
WE'RE HIDING OUT IN ENGLAND, YEAH?
IS JUST HIDING, KEEPING OUR FAMILIES SAFE--UT!
HRK! WHAT WE NEED IS A PLAN, LOVE!
MY UNCLE LOCH WENT TO L.A., BUT WHAT ABOUT WHEN HE COMES BACK?
CLANK
OR IS HE EVEN SAFE THAT FAR AWAY FROM US? HUP!
WHA--?
NICE, LANCE.
THANKS.
BUT, YEAH, WE AREN'T SURE IF THE FAE HAVE SPIES WATCHING EVERYONE--MERLIN DOESN'T EVEN KNOW...

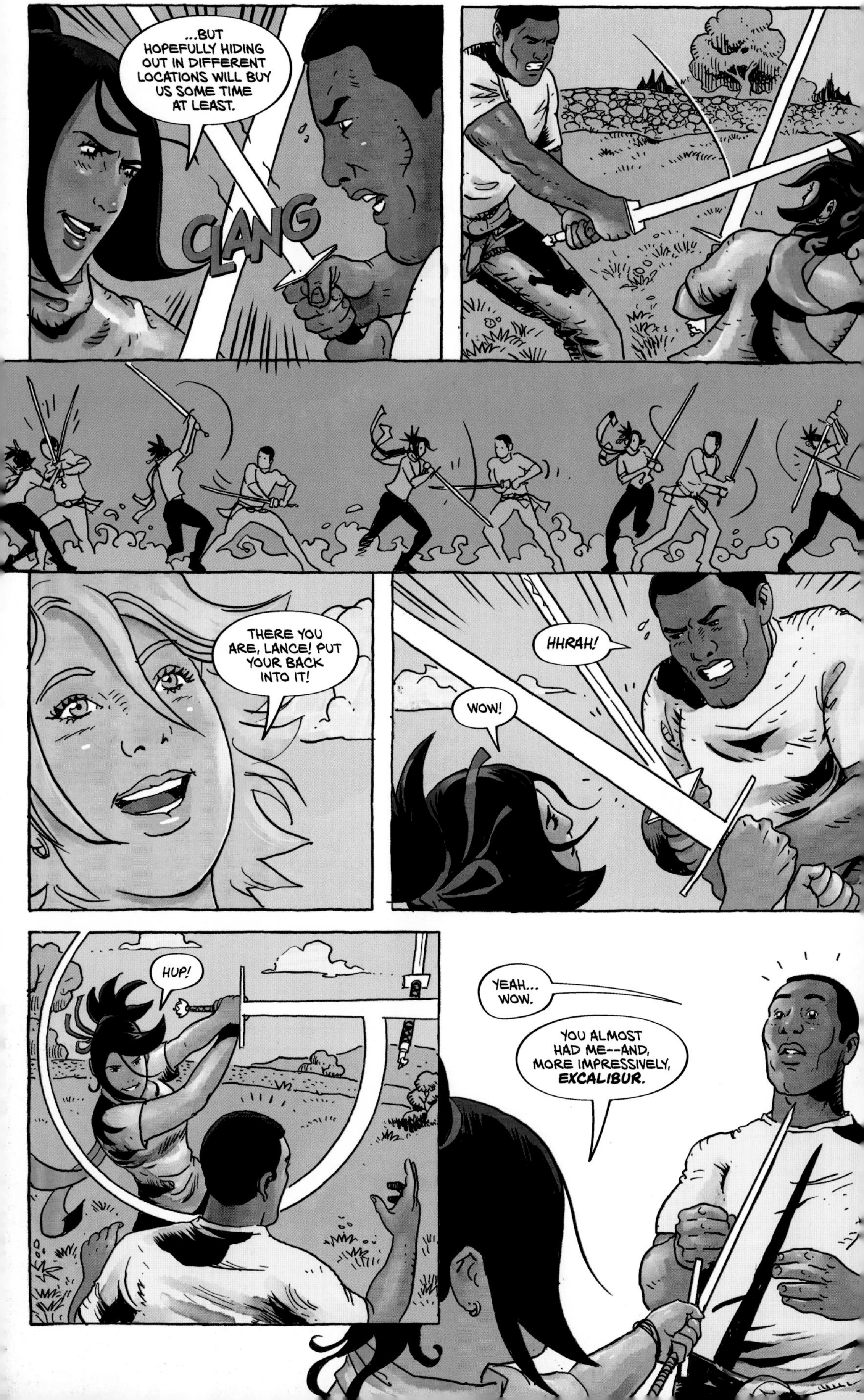
...BUT HOPEFULLY HIDING OUT IN DIFFERENT LOCATIONS WILL BUY US SOME TIME AT LEAST.
CLANG
THERE YOU ARE, LANCE! PUT YOUR BACK INTO IT!
HHRAH!
WOW!
HUP!
YEAH... WOW.
YOU ALMOST HAD ME--AND, MORE IMPRESSIVELY, **EXCALIBUR.**

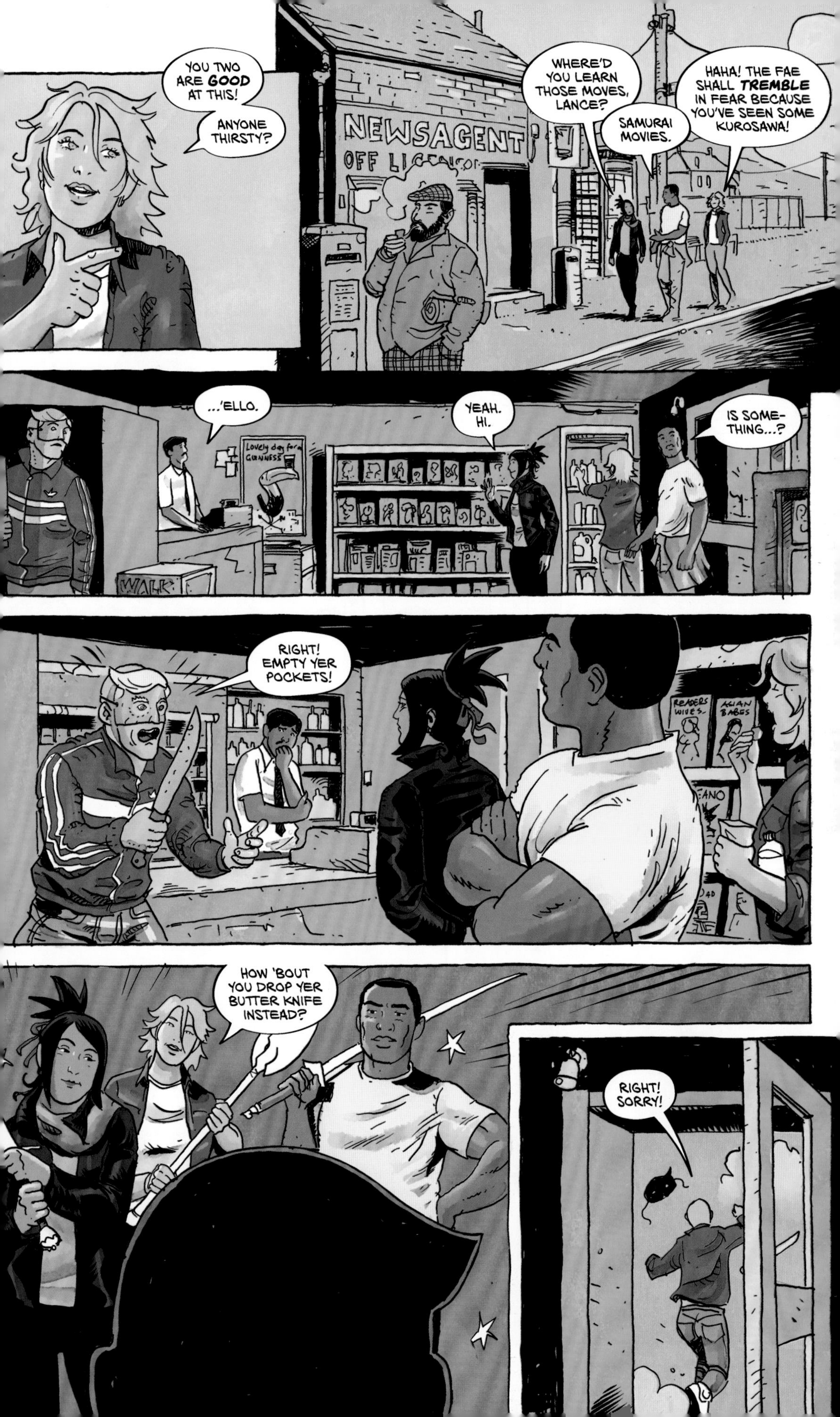
YOU TWO ARE GOOD AT THIS!
ANYONE THIRSTY?
NEWSAGENT
OFF LI...
WHERE'D YOU LEARN THOSE MOVES, LANCE?
SAMURAI MOVIES.
HAHA! THE FAE SHALL TREMBLE IN FEAR BECAUSE YOU'VE SEEN SOME KUROSAWA!
...'ELLO.
Lovely day for a GUINNESS
YEAH. HI.
IS SOMETHING...?
RIGHT! EMPTY YER POCKETS!
READERS WIVES
ASIAN BABES
HOW 'BOUT YOU DROP YER BUTTER KNIFE INSTEAD?
RIGHT! SORRY!

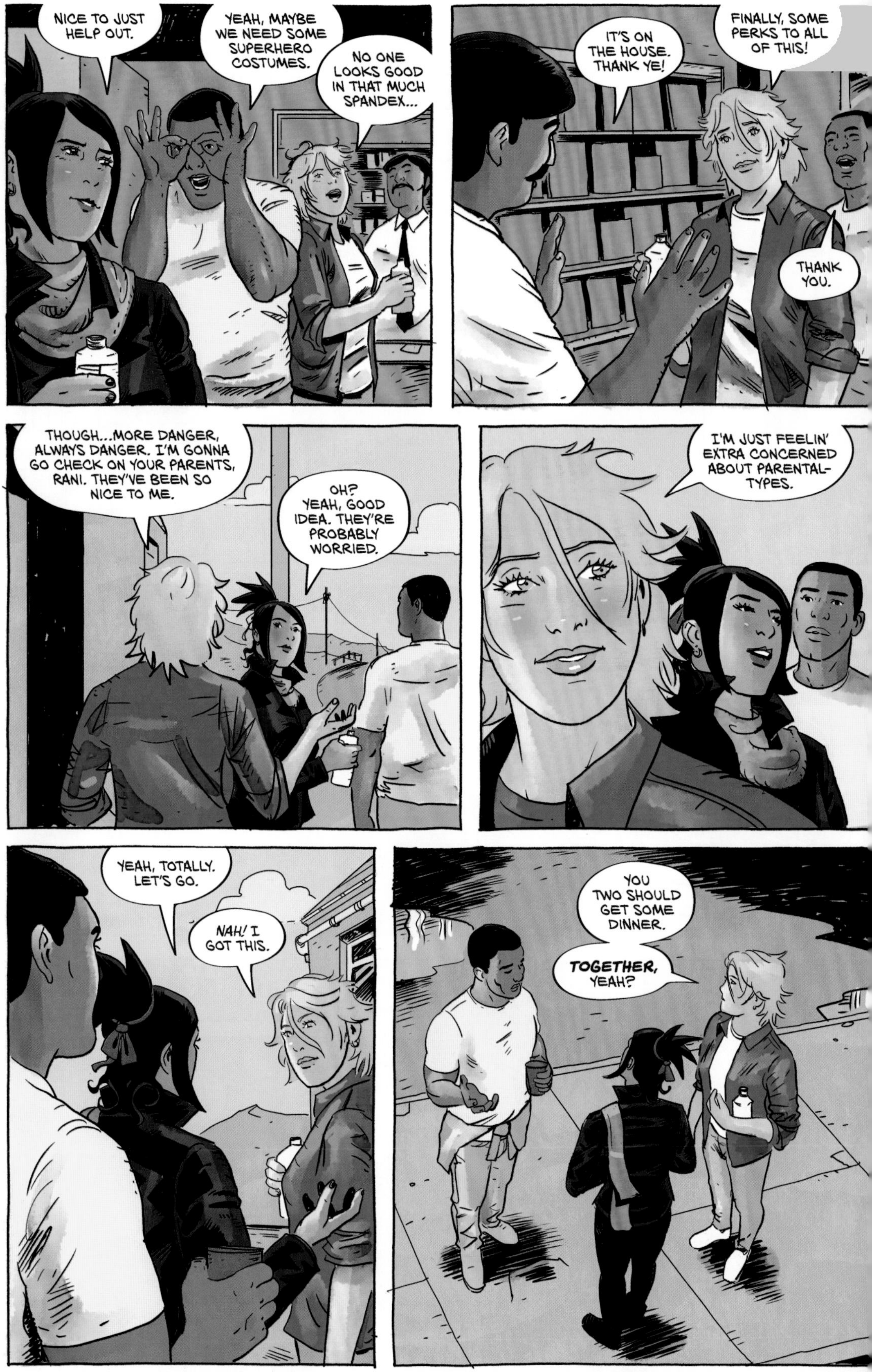
NICE TO JUST HELP OUT.
YEAH, MAYBE WE NEED SOME SUPERHERO COSTUMES.
NO ONE LOOKS GOOD IN THAT MUCH SPANDEX...
IT'S ON THE HOUSE. THANK YE!
FINALLY, SOME PERKS TO ALL OF THIS!
THANK YOU.
THOUGH...MORE DANGER, ALWAYS DANGER. I'M GONNA GO CHECK ON YOUR PARENTS, RANI. THEY'VE BEEN SO NICE TO ME.
OH? YEAH, GOOD IDEA. THEY'RE PROBABLY WORRIED.
I'M JUST FEELIN' EXTRA CONCERNED ABOUT PARENTAL-TYPES.
YEAH, TOTALLY. LET'S GO.
NAH! I GOT THIS.
YOU TWO SHOULD GET SOME DINNER.
TOGETHER, YEAH?

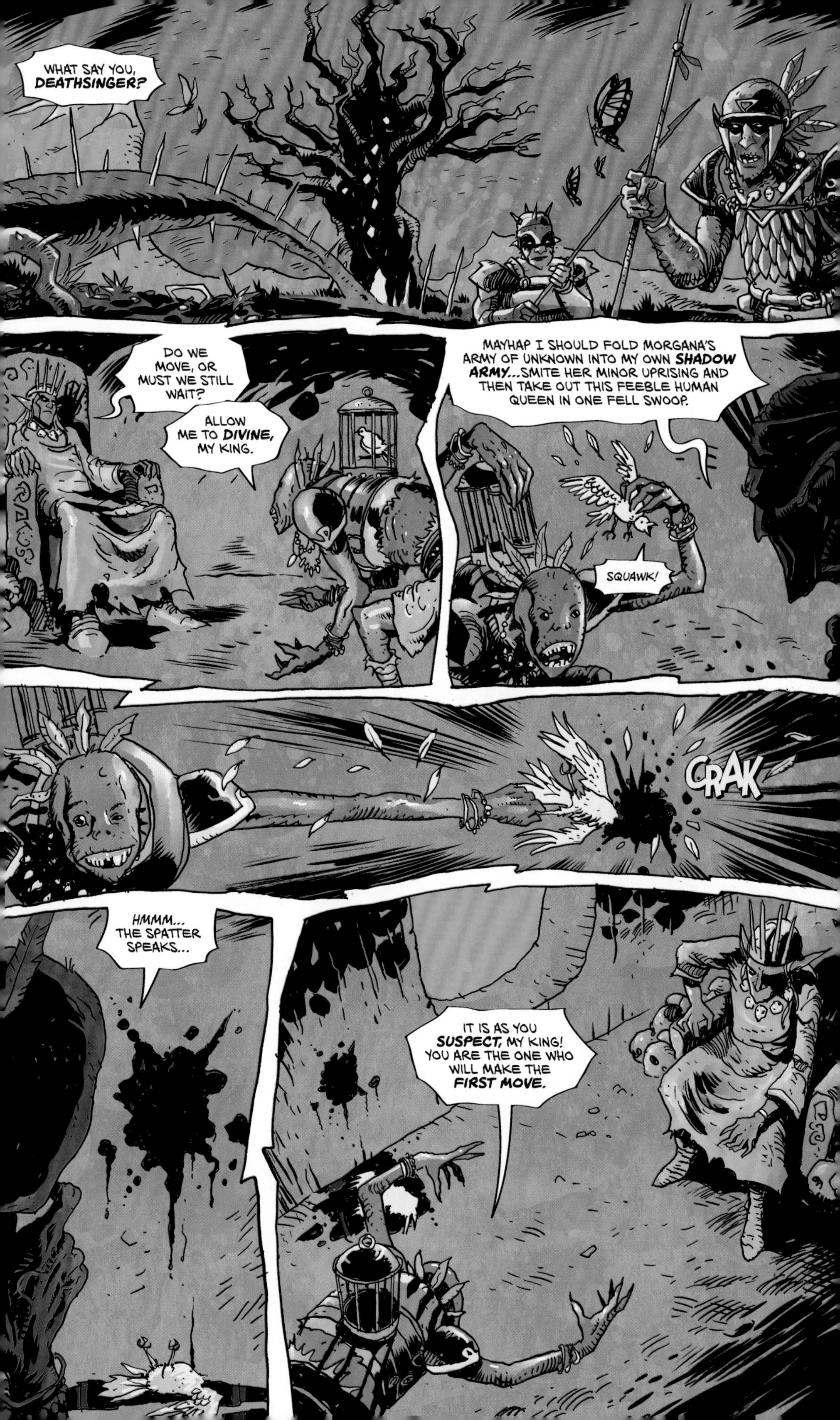
WHAT SAY YOU, DEATHSINGER?
DO WE MOVE, OR MUST WE STILL WAIT?
ALLOW ME TO DIVINE, MY KING.
MAYHAP I SHOULD FOLD MORGANA'S ARMY OF UNKNOWN INTO MY OWN SHADOW ARMY...SMITE HER MINOR UPRISING AND THEN TAKE OUT THIS FEEBLE HUMAN QUEEN IN ONE FELL SWOOP.
SQUAWK!
CRAK
HMMM... THE SPATTER SPEAKS...
IT IS AS YOU SUSPECT, MY KING! YOU ARE THE ONE WHO WILL MAKE THE FIRST MOVE.

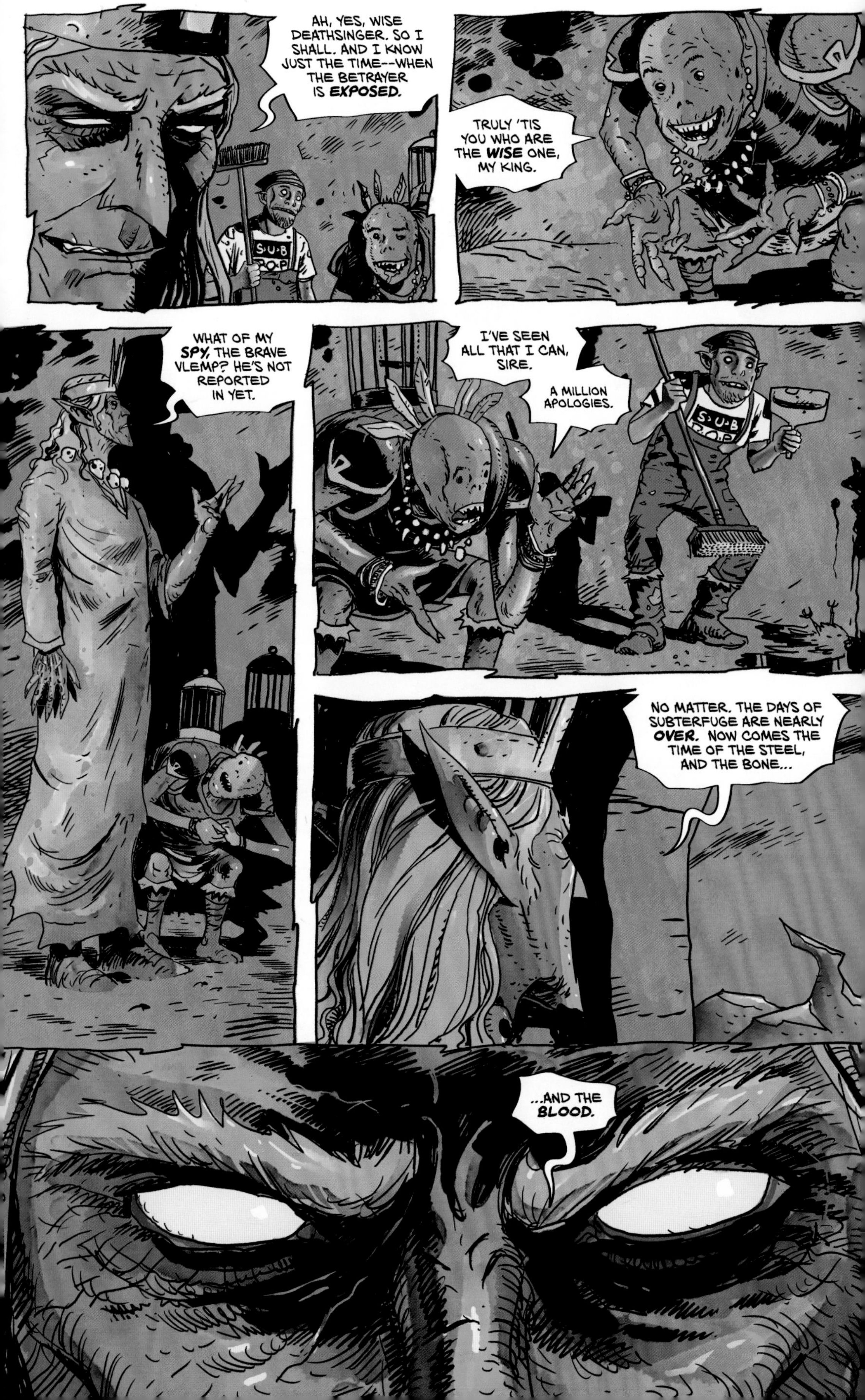

AH, YES, WISE DEATHSINGER. SO I SHALL. AND I KNOW JUST THE TIME--WHEN THE BETRAYER IS **EXPOSED.**
S·U·B
TRULY 'TIS YOU WHO ARE THE **WISE** ONE, MY KING.
WHAT OF MY **SPY,** THE BRAVE VLEMP? HE'S NOT REPORTED IN YET.
I'VE SEEN ALL THAT I CAN, SIRE.
A MILLION APOLOGIES.
S·U·B
NO MATTER. THE DAYS OF SUBTERFUGE ARE NEARLY **OVER.** NOW COMES THE TIME OF THE STEEL, AND THE BONE...
...AND THE **BLOOD.**

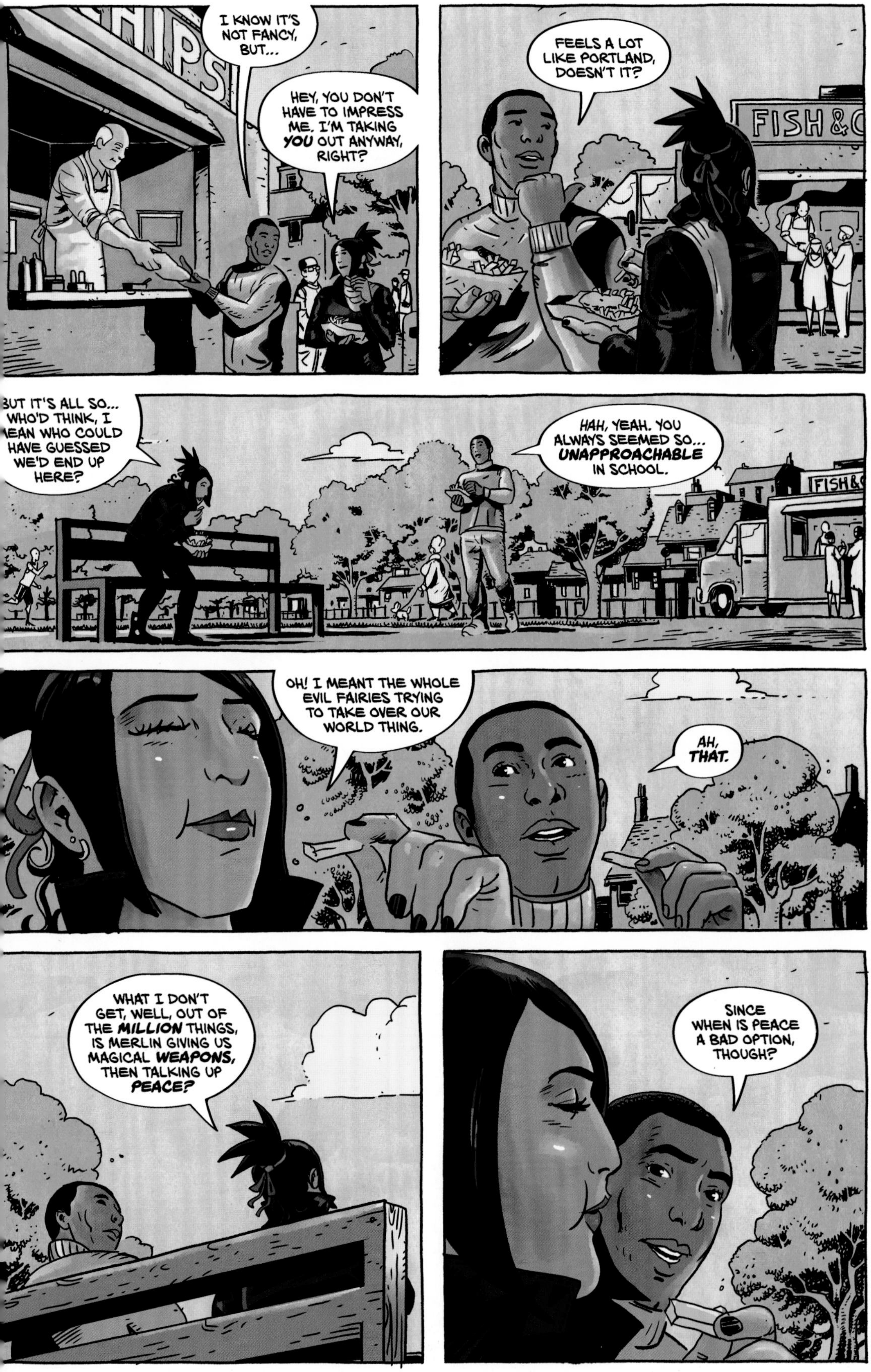

I KNOW IT'S NOT FANCY, BUT...
HEY, YOU DON'T HAVE TO IMPRESS ME. I'M TAKING *YOU* OUT ANYWAY, RIGHT?
CHIPS
FEELS A LOT LIKE PORTLAND, DOESN'T IT?
FISH &
BUT IT'S ALL SO... WHO'D THINK, I MEAN WHO COULD HAVE GUESSED WE'D END UP HERE?
HAH, YEAH. YOU ALWAYS SEEMED SO... ***UNAPPROACHABLE*** IN SCHOOL.
OH! I MEANT THE WHOLE EVIL FAIRIES TRYING TO TAKE OVER OUR WORLD THING.
AH, ***THAT.***
WHAT I DON'T GET, WELL, OUT OF THE ***MILLION*** THINGS, IS MERLIN GIVING US MAGICAL ***WEAPONS,*** THEN TALKING UP ***PEACE?***
SINCE WHEN IS PEACE A BAD OPTION, THOUGH?

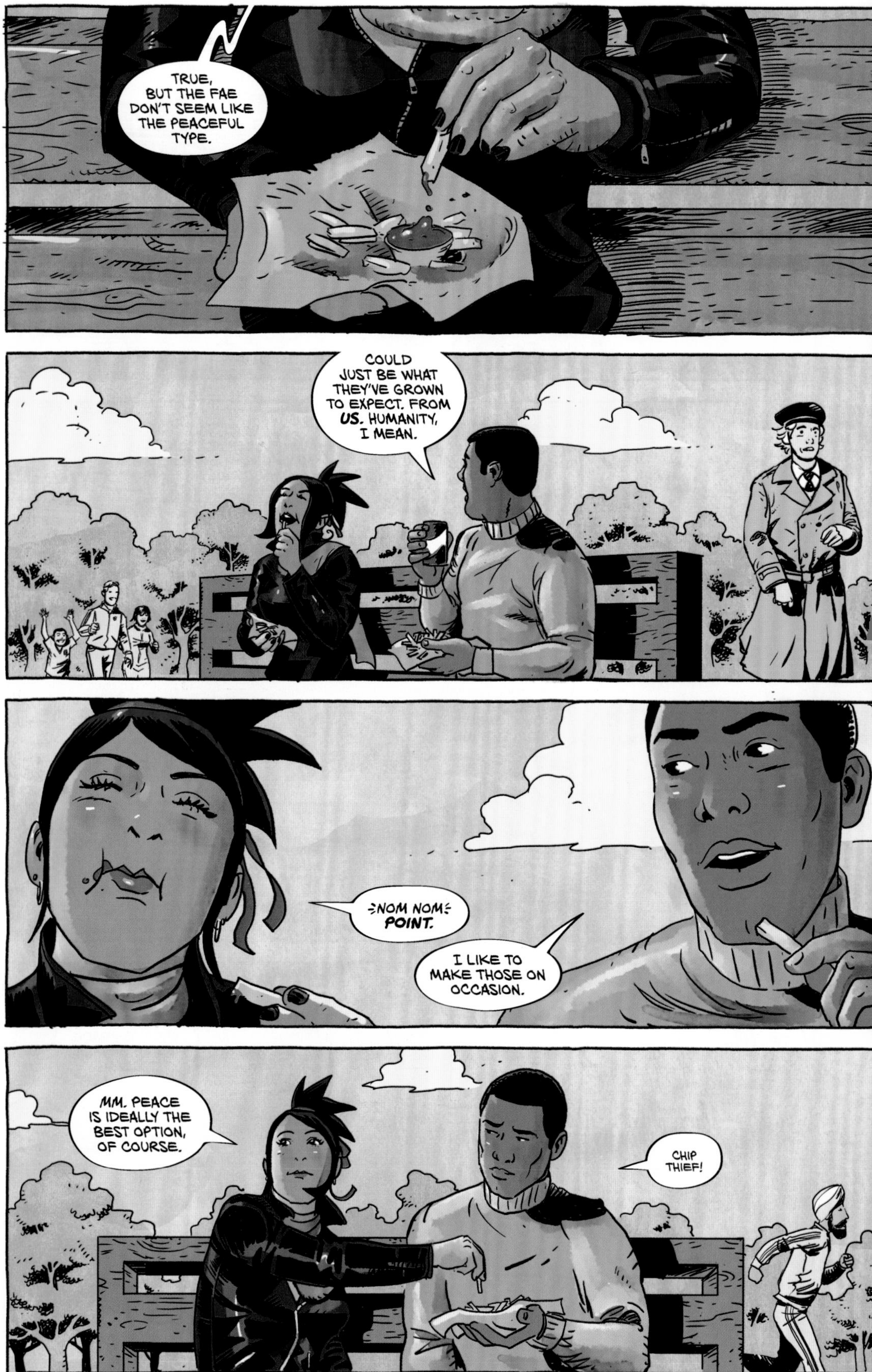
TRUE, BUT THE FAE DON'T SEEM LIKE THE PEACEFUL TYPE.
COULD JUST BE WHAT THEY'VE GROWN TO EXPECT. FROM US. HUMANITY, I MEAN.
NOM NOM POINT.
I LIKE TO MAKE THOSE ON OCCASION.
MM. PEACE IS IDEALLY THE BEST OPTION, OF COURSE.
CHIP THIEF!

LANCE, SHOULD WE EVEN BE TRYING TO, UH...

DATE?

YEAH, *THAT*. I LIKE YOU AND GWEN BOTH, BUT THERE'S *SO MUCH* AT STAKE.

DOES LIFE STOP DURING WARTIME?

I DUNNO. MAYBE. NEVER RAN A WAR BEFORE, OUTSIDE OF A CHESSBOARD.

BUT THOSE WERE...GAMES. THIS IS *REAL*. I MEAN, CAN WE EVEN HAVE A SOCIAL LIFE, EVEN WITH EACH OTHER--

AND GWEN.

--AND GWEN, YEAH, WITH ALL THAT'S HAPPENING? WHERE DO WE EVEN GO FROM HERE?

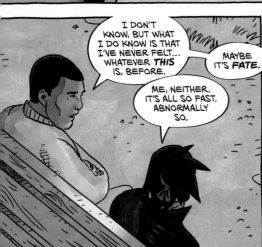

I DON'T KNOW, BUT WHAT I DO KNOW IS THAT I'VE NEVER FELT... WHATEVER *THIS* IS, BEFORE.

MAYBE IT'S *FATE*.

ME, NEITHER. IT'S ALL SO FAST. ABNORMALLY SO.

I DON'T BELIEVE IN THAT SHIT.

THIS FROM THE GIRL WHO LITERALLY PULLED THE *SWORD* FROM THE *STONE*.

I'M GOING TO KISS YOU NOW. IS THAT...DO YOU ENJOY IT?

SOMETIMES. NOW. YEAH.

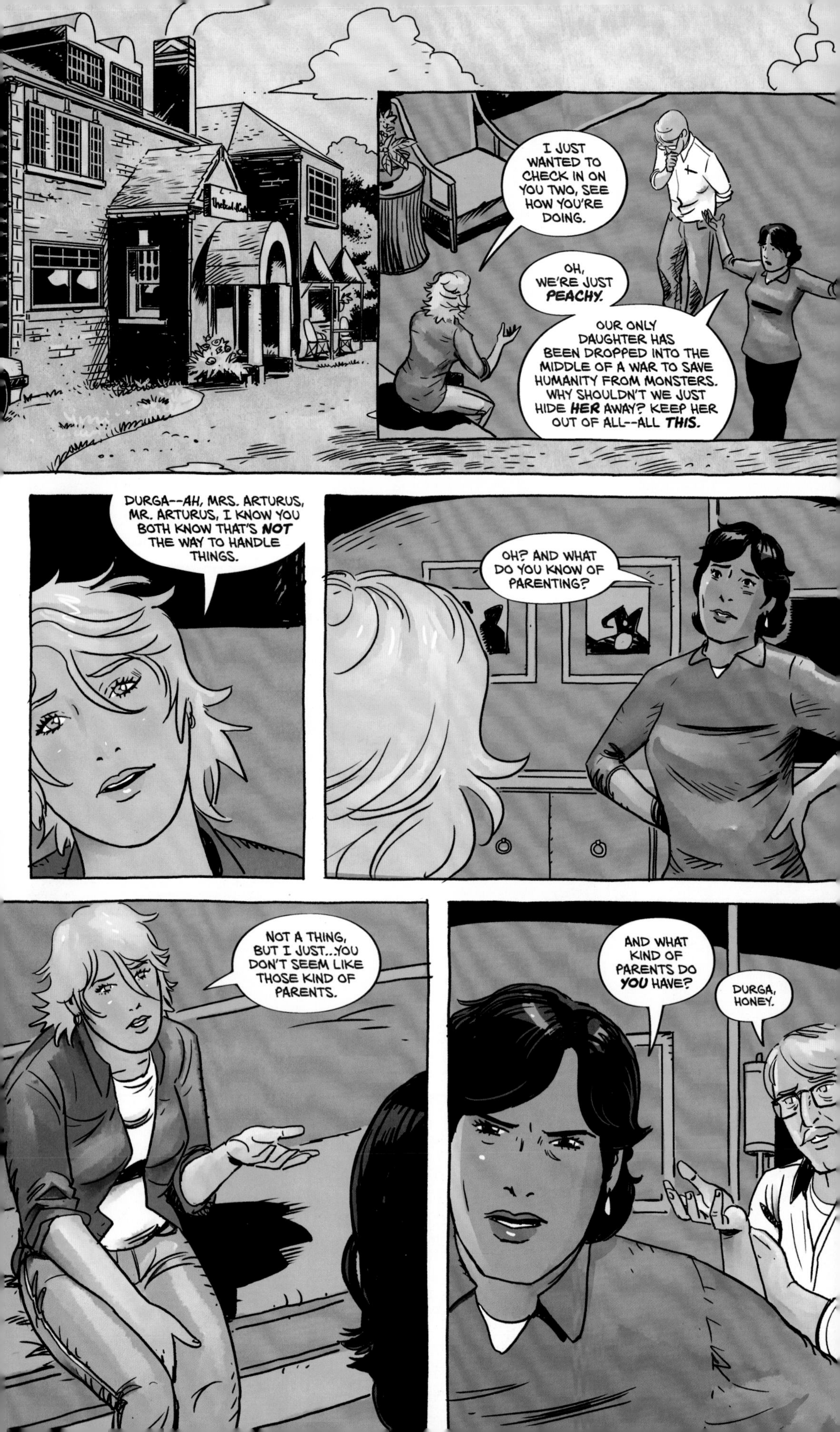
I JUST WANTED TO CHECK IN ON YOU TWO, SEE HOW YOU'RE DOING.
OH, WE'RE JUST *PEACHY.*
OUR ONLY DAUGHTER HAS BEEN DROPPED INTO THE MIDDLE OF A WAR TO SAVE HUMANITY FROM MONSTERS. WHY SHOULDN'T WE JUST HIDE **HER** AWAY? KEEP HER OUT OF ALL--ALL **THIS.**
DURGA--*AH*, MRS. ARTURUS, MR. ARTURUS, I KNOW YOU BOTH KNOW THAT'S **NOT** THE WAY TO HANDLE THINGS.
OH? AND WHAT DO YOU KNOW OF PARENTING?
NOT A THING, BUT I JUST...YOU DON'T SEEM LIKE THOSE KIND OF PARENTS.
AND WHAT KIND OF PARENTS DO **YOU** HAVE?
DURGA, HONEY.

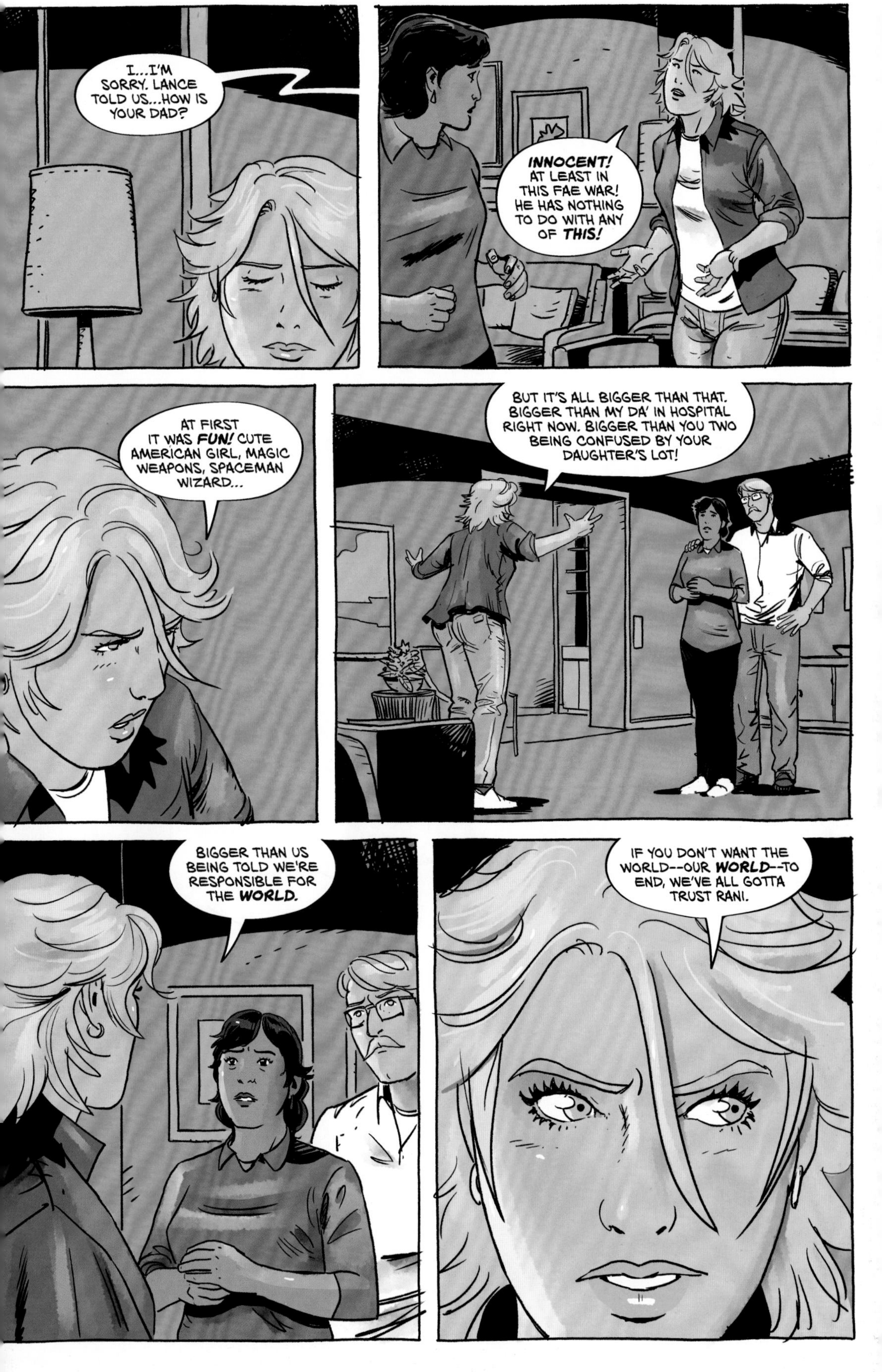
I...I'M SORRY. LANCE TOLD US...HOW IS YOUR DAD?
INNOCENT! AT LEAST IN THIS FAE WAR! HE HAS NOTHING TO DO WITH ANY OF THIS!
AT FIRST IT WAS FUN! CUTE AMERICAN GIRL, MAGIC WEAPONS, SPACEMAN WIZARD...
BUT IT'S ALL BIGGER THAN THAT. BIGGER THAN MY DA' IN HOSPITAL RIGHT NOW. BIGGER THAN YOU TWO BEING CONFUSED BY YOUR DAUGHTER'S LOT!
BIGGER THAN US BEING TOLD WE'RE RESPONSIBLE FOR THE WORLD.
IF YOU DON'T WANT THE WORLD--OUR WORLD--TO END, WE'VE ALL GOTTA TRUST RANI.

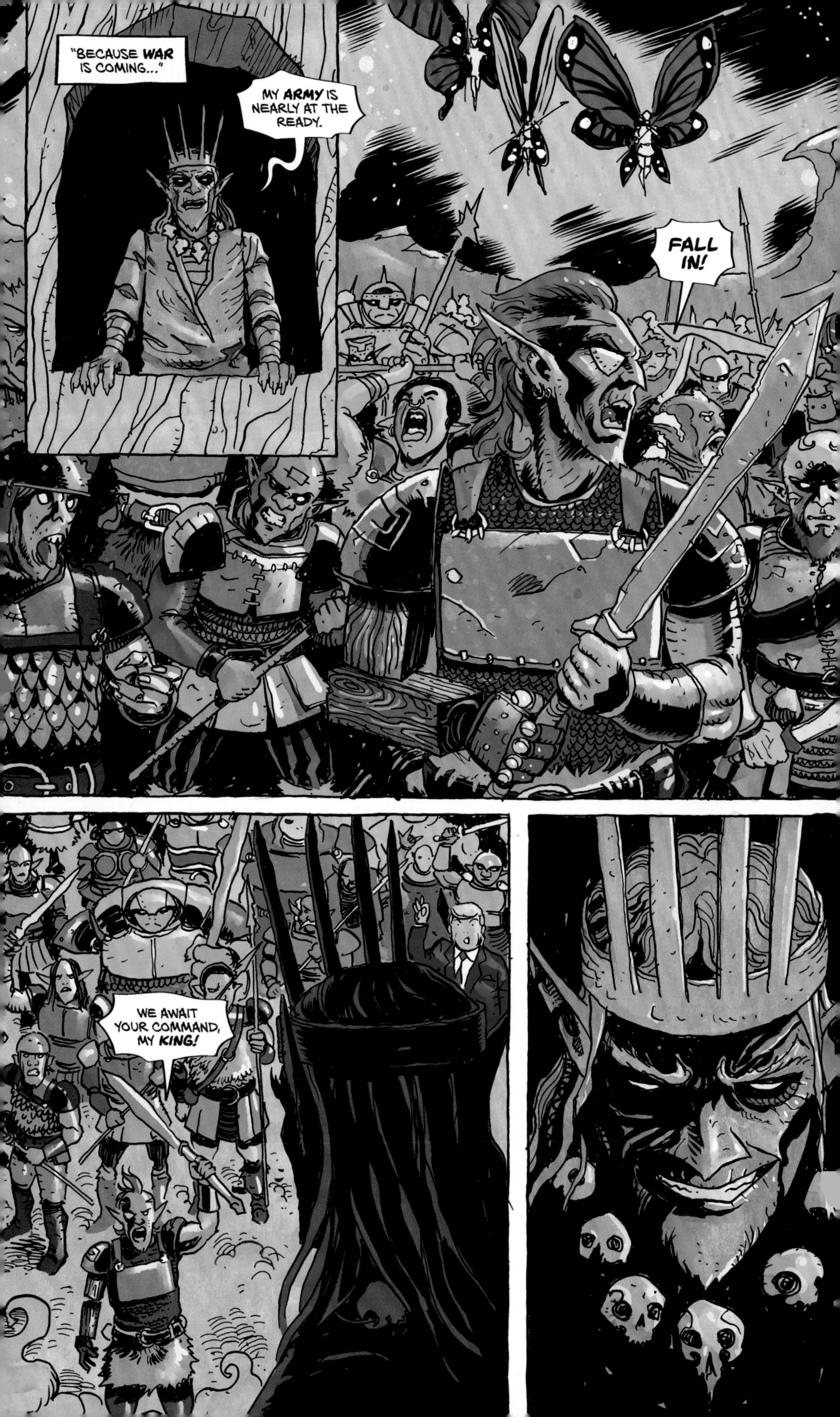
"BECAUSE WAR IS COMING..."
MY ARMY IS NEARLY AT THE READY.
FALL IN!
WE AWAIT YOUR COMMAND, MY KING!

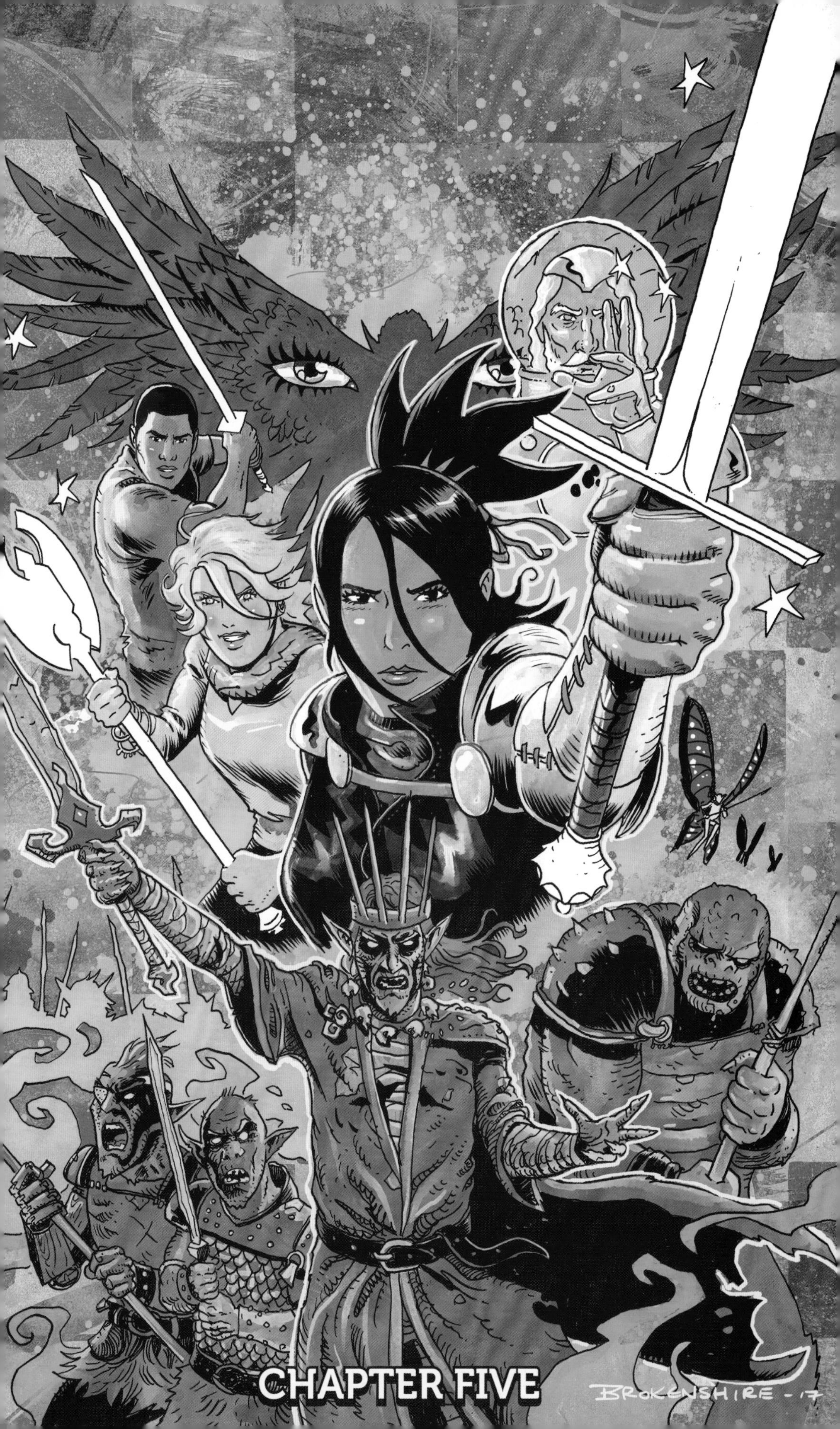
BROKENSHIRE - 17

CHAPTER FIVE

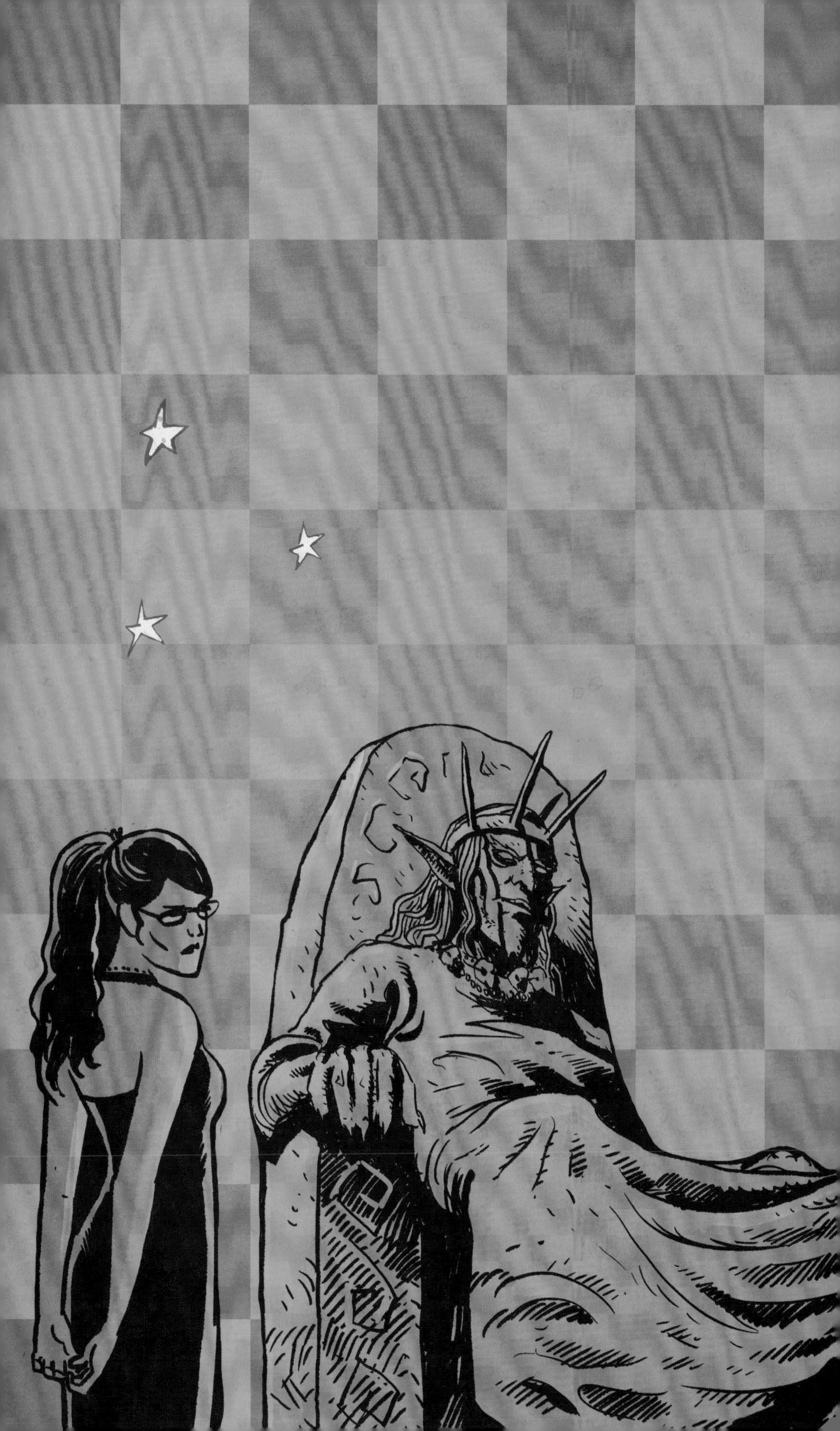

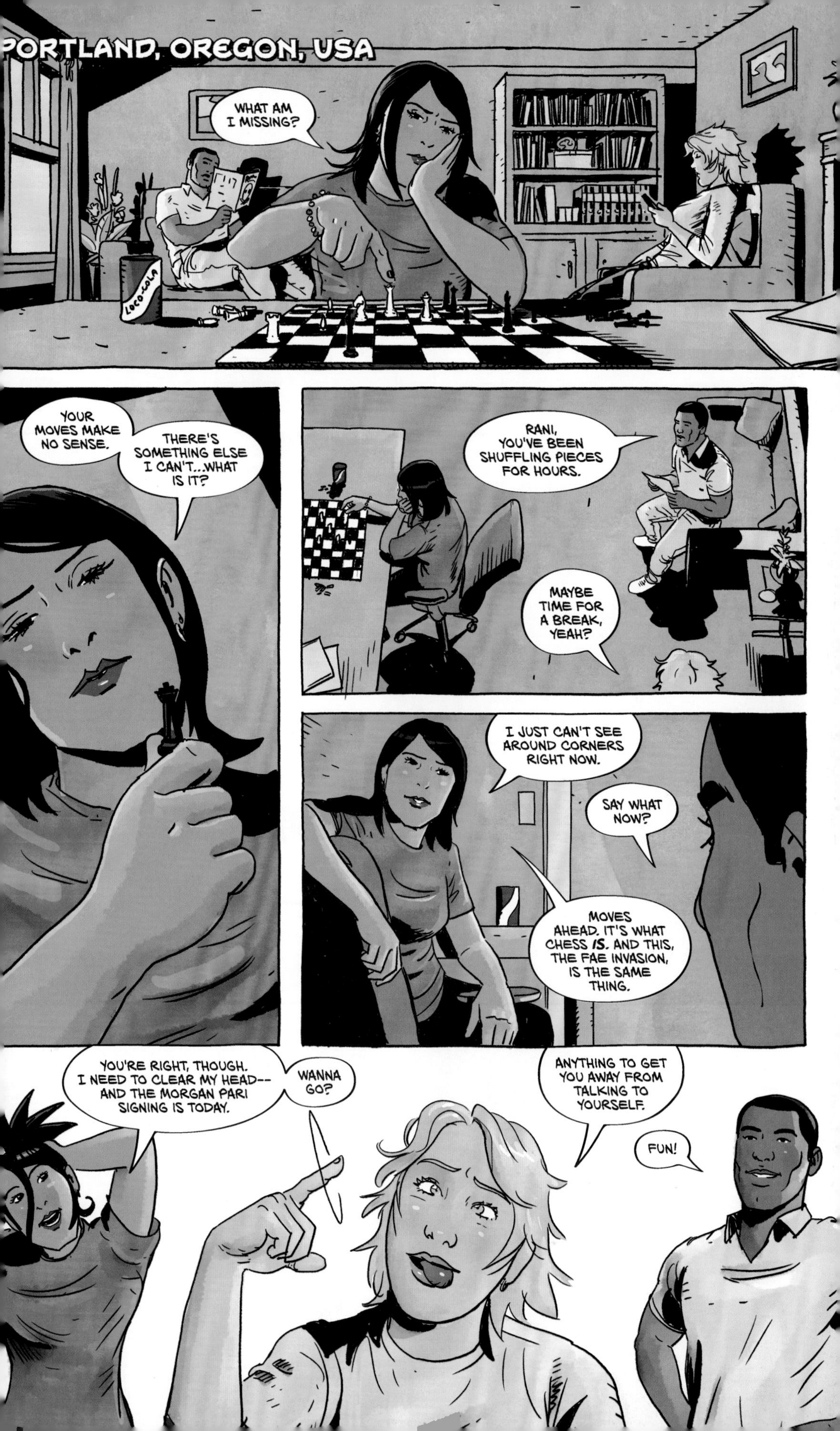
PORTLAND, OREGON, USA
WHAT AM I MISSING?
LOCO-COLA
YOUR MOVES MAKE NO SENSE.
THERE'S SOMETHING ELSE I CAN'T...WHAT IS IT?
RANI, YOU'VE BEEN SHUFFLING PIECES FOR HOURS.
MAYBE TIME FOR A BREAK, YEAH?
I JUST CAN'T SEE AROUND CORNERS RIGHT NOW.
SAY WHAT NOW?
MOVES AHEAD. IT'S WHAT CHESS *IS.* AND THIS, THE FAE INVASION, IS THE SAME THING.
YOU'RE RIGHT, THOUGH. I NEED TO CLEAR MY HEAD-- AND THE MORGAN PARI SIGNING IS TODAY.
WANNA GO?
ANYTHING TO GET YOU AWAY FROM TALKING TO YOURSELF.
FUN!

MORGAN PARI'S HOTEL

WHAT'S THIS?

PENS! FOR, *UH,* FOR SIGNING YOUR BOOKS?

HOOBOY...

I BROUGHT MY LUCKY PEN BECAUSE THIS **HAS** TO BE A GOOD SIGNING.

IT **WILL** BE. THE CROWD IS EXCITED. *LOST FAE* IS STILL A BEST-SELLER AND--

THAT WAS MY **LAST** BOOK. *TERMINAL WINGS* IS UNDER-PERFORMING.

IT'S DOING FINE, MORGAN, JUST A DENSER READ.

YOU'VE DONE THIS A THOUSAND TIMES. WHY ARE YOU STRESSING?

THIS ONE'S IMPORTANT, IS ALL. I DON'T WANT TO LET MY FANS DOWN. MY ARMY.

ARMY?

OF FANS, BETTY! THERE ARE A LOT OF THEM. IT'LL B **FINE.**

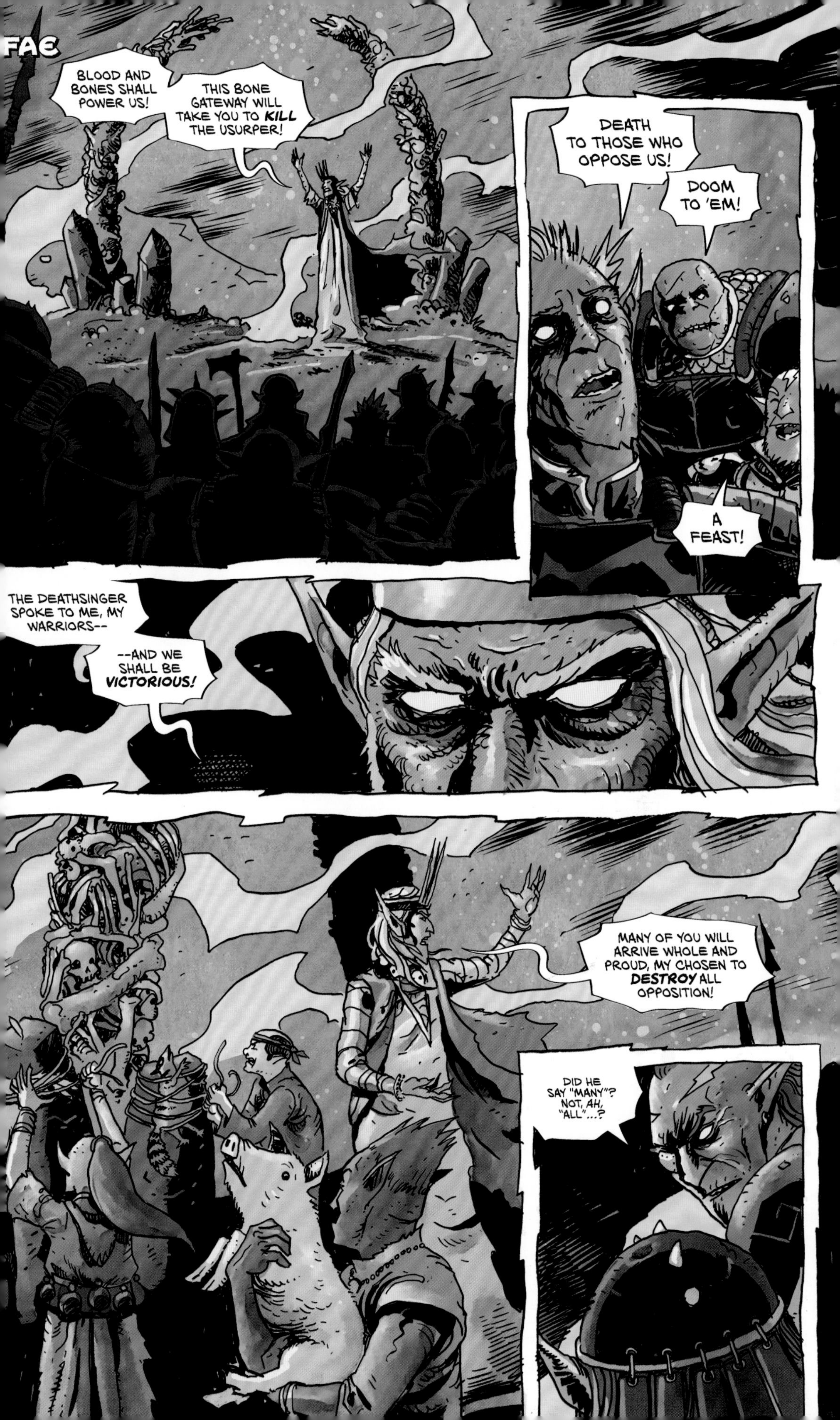
BLOOD AND BONES SHALL POWER US!
THIS BONE GATEWAY WILL TAKE YOU TO **KILL** THE USURPER!
DEATH TO THOSE WHO OPPOSE US!
DOOM TO 'EM!
A FEAST!
THE DEATHSINGER SPOKE TO ME, MY WARRIORS--
--AND WE SHALL BE **VICTORIOUS!**
MANY OF YOU WILL ARRIVE WHOLE AND PROUD, MY CHOSEN TO **DESTROY** ALL OPPOSITION!
DID HE SAY "MANY"? NOT, *AH,* "ALL"...?

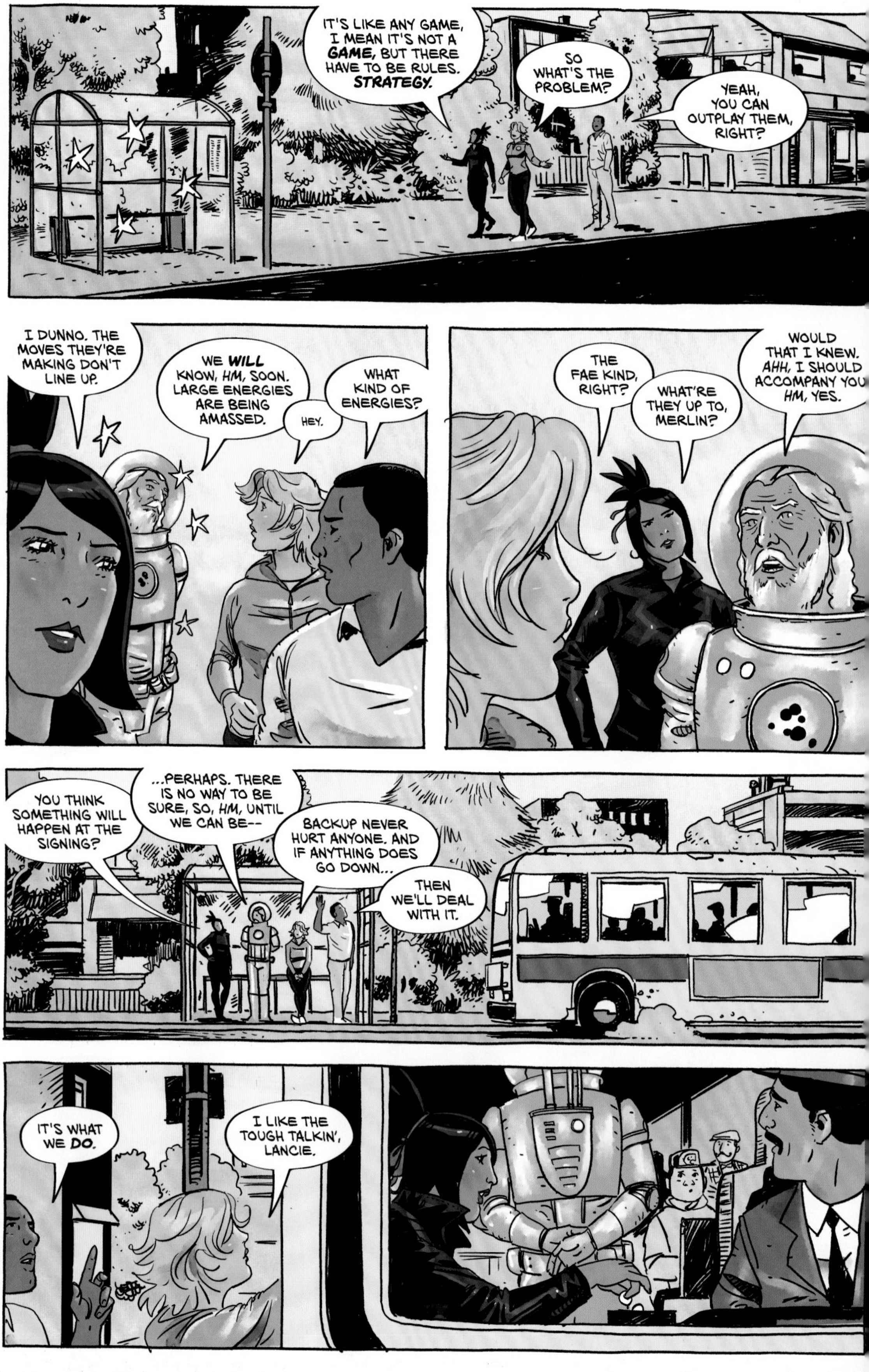
IT'S LIKE ANY GAME, I MEAN IT'S NOT A GAME, BUT THERE HAVE TO BE RULES. STRATEGY.
SO WHAT'S THE PROBLEM?
YEAH, YOU CAN OUTPLAY THEM, RIGHT?
I DUNNO. THE MOVES THEY'RE MAKING DON'T LINE UP.
WE WILL KNOW, HM, SOON. LARGE ENERGIES ARE BEING AMASSED.
HEY.
WHAT KIND OF ENERGIES?
THE FAE KIND, RIGHT?
WHAT'RE THEY UP TO, MERLIN?
WOULD THAT I KNEW. AHH, I SHOULD ACCOMPANY YOU HM, YES.
YOU THINK SOMETHING WILL HAPPEN AT THE SIGNING?
...PERHAPS. THERE IS NO WAY TO BE SURE, SO, HM, UNTIL WE CAN BE--
BACKUP NEVER HURT ANYONE. AND IF ANYTHING DOES GO DOWN...
THEN WE'LL DEAL WITH IT.
IT'S WHAT WE DO.
I LIKE THE TOUGH TALKIN', LANCIE.

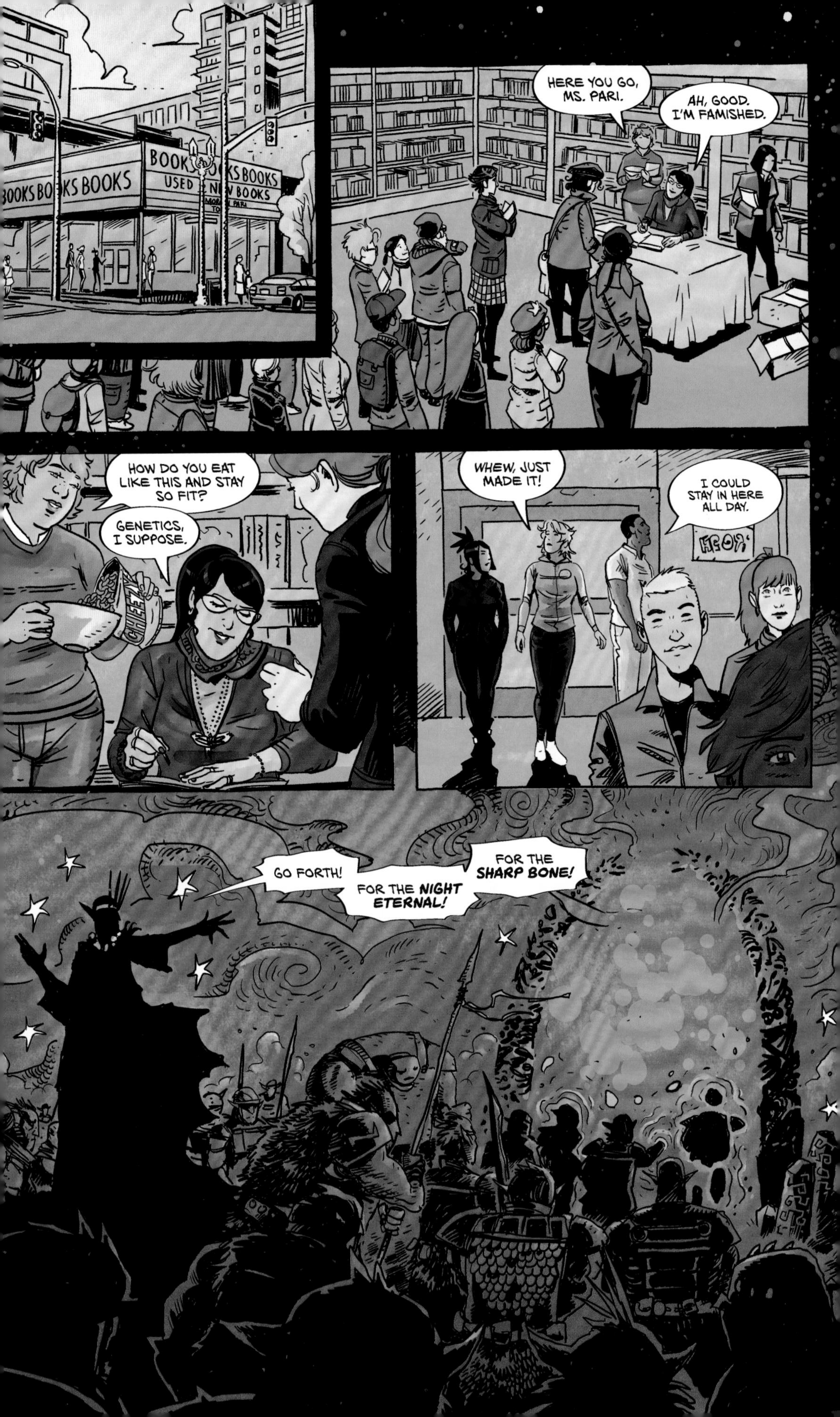
BOOKS BOOKS BOOKS
BOOKS BOOKS BOOKS
USED NEW BOOKS
HERE YOU GO, MS. PARI.
AH, GOOD. I'M FAMISHED.
HOW DO YOU EAT LIKE THIS AND STAY SO FIT?
GENETICS, I SUPPOSE.
WHEW, JUST MADE IT!
I COULD STAY IN HERE ALL DAY.
GO FORTH!
FOR THE NIGHT ETERNAL!
FOR THE SHARP BONE!

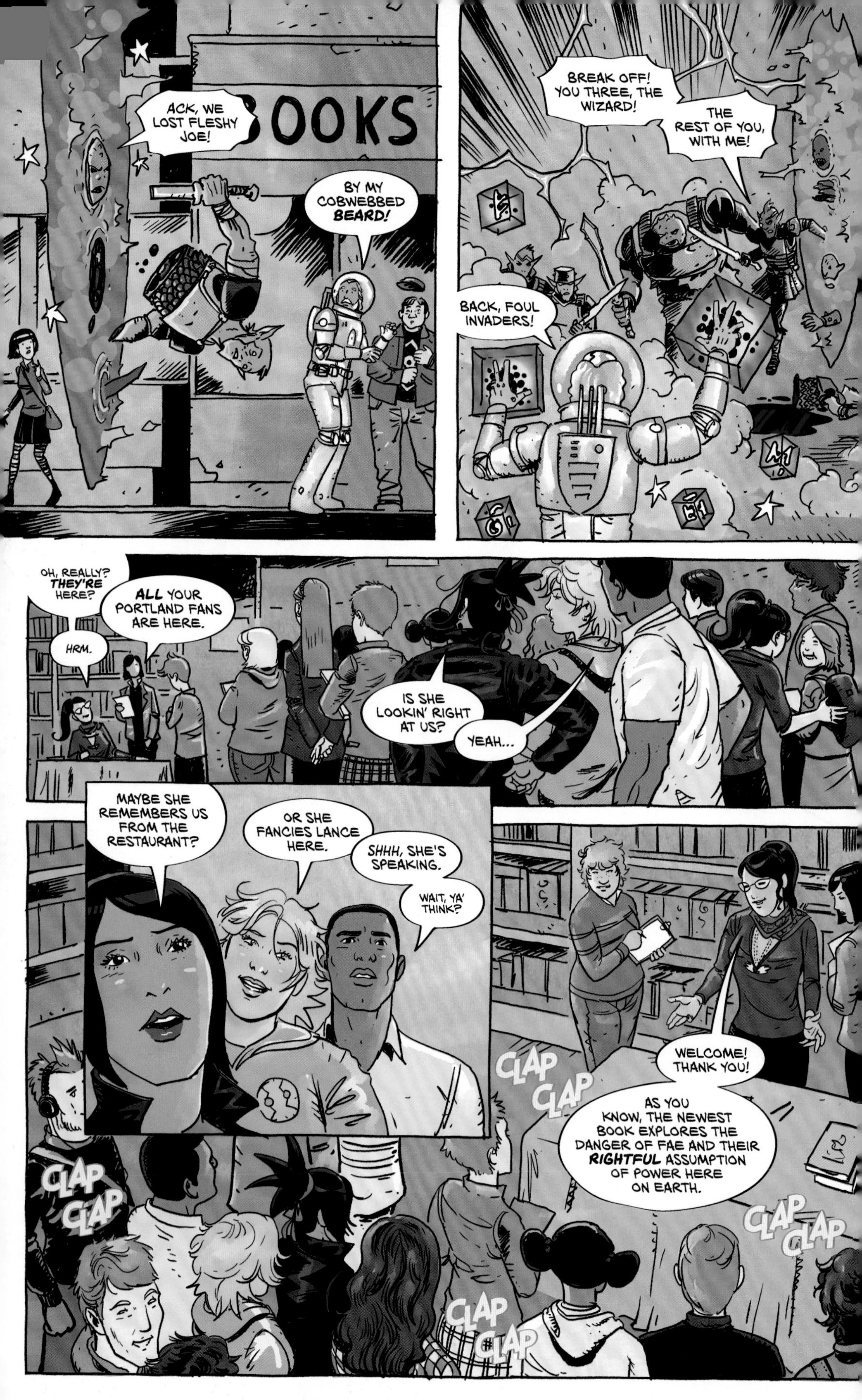

BOOKS
ACK, WE LOST FLESHY JOE!
BY MY COBWEBBED **BEARD!**
BREAK OFF! YOU THREE, THE WIZARD!
THE REST OF YOU, WITH ME!
BACK, FOUL INVADERS!
OH, REALLY? **THEY'RE** HERE?
ALL YOUR PORTLAND FANS ARE HERE.
HRM.
IS SHE LOOKIN' RIGHT AT US?
YEAH...
MAYBE SHE REMEMBERS US FROM THE RESTAURANT?
OR SHE FANCIES LANCE HERE.
SHHH, SHE'S SPEAKING.
WAIT, YA' THINK?
WELCOME! THANK YOU!
AS YOU KNOW, THE NEWEST BOOK EXPLORES THE DANGER OF FAE AND THEIR **RIGHTFUL** ASSUMPTION OF POWER HERE ON EARTH.
CLAP CLAP
CLAP CLAP
CLAP CLAP
CLAP CLAP

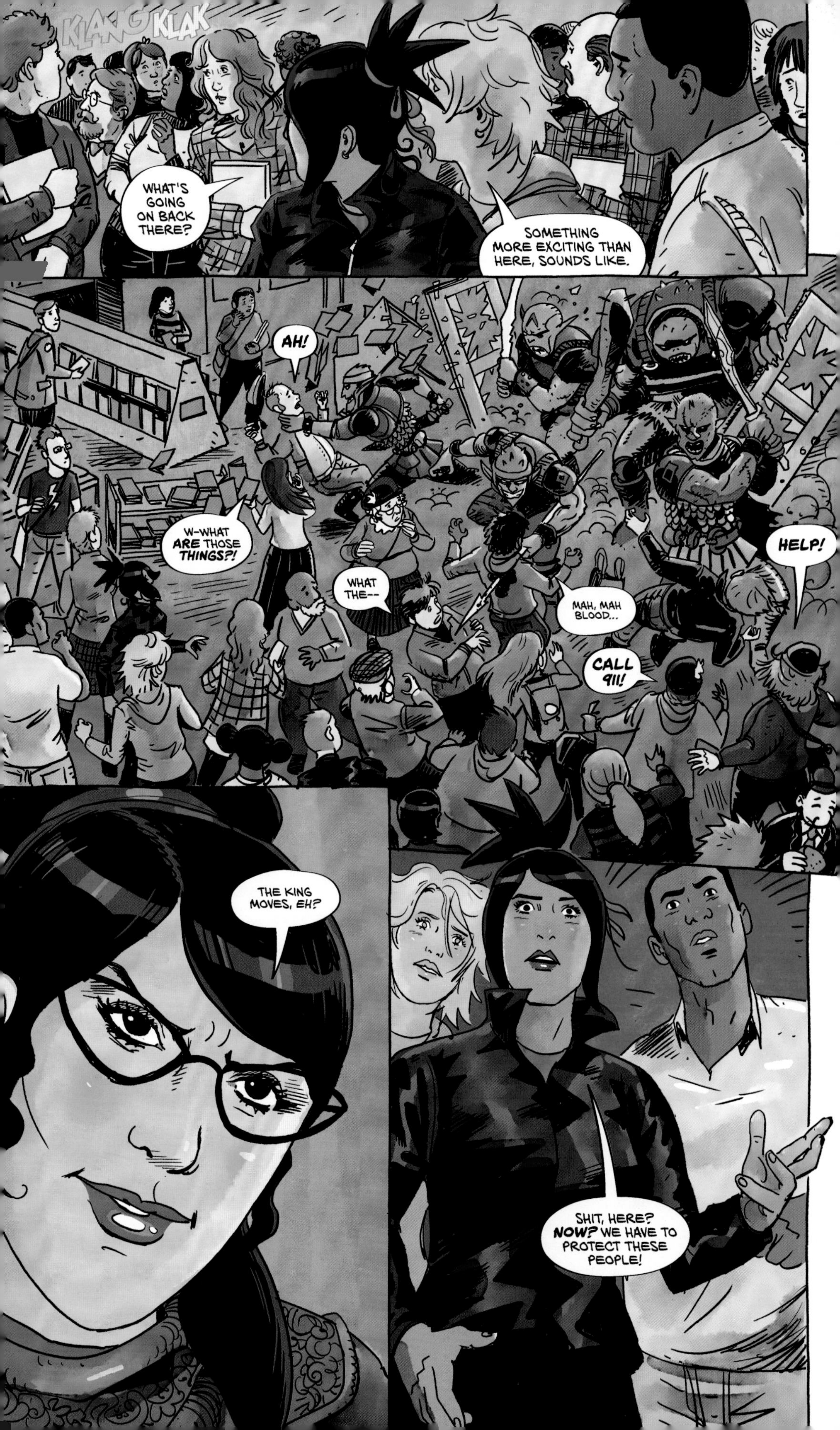
KLANG KLAK
WHAT'S GOING ON BACK THERE?
SOMETHING MORE EXCITING THAN HERE, SOUNDS LIKE.
AH!
W-WHAT ARE THOSE THINGS?!
WHAT THE--
MAH, MAH BLOOD...
CALL 911!
HELP!
THE KING MOVES, EH?
SHIT, HERE? NOW? WE HAVE TO PROTECT THESE PEOPLE!

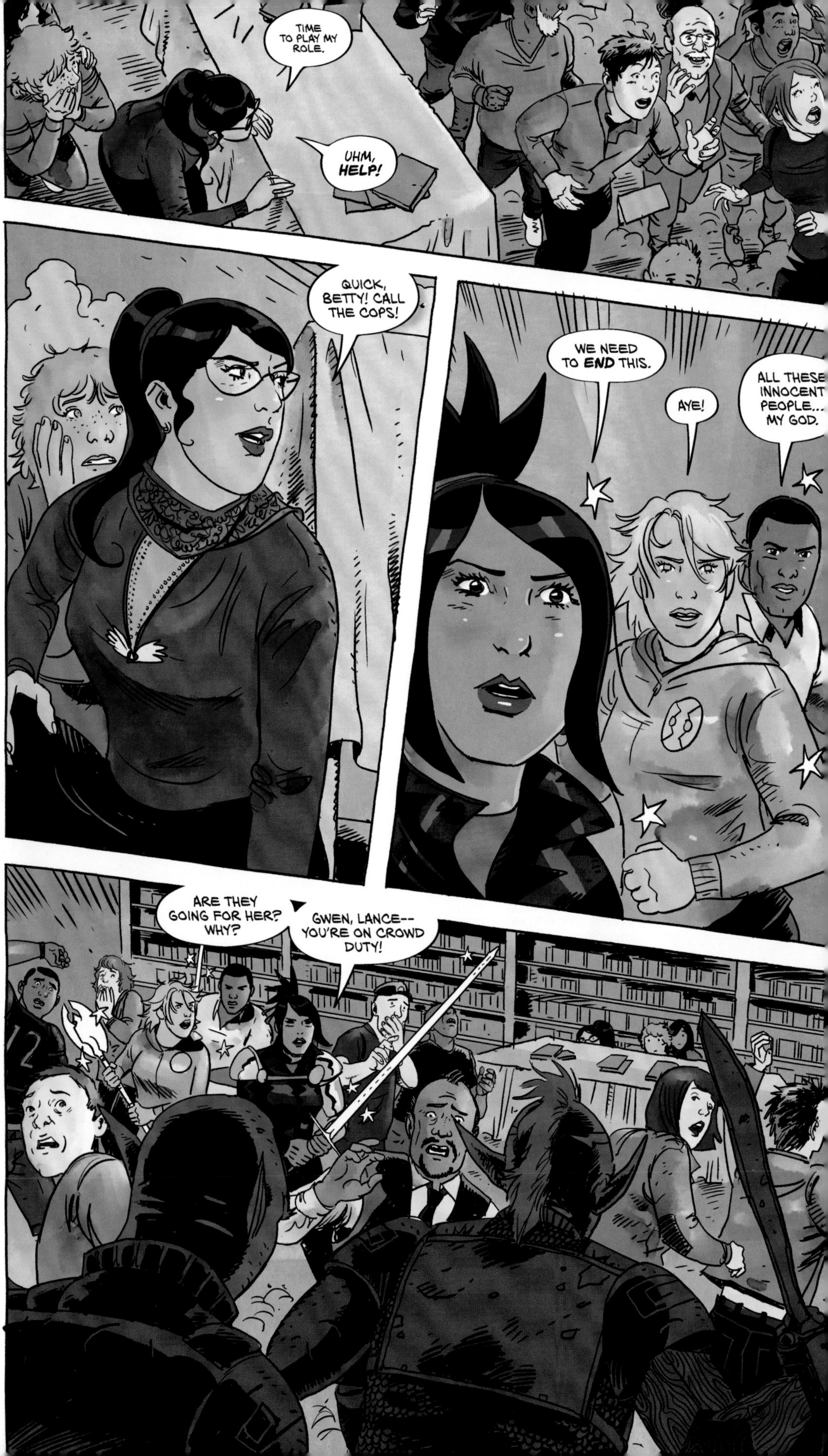
TIME TO PLAY MY ROLE.
UHM, **HELP!**
QUICK, BETTY! CALL THE COPS!
WE NEED TO **END** THIS.
AYE!
ALL THESE INNOCENT PEOPLE... MY GOD.
ARE THEY GOING FOR HER? WHY?
GWEN, LANCE-- YOU'RE ON CROWD DUTY!

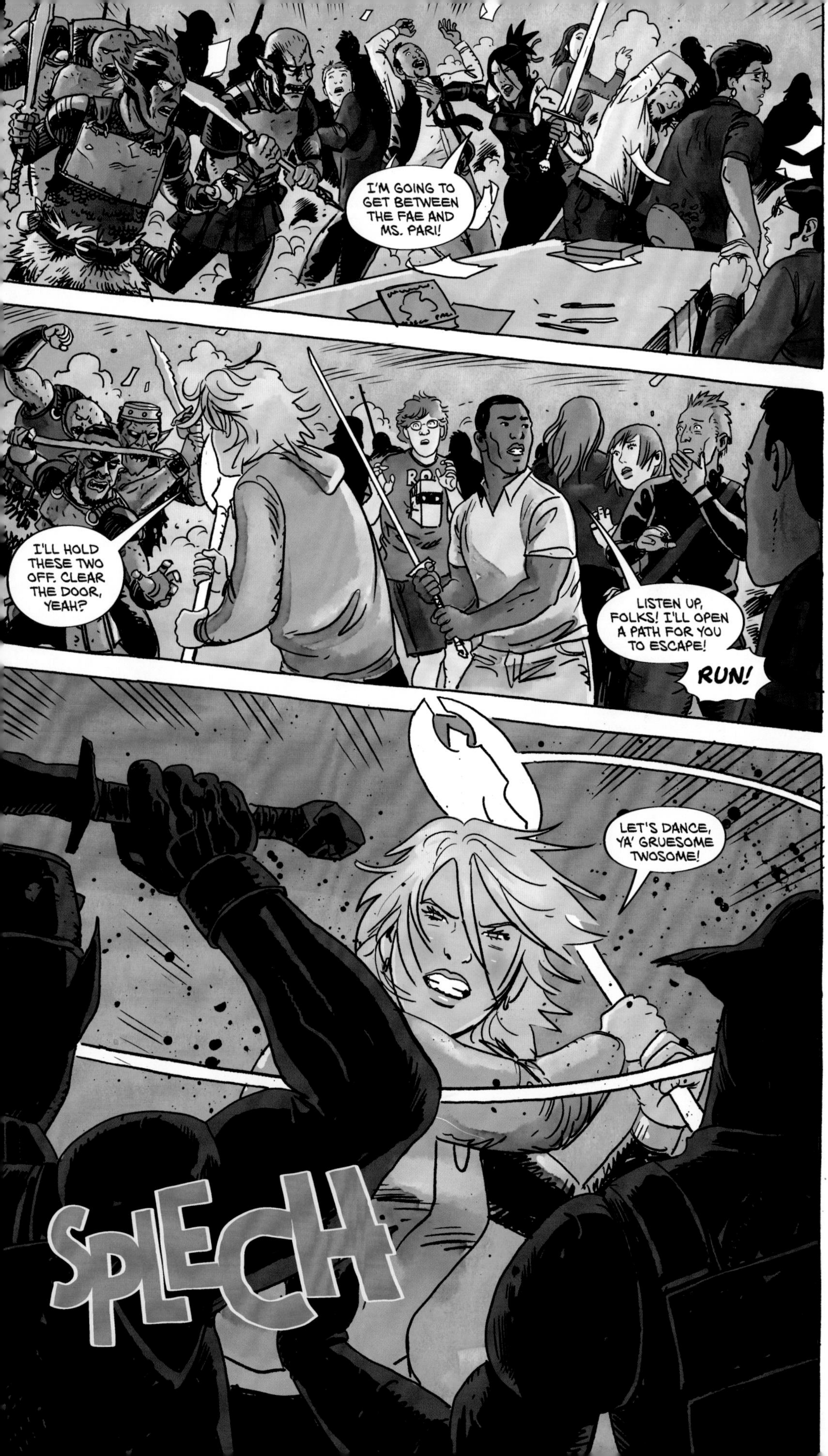
I'M GOING TO GET BETWEEN THE FAE AND MS. PARI!
I'LL HOLD THESE TWO OFF. CLEAR THE DOOR, YEAH?
LISTEN UP, FOLKS! I'LL OPEN A PATH FOR YOU TO ESCAPE!
RUN!
LET'S DANCE, YA' GRUESOME TWOSOME!
SPLECH

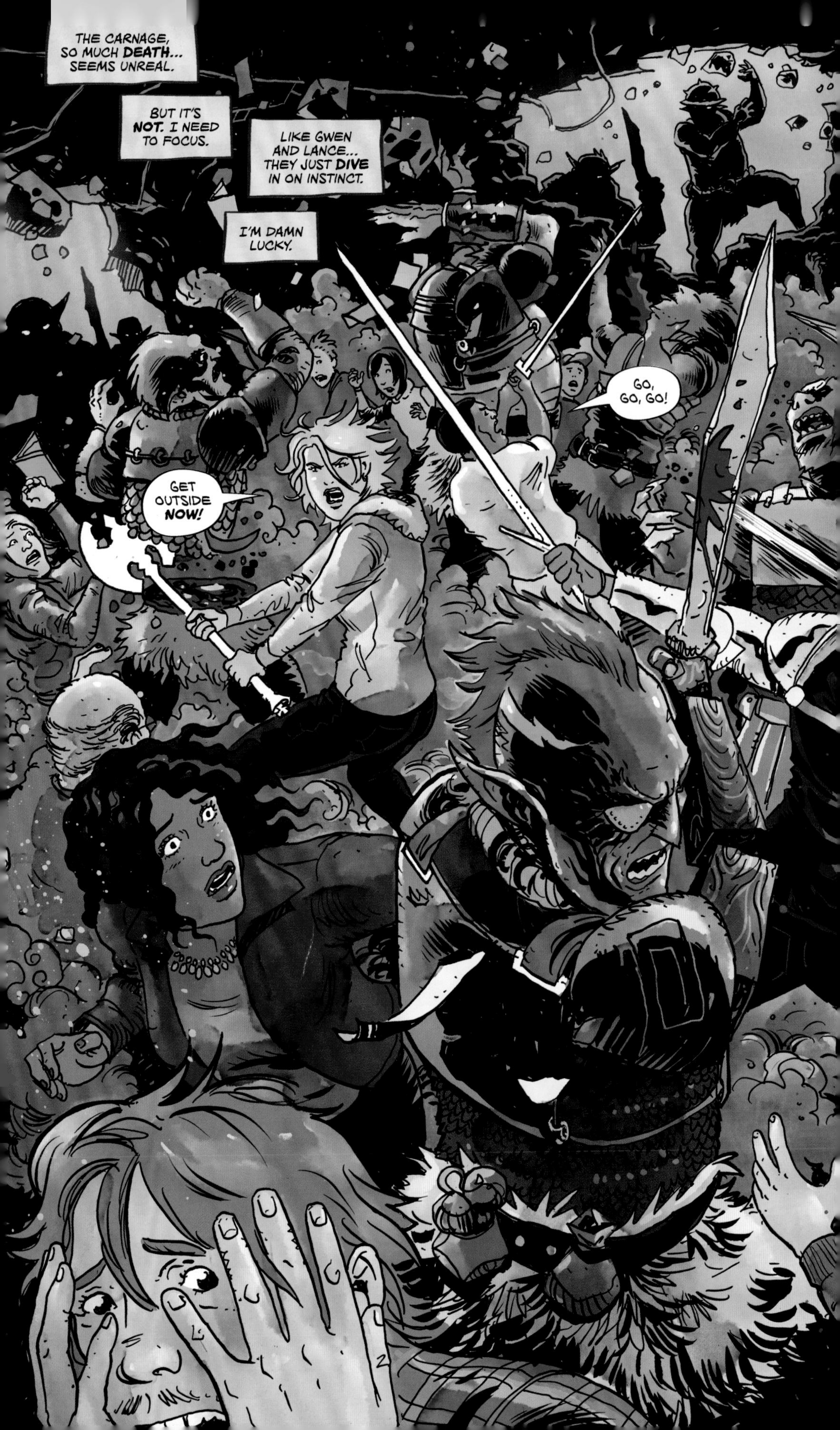
THE CARNAGE, SO MUCH DEATH... SEEMS UNREAL.
BUT IT'S NOT. I NEED TO FOCUS.
LIKE GWEN AND LANCE... THEY JUST DIVE IN ON INSTINCT.
I'M DAMN LUCKY.
GO, GO, GO!
GET OUTSIDE NOW!

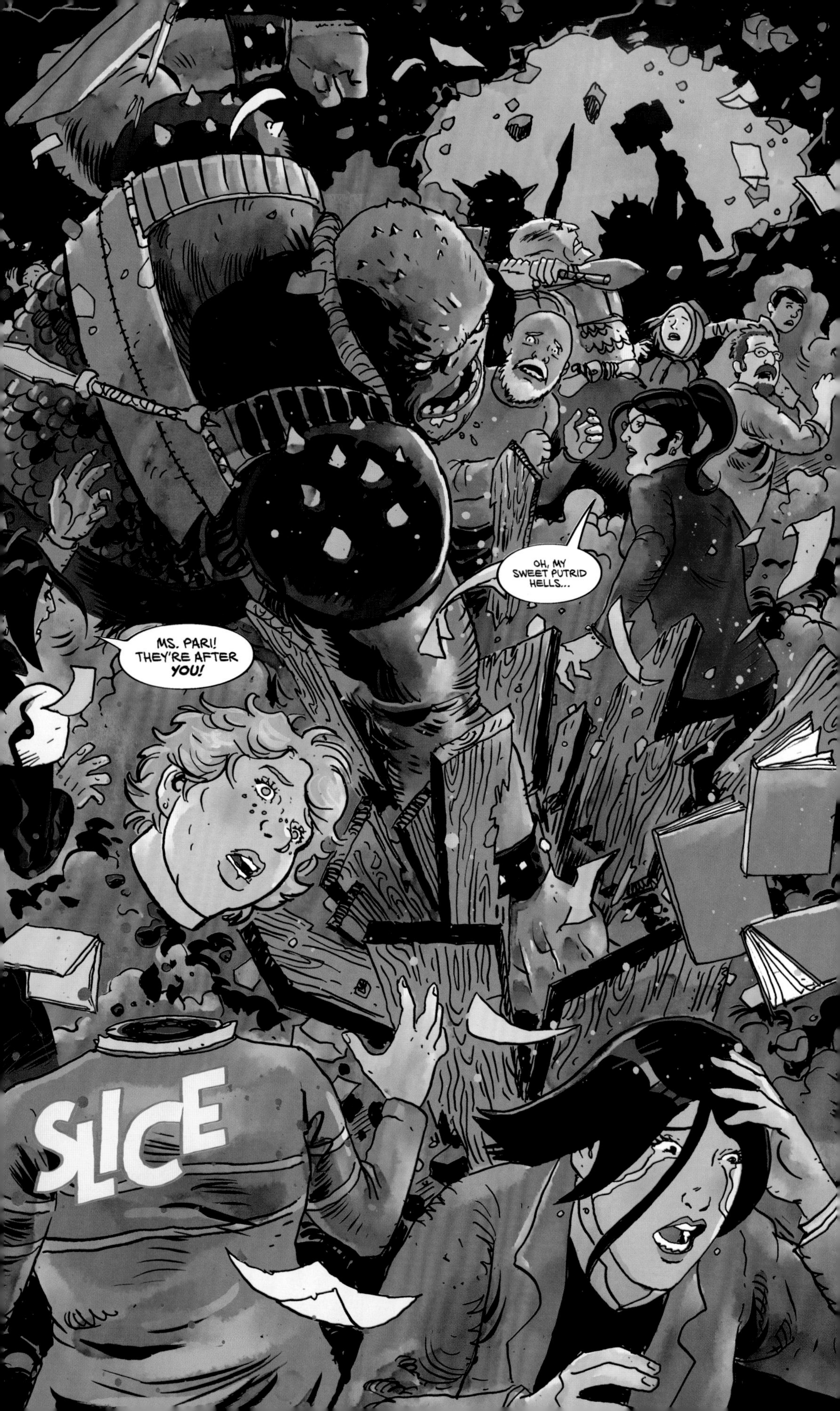
OH, MY SWEET PUTRID HELLS...
MS. PARI! THEY'RE AFTER YOU!
SLICE

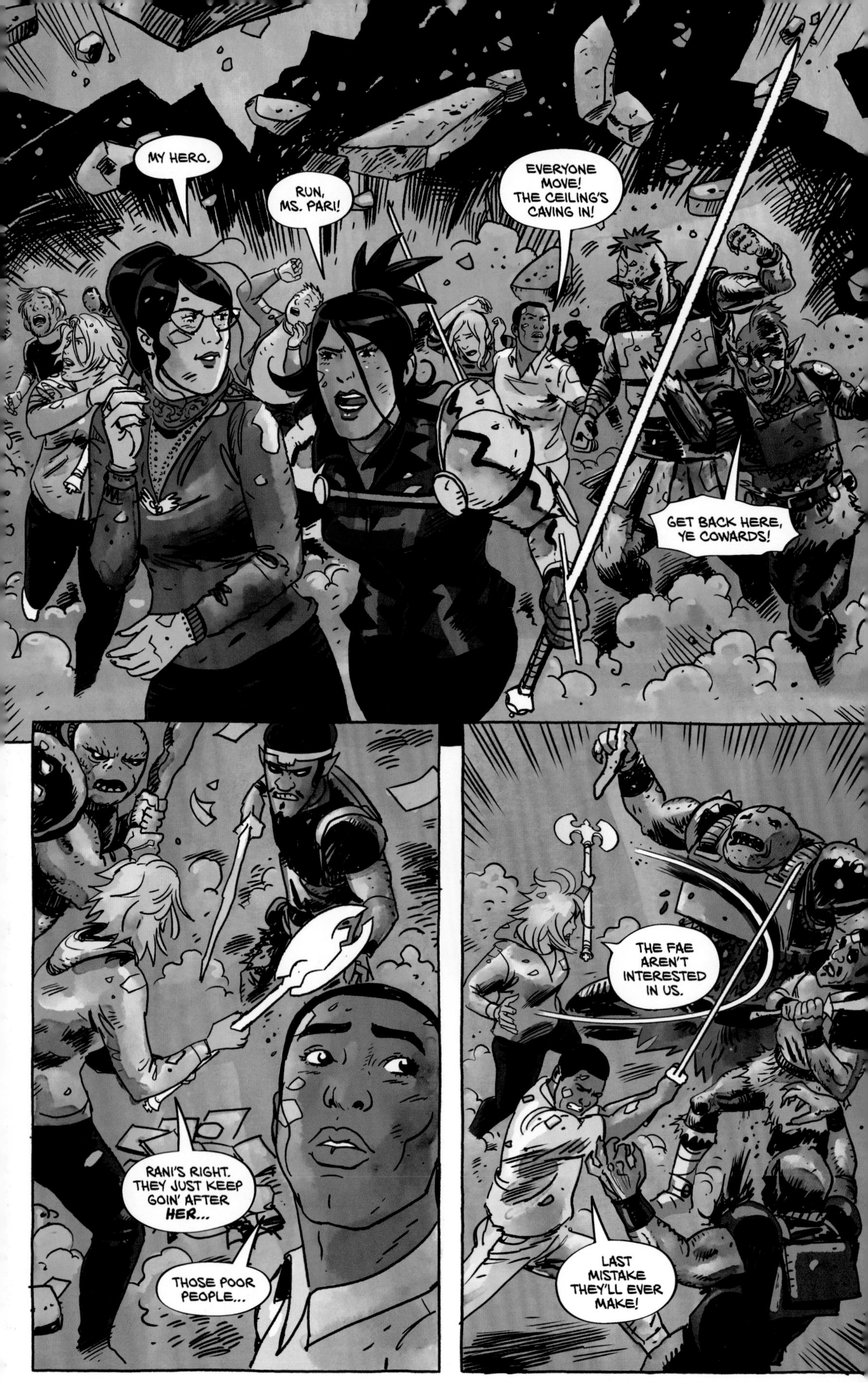
MY HERO.
RUN, MS. PARI!
EVERYONE MOVE! THE CEILING'S CAVING IN!
GET BACK HERE, YE COWARDS!
RANI'S RIGHT. THEY JUST KEEP GOIN' AFTER HER...
THOSE POOR PEOPLE...
THE FAE AREN'T INTERESTED IN US.
LAST MISTAKE THEY'LL EVER MAKE!

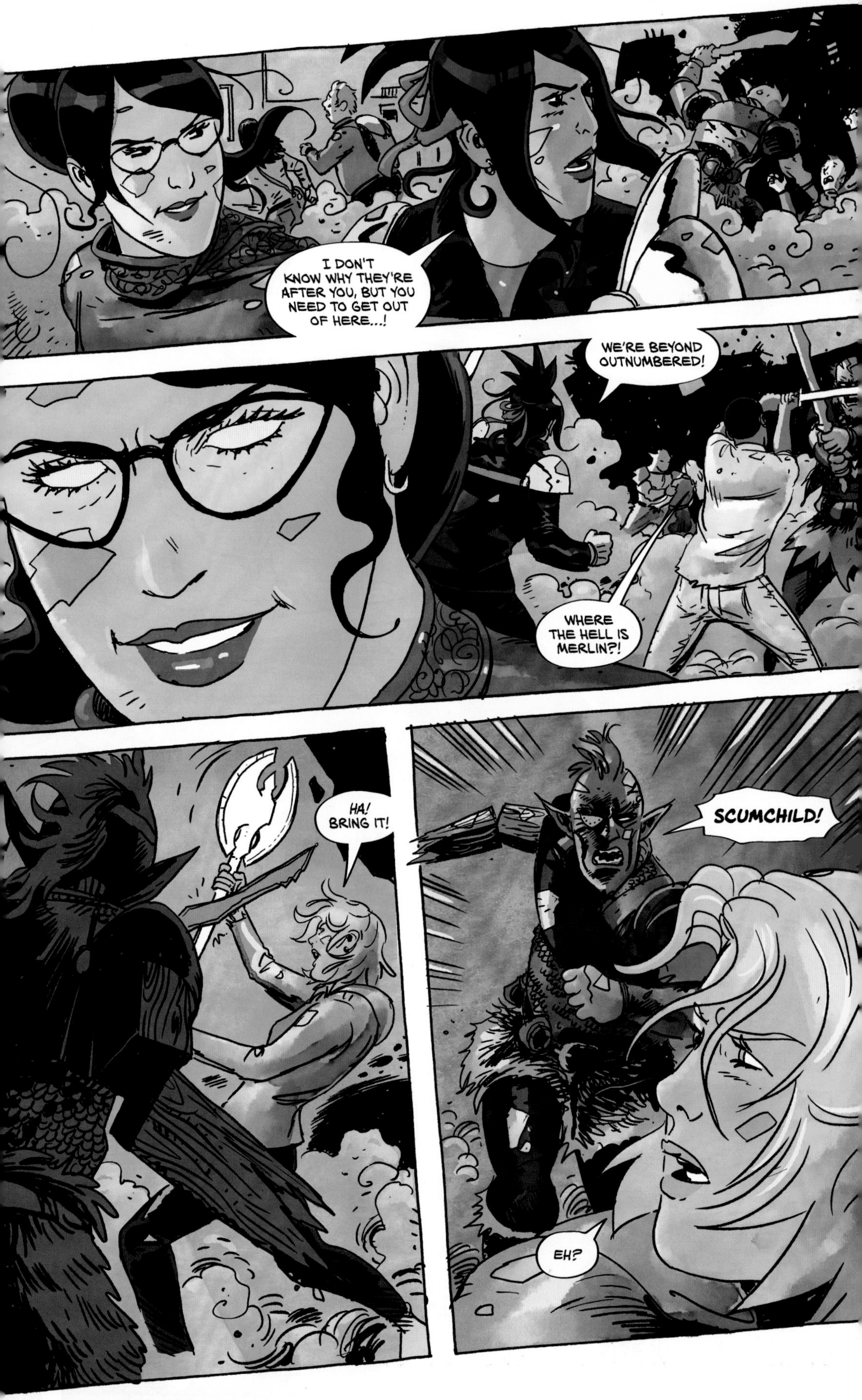

I DON'T KNOW WHY THEY'RE AFTER YOU, BUT YOU NEED TO GET OUT OF HERE...!
WE'RE BEYOND OUTNUMBERED!
WHERE THE HELL IS MERLIN?!
HA! BRING IT!
SCUMCHILD!
EH?

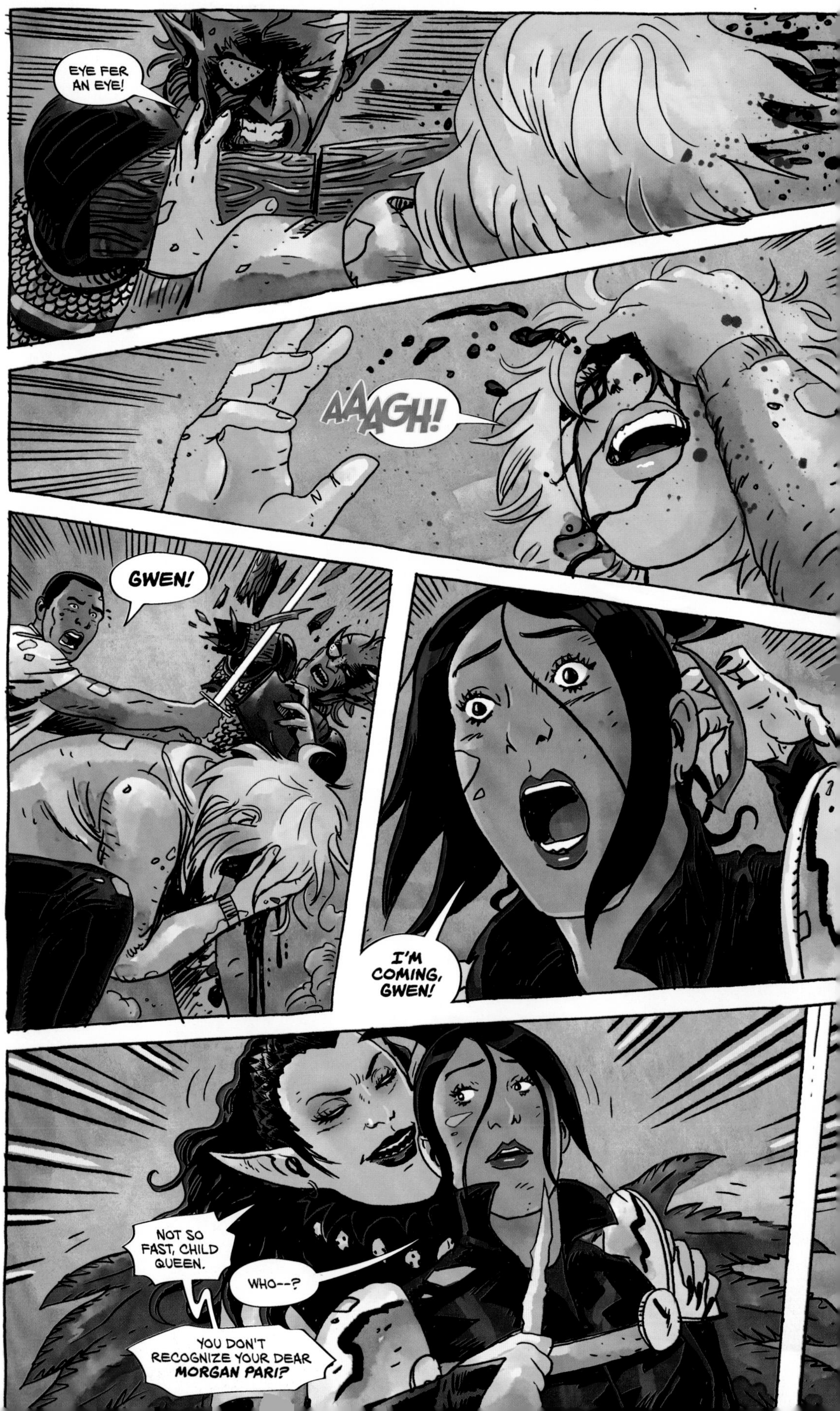
EYE FER AN EYE!
AAAGH!
GWEN!
I'M COMING, GWEN!
NOT SO FAST, CHILD QUEEN.
WHO--?
YOU DON'T RECOGNIZE YOUR DEAR MORGAN PARI?

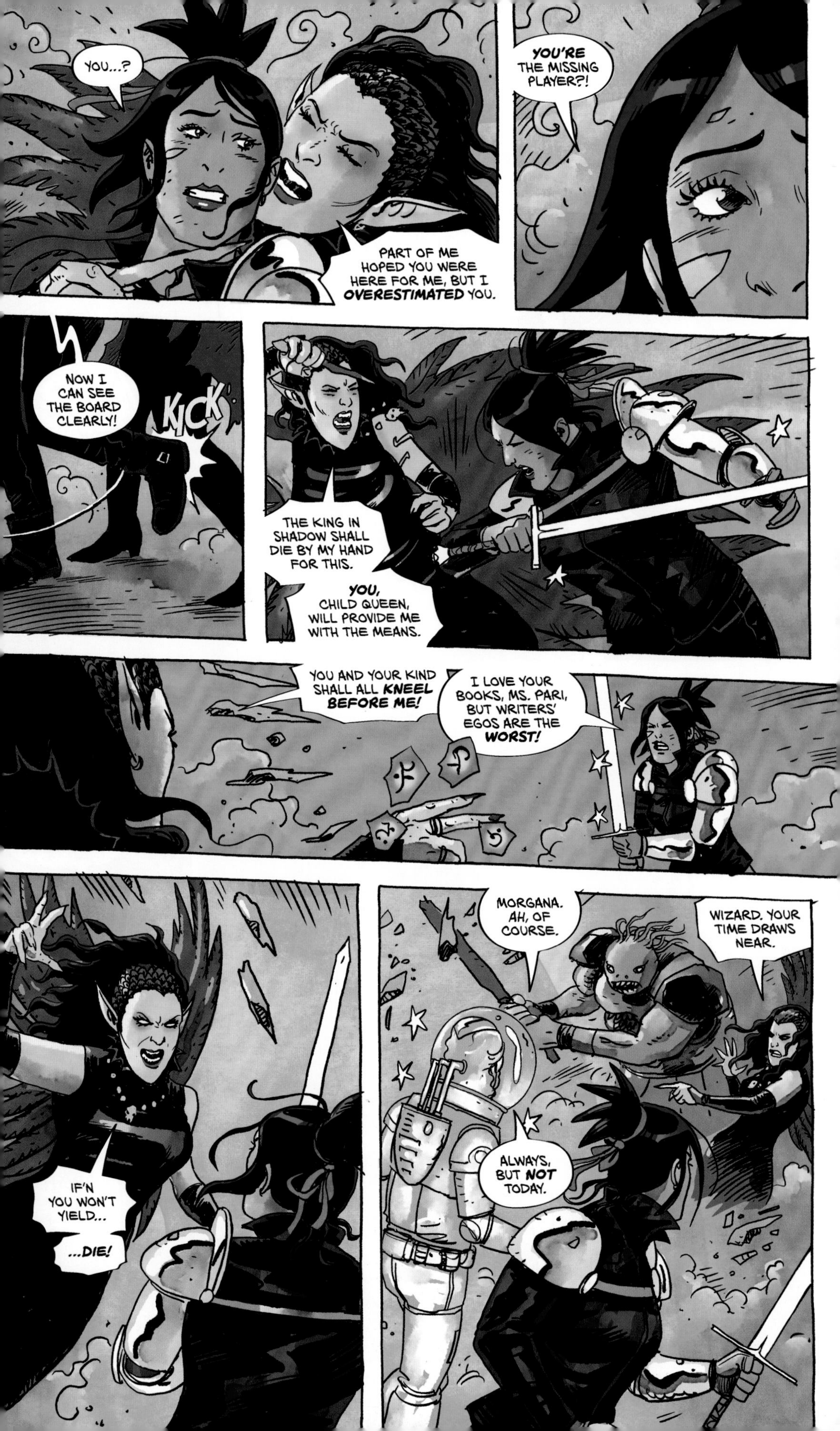
YOU...?
PART OF ME HOPED YOU WERE HERE FOR ME, BUT I **OVERESTIMATED** YOU.
YOU'RE THE MISSING PLAYER?!
NOW I CAN SEE THE BOARD CLEARLY!
KICK
THE KING IN SHADOW SHALL DIE BY MY HAND FOR THIS.
YOU, CHILD QUEEN, WILL PROVIDE ME WITH THE MEANS.
YOU AND YOUR KIND SHALL ALL **KNEEL BEFORE ME!**
I LOVE YOUR BOOKS, MS. PARI, BUT WRITERS' EGOS ARE THE **WORST!**
IF'N YOU WON'T YIELD...
...DIE!
MORGANA. AH, OF COURSE.
WIZARD. YOUR TIME DRAWS NEAR.
ALWAYS, BUT **NOT** TODAY.

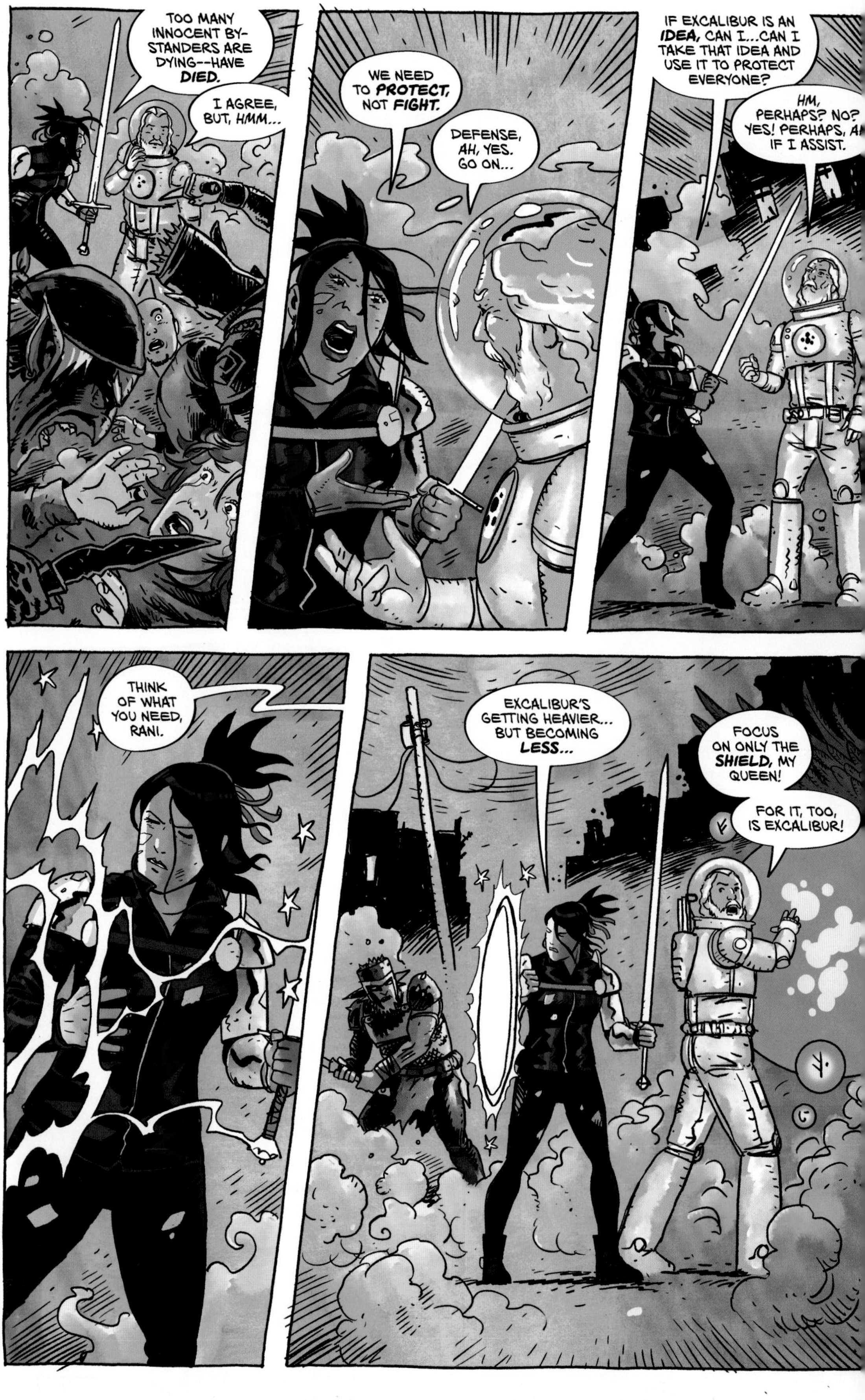
TOO MANY INNOCENT BY-STANDERS ARE DYING--HAVE **DIED.**
I AGREE, BUT, HMM...
WE NEED TO **PROTECT,** NOT **FIGHT.**
DEFENSE, AH, YES. GO ON...
IF EXCALIBUR IS AN **IDEA,** CAN I...CAN I TAKE THAT IDEA AND USE IT TO PROTECT EVERYONE?
HM, PERHAPS? NO? YES! PERHAPS, A
IF I ASSIST.
THINK OF WHAT YOU NEED, RANI.
EXCALIBUR'S GETTING HEAVIER... BUT BECOMING **LESS...**
FOCUS ON ONLY THE **SHIELD,** MY QUEEN!
FOR IT, TOO, IS EXCALIBUR!

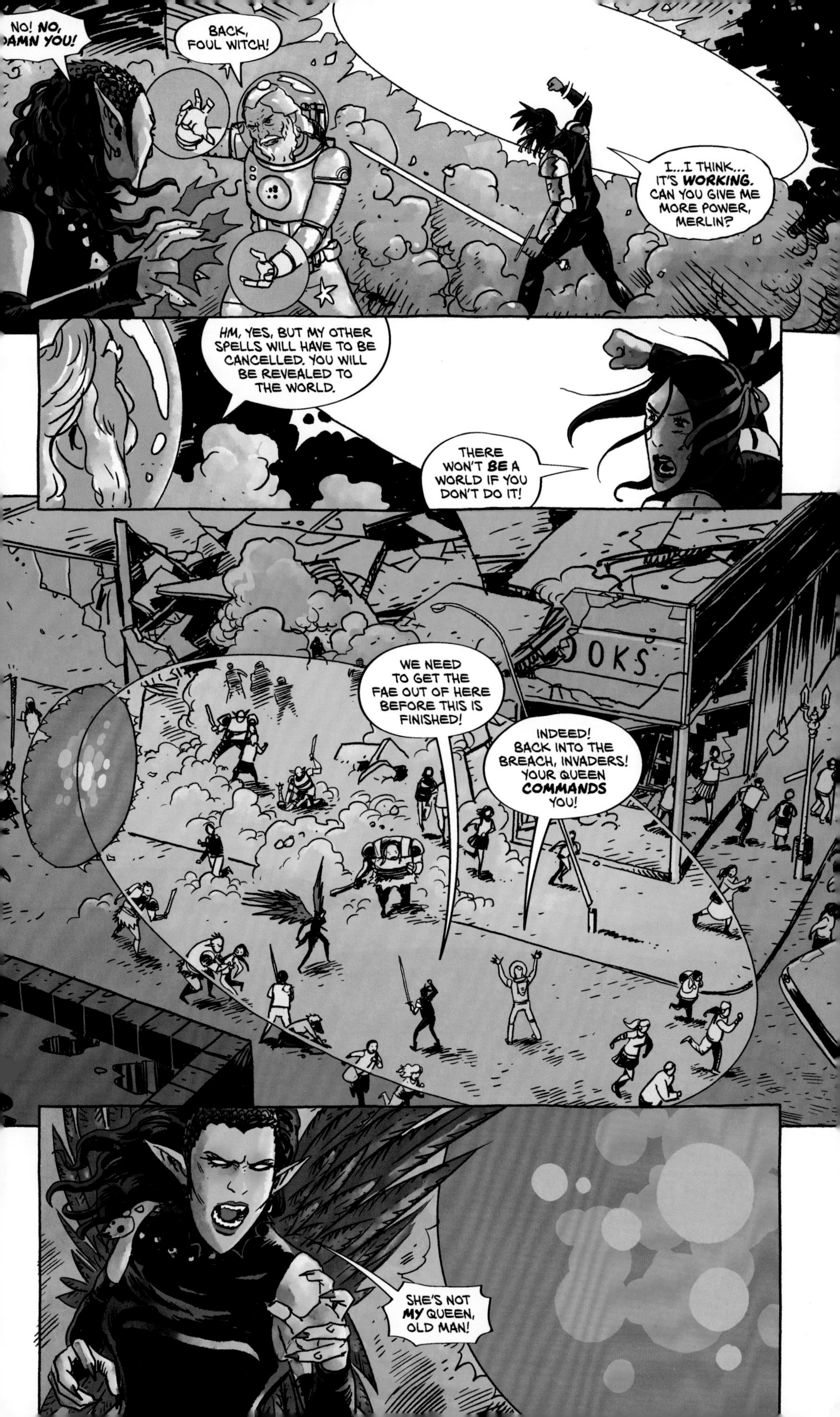

NO! NO, DAMN YOU!
BACK, FOUL WITCH!
I...I THINK... IT'S **WORKING.** CAN YOU GIVE ME MORE POWER, MERLIN?
HM, YES, BUT MY OTHER SPELLS WILL HAVE TO BE CANCELLED. YOU WILL BE REVEALED TO THE WORLD.
THERE WON'T **BE** A WORLD IF YOU DON'T DO IT!
OOKS
WE NEED TO GET THE FAE OUT OF HERE BEFORE THIS IS FINISHED!
INDEED! BACK INTO THE BREACH, INVADERS! YOUR QUEEN **COMMANDS** YOU!
SHE'S NOT **MY** QUEEN, OLD MAN!

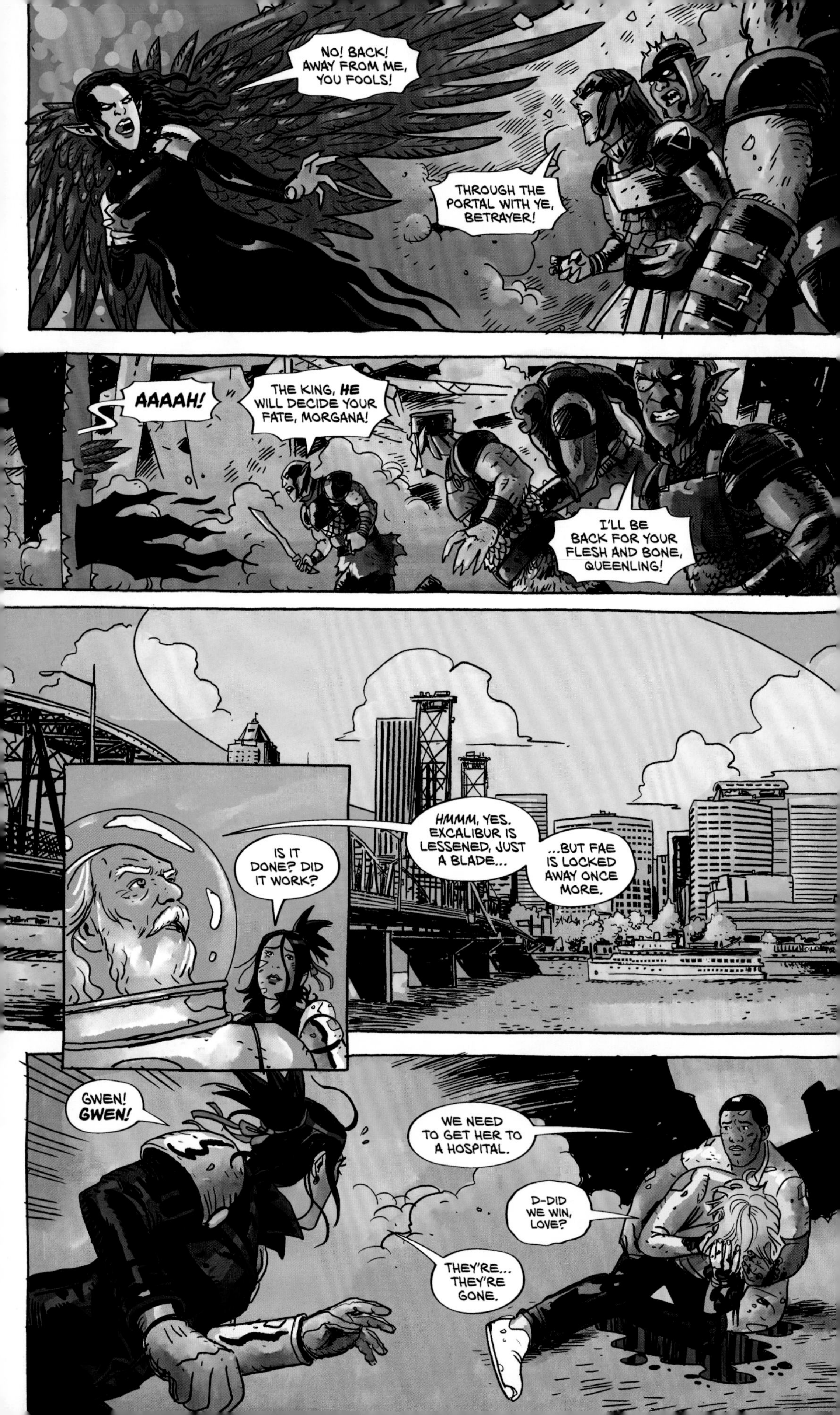
NO! BACK! AWAY FROM ME, YOU FOOLS!
THROUGH THE PORTAL WITH YE, BETRAYER!
AAAAH!
THE KING, HE WILL DECIDE YOUR FATE, MORGANA!
I'LL BE BACK FOR YOUR FLESH AND BONE, QUEENLING!
IS IT DONE? DID IT WORK?
HMMM, YES. EXCALIBUR IS LESSENED, JUST A BLADE...
...BUT FAE IS LOCKED AWAY ONCE MORE.
GWEN! GWEN!
WE NEED TO GET HER TO A HOSPITAL.
D-DID WE WIN, LOVE?
THEY'RE... THEY'RE GONE.

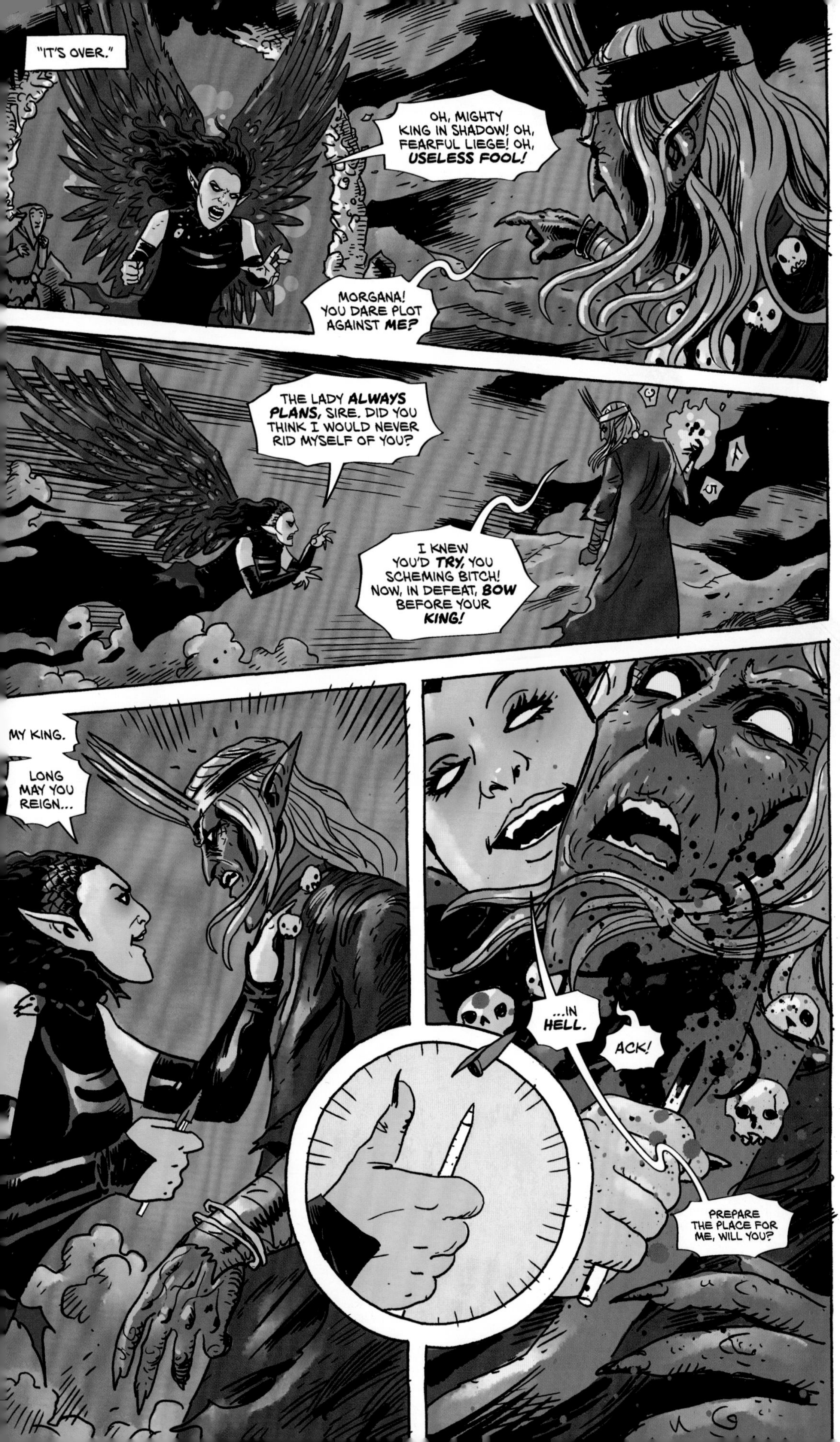
"IT'S OVER."
OH, MIGHTY KING IN SHADOW! OH, FEARFUL LIEGE! OH, USELESS FOOL!
MORGANA! YOU DARE PLOT AGAINST ME?
THE LADY ALWAYS PLANS, SIRE. DID YOU THINK I WOULD NEVER RID MYSELF OF YOU?
I KNEW YOU'D TRY, YOU SCHEMING BITCH! NOW, IN DEFEAT, BOW BEFORE YOUR KING!
MY KING.
LONG MAY YOU REIGN...
...IN HELL.
ACK!
PREPARE THE PLACE FOR ME, WILL YOU?

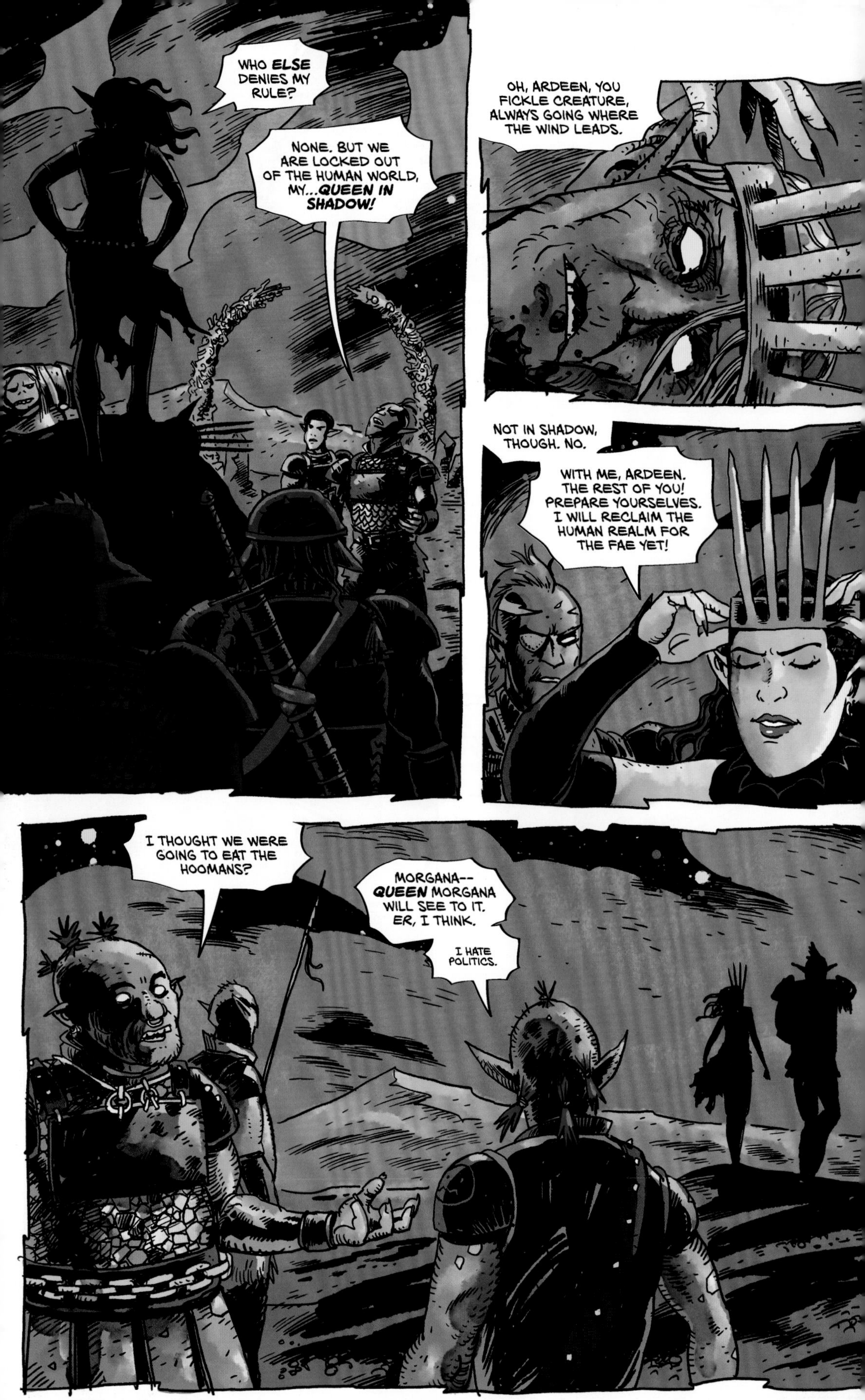
WHO ELSE DENIES MY RULE?
NONE. BUT WE ARE LOCKED OUT OF THE HUMAN WORLD, MY...QUEEN IN SHADOW!
OH, ARDEEN, YOU FICKLE CREATURE, ALWAYS GOING WHERE THE WIND LEADS.
NOT IN SHADOW, THOUGH. NO.
WITH ME, ARDEEN. THE REST OF YOU! PREPARE YOURSELVES. I WILL RECLAIM THE HUMAN REALM FOR THE FAE YET!
I THOUGHT WE WERE GOING TO EAT THE HOOMANS?
MORGANA-- QUEEN MORGANA WILL SEE TO IT. ER, I THINK.
I HATE POLITICS.

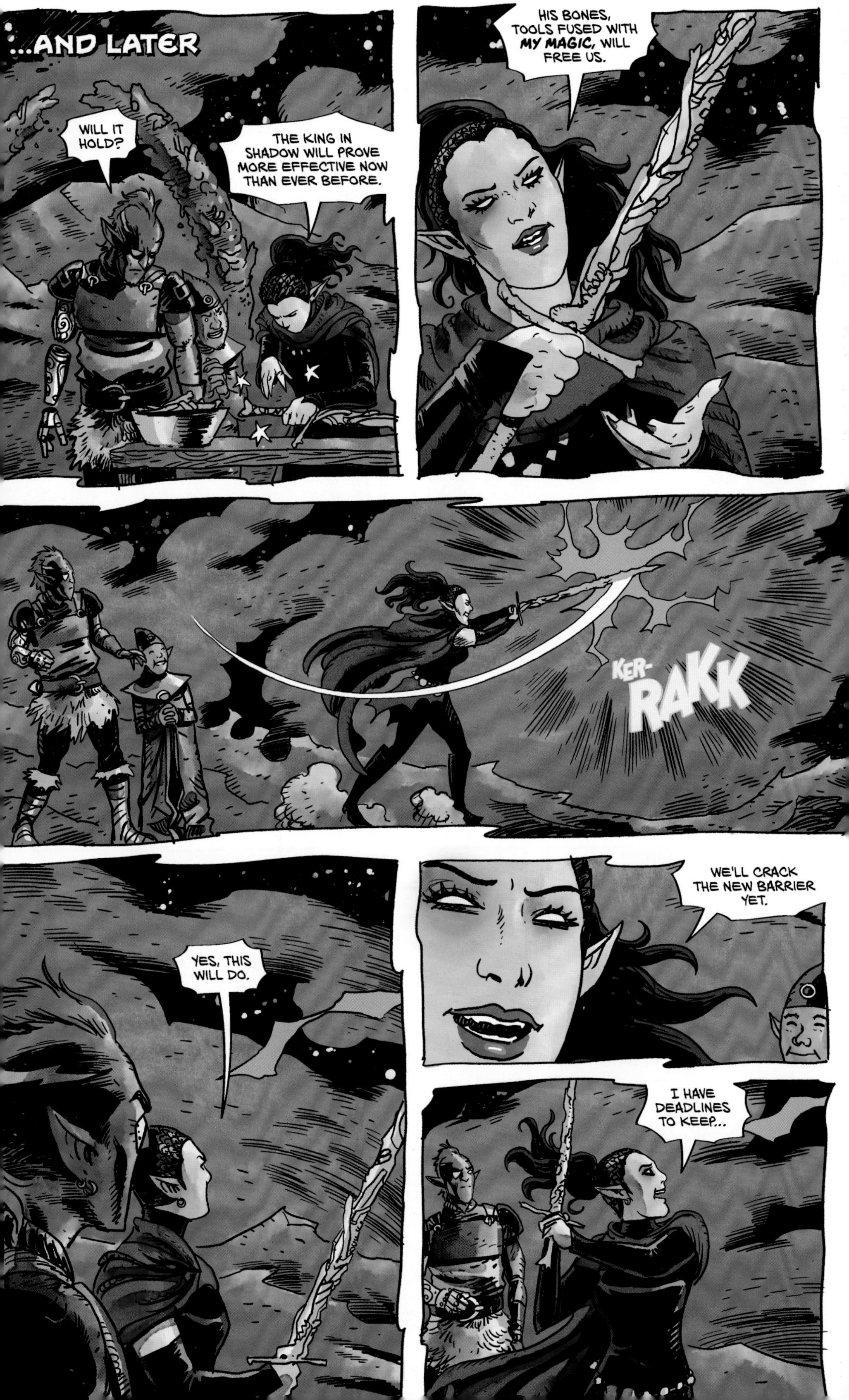
...AND LATER
WILL IT HOLD?
THE KING IN SHADOW WILL PROVE MORE EFFECTIVE NOW THAN EVER BEFORE.
HIS BONES, TOOLS FUSED WITH MY MAGIC, WILL FREE US.
KER-RAKK
YES, THIS WILL DO.
WE'LL CRACK THE NEW BARRIER YET.
I HAVE DEADLINES TO KEEP...

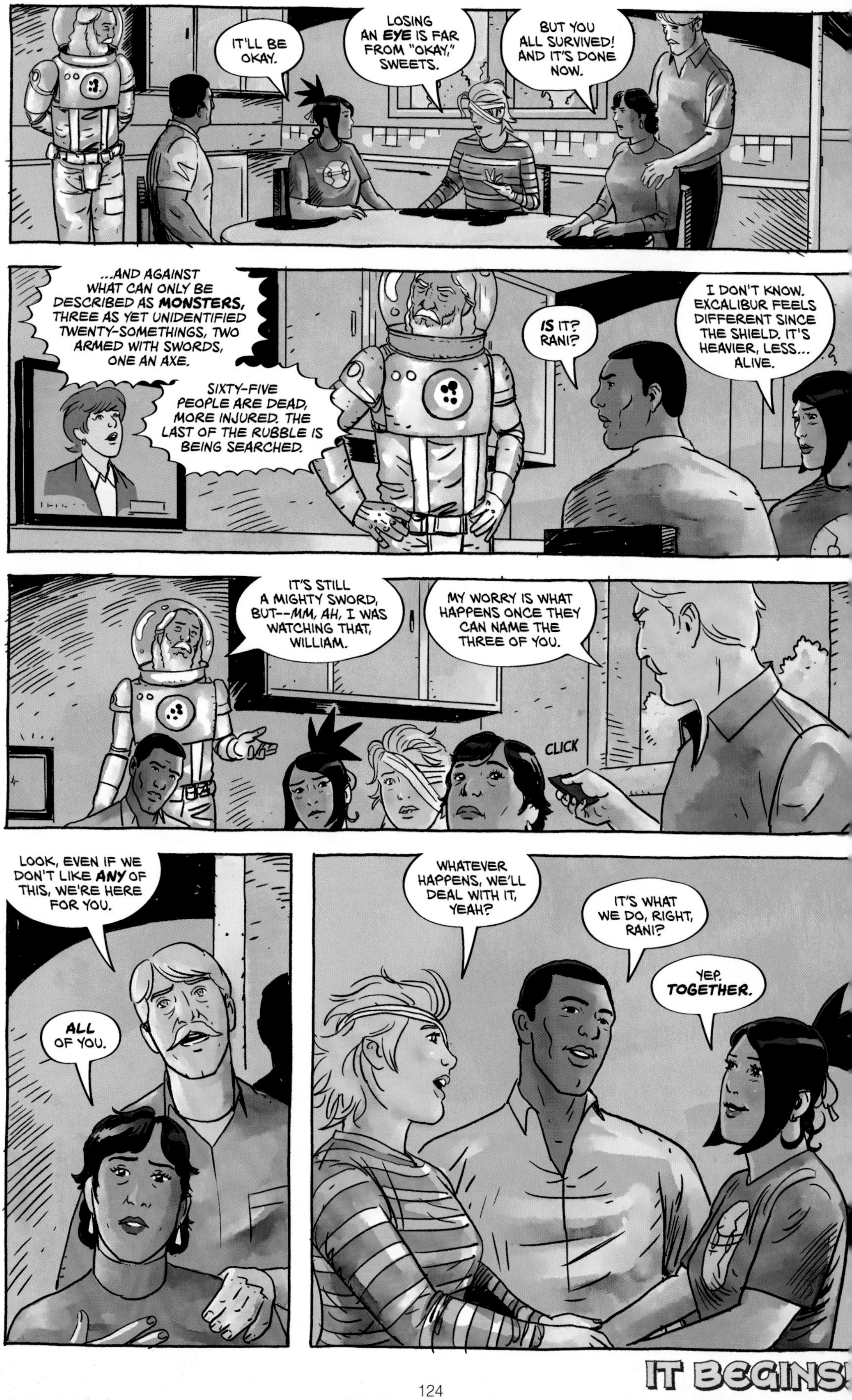
IT'LL BE OKAY.
LOSING AN EYE IS FAR FROM "OKAY," SWEETS.
BUT YOU ALL SURVIVED! AND IT'S DONE NOW.
...AND AGAINST WHAT CAN ONLY BE DESCRIBED AS MONSTERS, THREE AS YET UNIDENTIFIED TWENTY-SOMETHINGS, TWO ARMED WITH SWORDS, ONE AN AXE.
SIXTY-FIVE PEOPLE ARE DEAD, MORE INJURED. THE LAST OF THE RUBBLE IS BEING SEARCHED.
IS IT? RANI?
I DON'T KNOW. EXCALIBUR FEELS DIFFERENT SINCE THE SHIELD. IT'S HEAVIER, LESS... ALIVE.
IT'S STILL A MIGHTY SWORD, BUT--MM, AH, I WAS WATCHING THAT, WILLIAM.
MY WORRY IS WHAT HAPPENS ONCE THEY CAN NAME THE THREE OF YOU.
CLICK
LOOK, EVEN IF WE DON'T LIKE ANY OF THIS, WE'RE HERE FOR YOU.
ALL OF YOU.
WHATEVER HAPPENS, WE'LL DEAL WITH IT, YEAH?
IT'S WHAT WE DO, RIGHT, RANI?
YEP. TOGETHER.
IT BEGINS!

the once and future QUEEN

EXTRAS

NOTES BY
Adam, D.J., and Nick

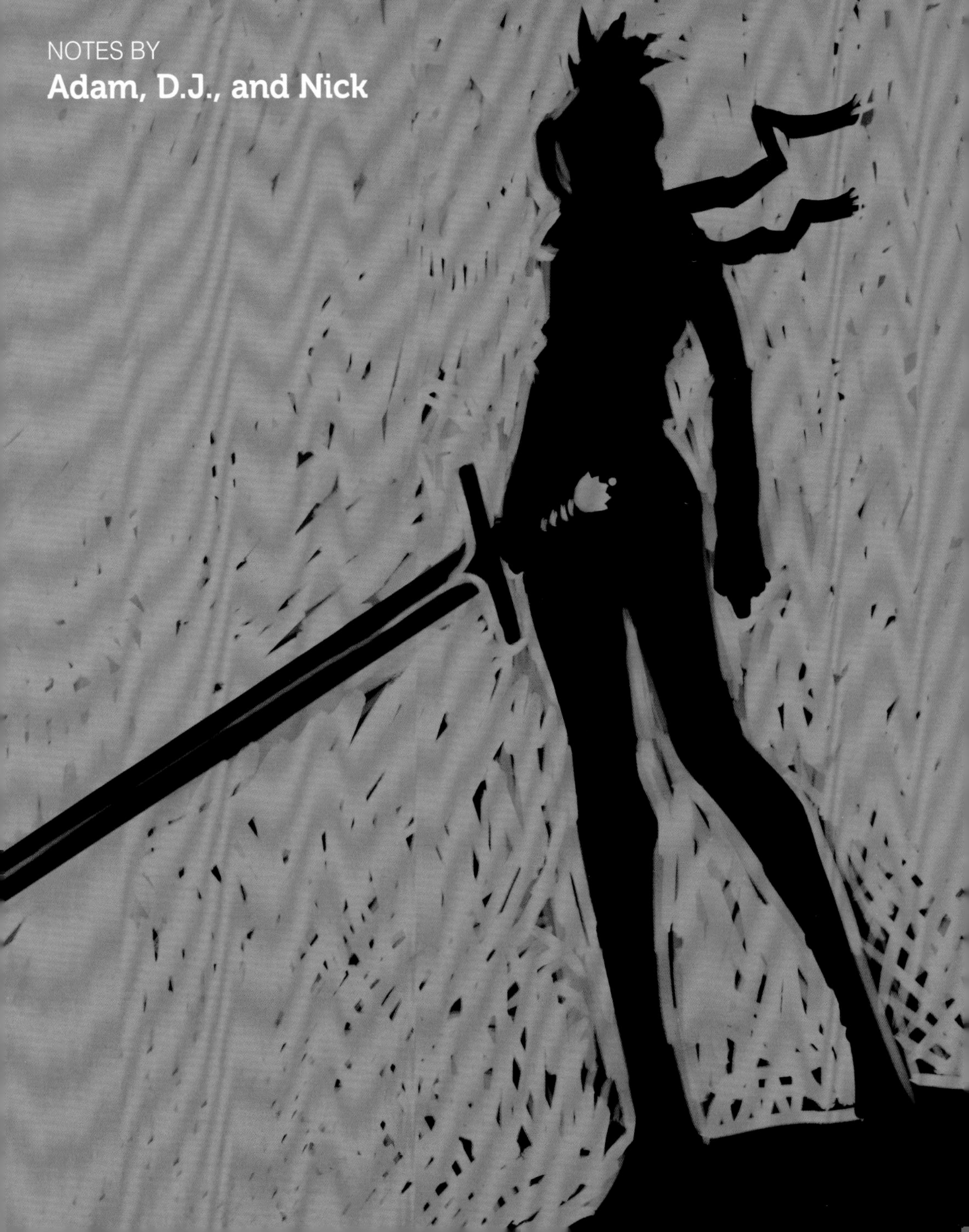

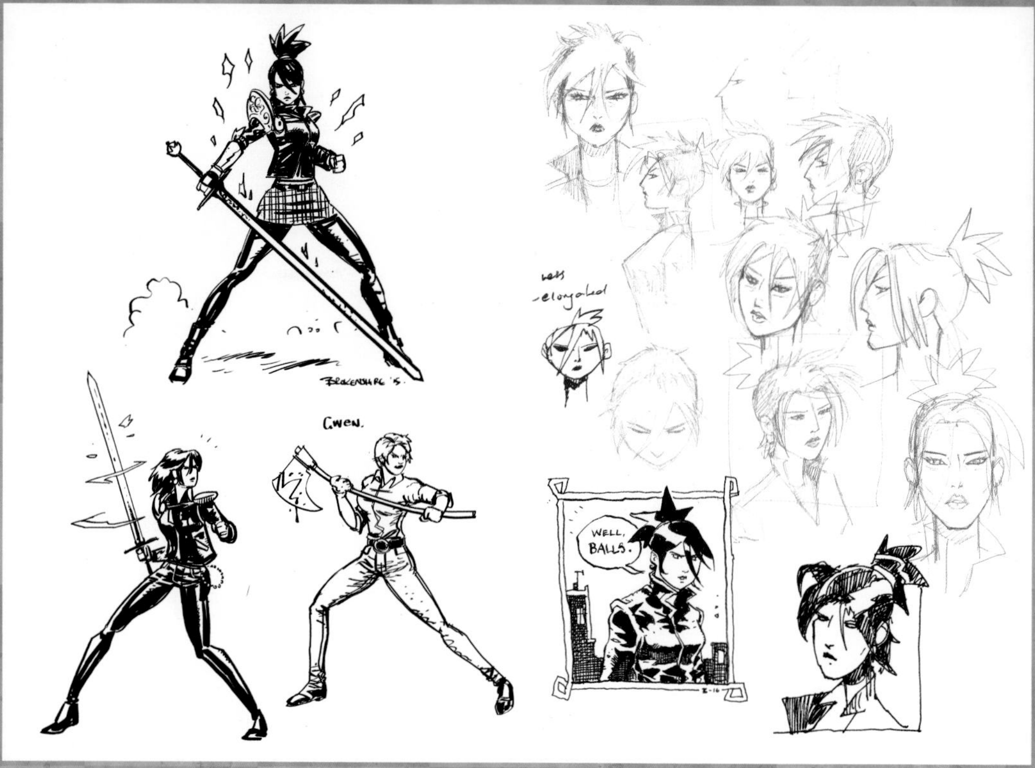
GWEN.
WELL, BALLS.

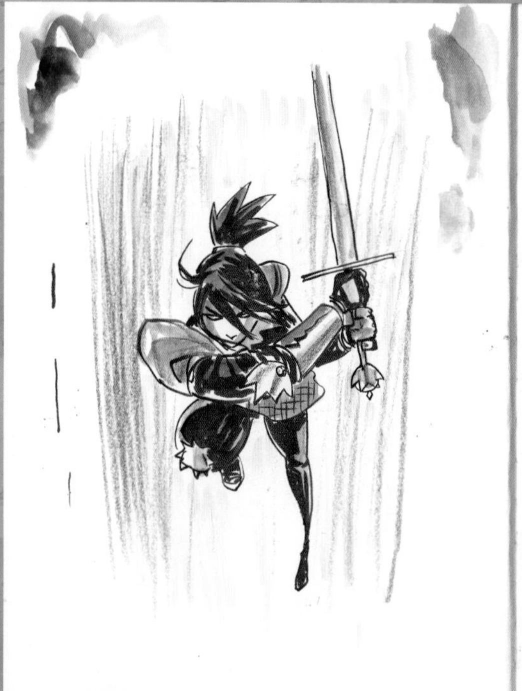

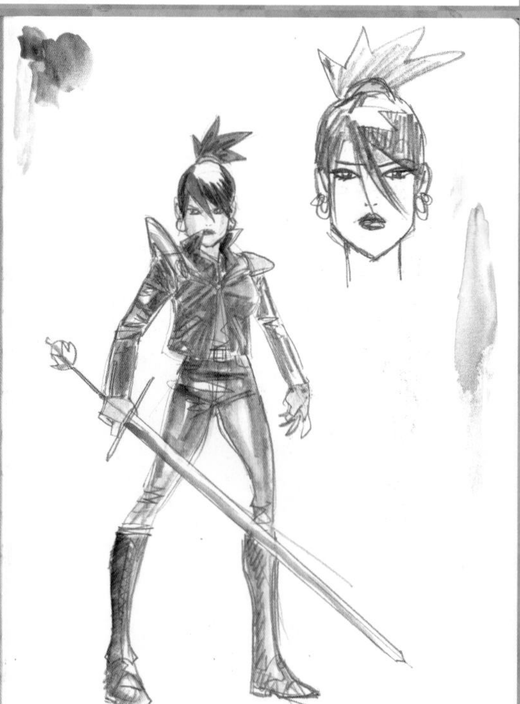

The previous page is the pitch cover featuring Frank's original logo, with the flag behind it based on old pulp novels. We moved away from that banner look for a cleaner logo space. On this page we have Nick's early takes on Rani (with a hint of Gwen). He had an instant feel for the character. The hair as crown idea and the punk/armor look were keys that helped us all unlock our hero's potential. Nick does endless tests and studies for lead characters, sharing them so we can hone in on look and personality.

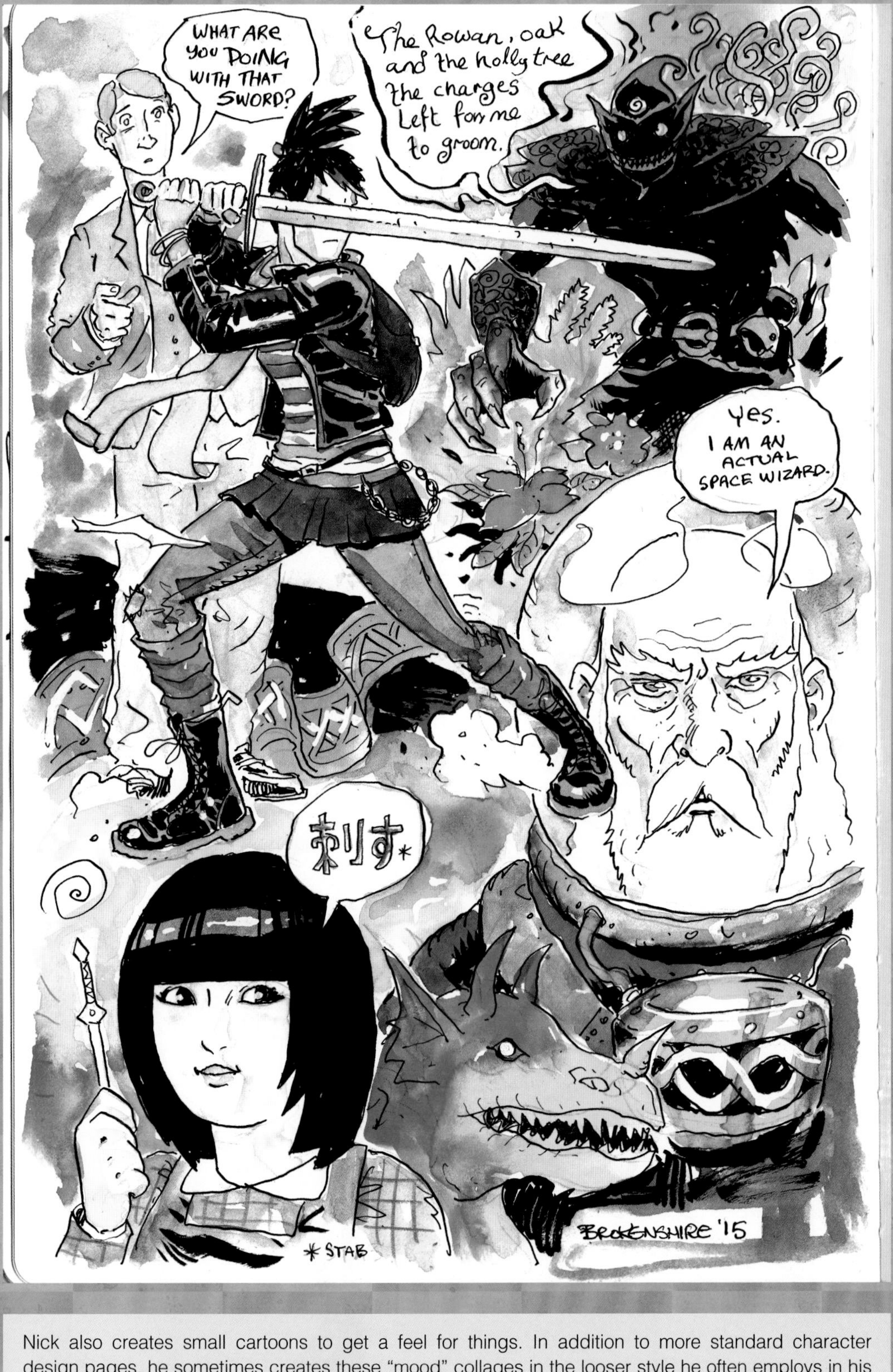
WHAT ARE YOU DOING WITH THAT SWORD?
The Rowan, oak and the holly tree The charges Left for me to groom.
YES. I AM AN ACTUAL SPACE WIZARD.
ありす*
*STAB
BROKENSHIRE '15

Nick also creates small cartoons to get a feel for things. In addition to more standard character design pages, he sometimes creates these "mood" collages in the looser style he often employs in his sketchbooks. Some of the characters presented here look pretty familiar, like Rani and this earlier version of "Spaceman Merlin." As for the knife-wielding girl in the lower left, the worried fella, the dark Fae, and the dragon, well, only Nick knows who they are—for now, at least.

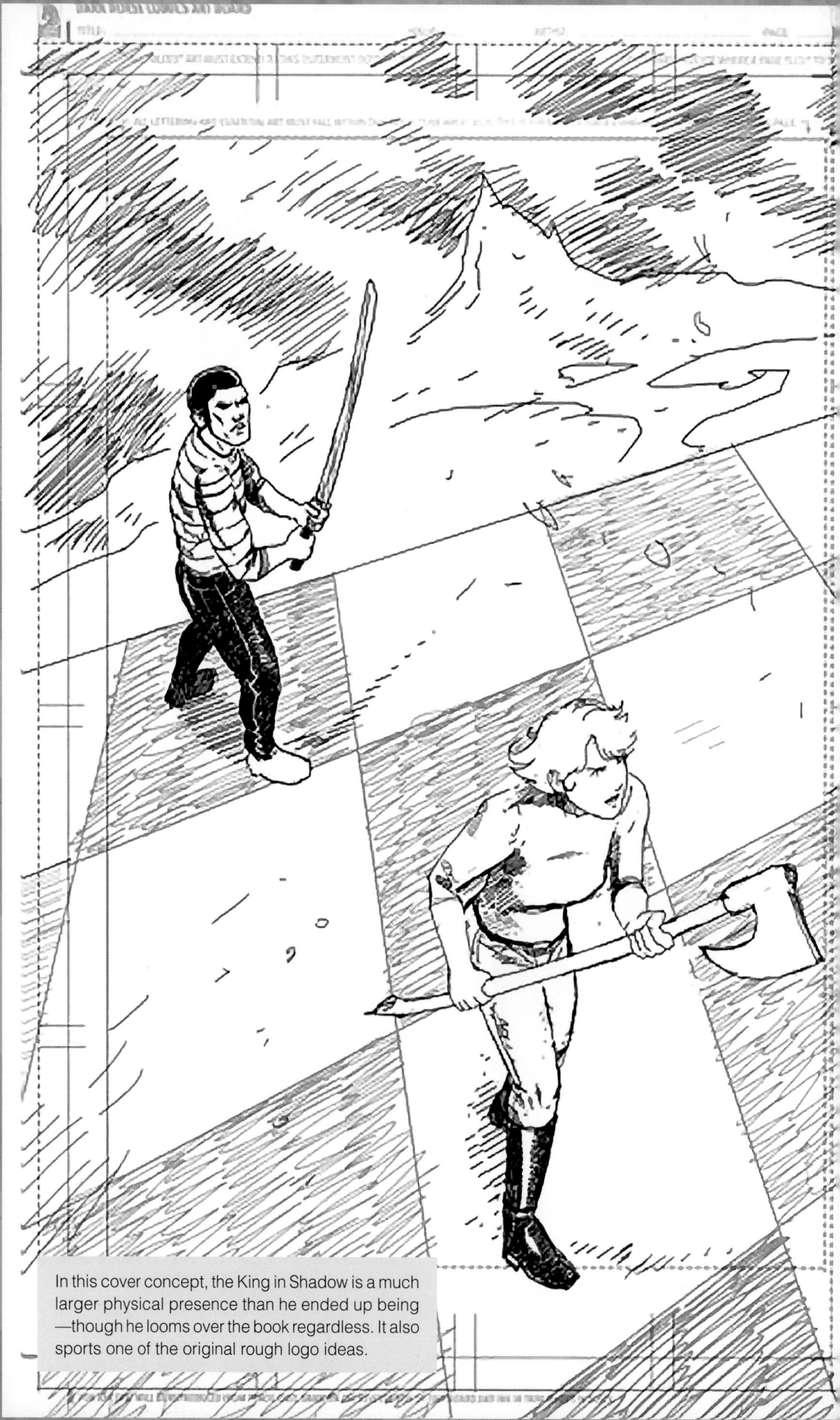

In this cover concept, the King in Shadow is a much larger physical presence than he ended up being—though he looms over the book regardless. It also sports one of the original rough logo ideas.

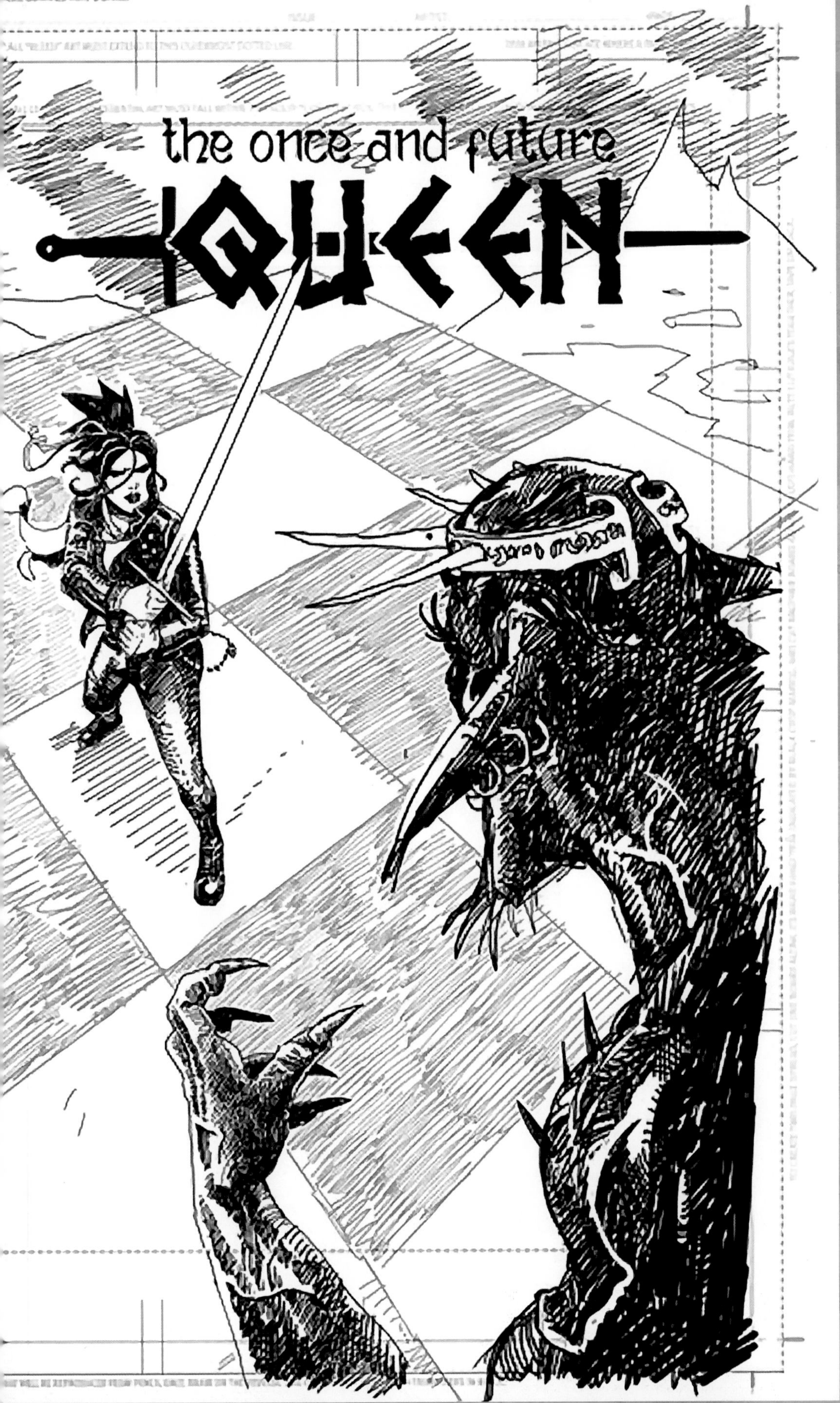
the once and future
QUEEN

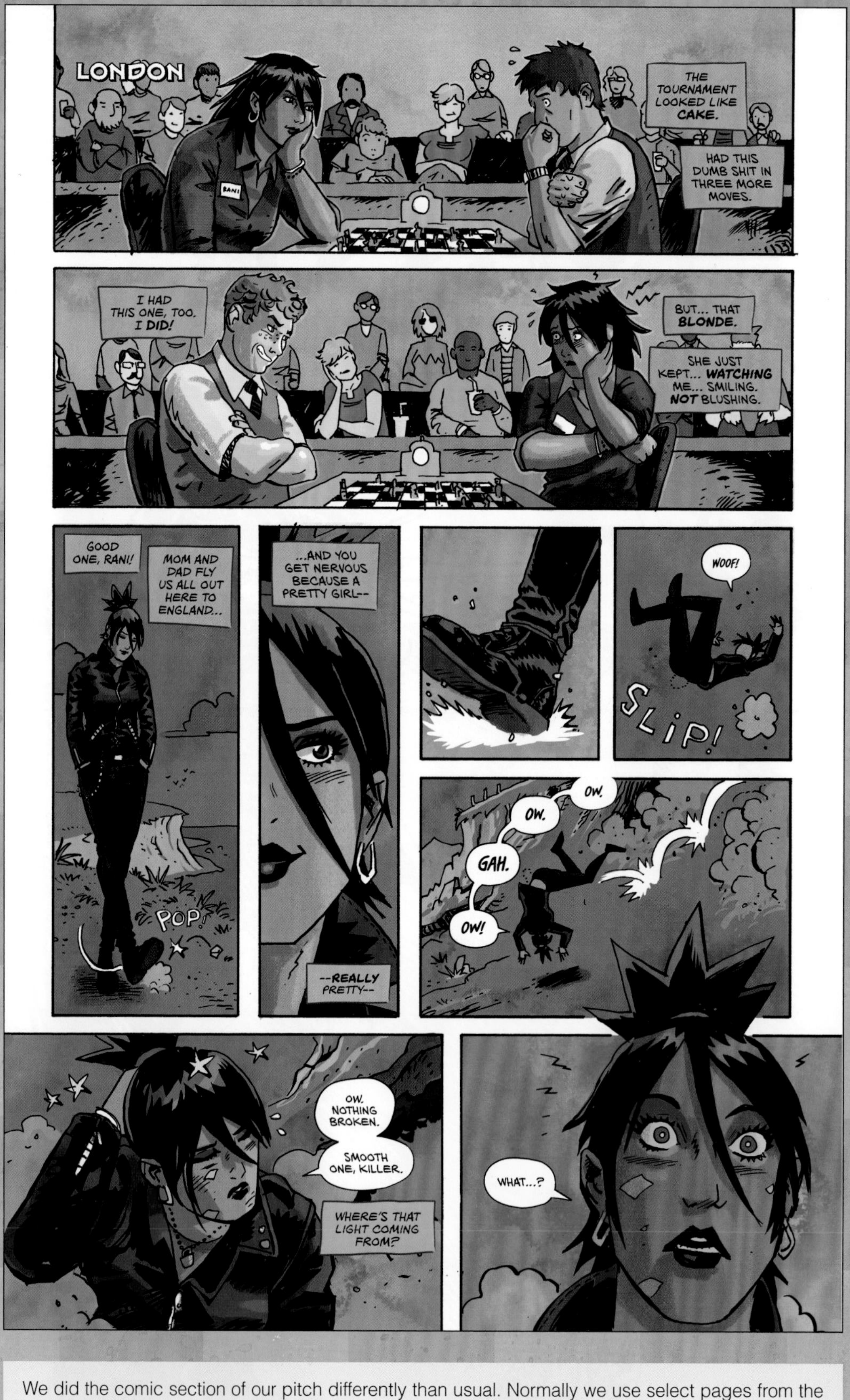
LONDON
THE TOURNAMENT LOOKED LIKE CAKE.
HAD THIS DUMB SHIT IN THREE MORE MOVES.
RANI
I HAD THIS ONE, TOO. I DID!
BUT... THAT BLONDE.
SHE JUST KEPT... WATCHING ME... SMILING. NOT BLUSHING.
GOOD ONE, RANI!
MOM AND DAD FLY US ALL OUT HERE TO ENGLAND...
POP!
...AND YOU GET NERVOUS BECAUSE A PRETTY GIRL--
--REALLY PRETTY--
WOOF!
SLIP!
OW.
OW.
GAH.
OW!
OW. NOTHING BROKEN.
SMOOTH ONE, KILLER.
WHERE'S THAT LIGHT COMING FROM?
WHAT...?

We did the comic section of our pitch differently than usual. Normally we use select pages from the script, if not a full issue. With *Queen*, we made a mini-comic to show the complete story in brief. Doing it this way helped us refine scenes later in the actual book.

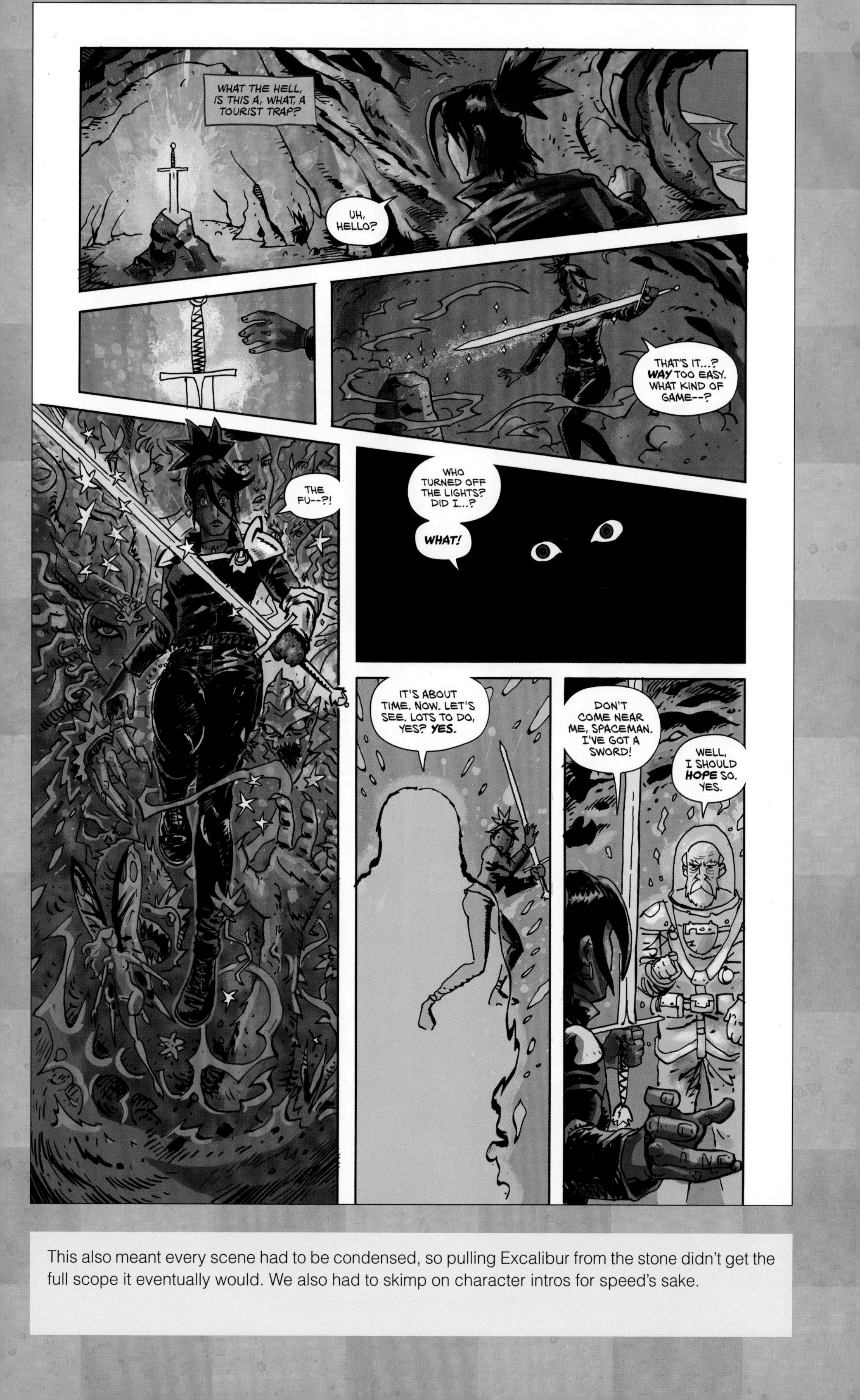
WHAT THE HELL, IS THIS A, WHAT, A TOURIST TRAP?
UH, HELLO?
THAT'S IT...? WAY TOO EASY. WHAT KIND OF GAME--?
THE FU--?!
WHO TURNED OFF THE LIGHTS? DID I...?
WHAT!
IT'S ABOUT TIME. NOW. LET'S SEE. LOTS TO DO, YES? YES.
DON'T COME NEAR ME, SPACEMAN. I'VE GOT A SWORD!
WELL, I SHOULD HOPE SO. YES.

This also meant every scene had to be condensed, so pulling Excalibur from the stone didn't get the full scope it eventually would. We also had to skimp on character intros for speed's sake.

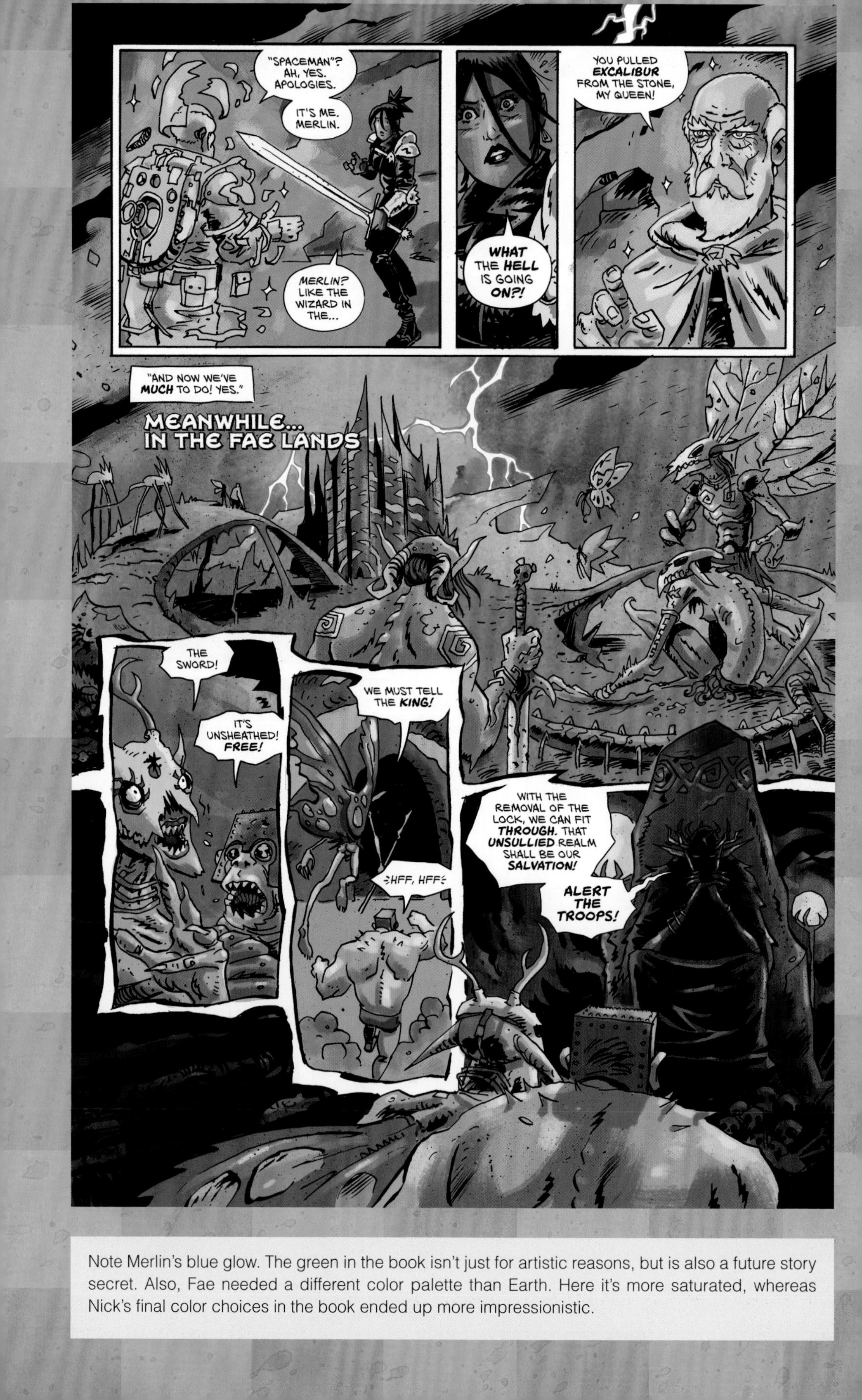
"SPACEMAN"? AH, YES. APOLOGIES.
IT'S ME. MERLIN.
MERLIN? LIKE THE WIZARD IN THE...
WHAT THE HELL IS GOING ON?!
YOU PULLED EXCALIBUR FROM THE STONE, MY QUEEN!
"AND NOW WE'VE MUCH TO DO! YES."
MEANWHILE... IN THE FAE LANDS
THE SWORD!
IT'S UNSHEATHED! FREE!
WE MUST TELL THE KING!
HFF, HFF
WITH THE REMOVAL OF THE LOCK, WE CAN FIT THROUGH. THAT UNSULLIED REALM SHALL BE OUR SALVATION!
ALERT THE TROOPS!

Note Merlin's blue glow. The green in the book isn't just for artistic reasons, but is also a future story secret. Also, Fae needed a different color palette than Earth. Here it's more saturated, whereas Nick's final color choices in the book ended up more impressionistic.

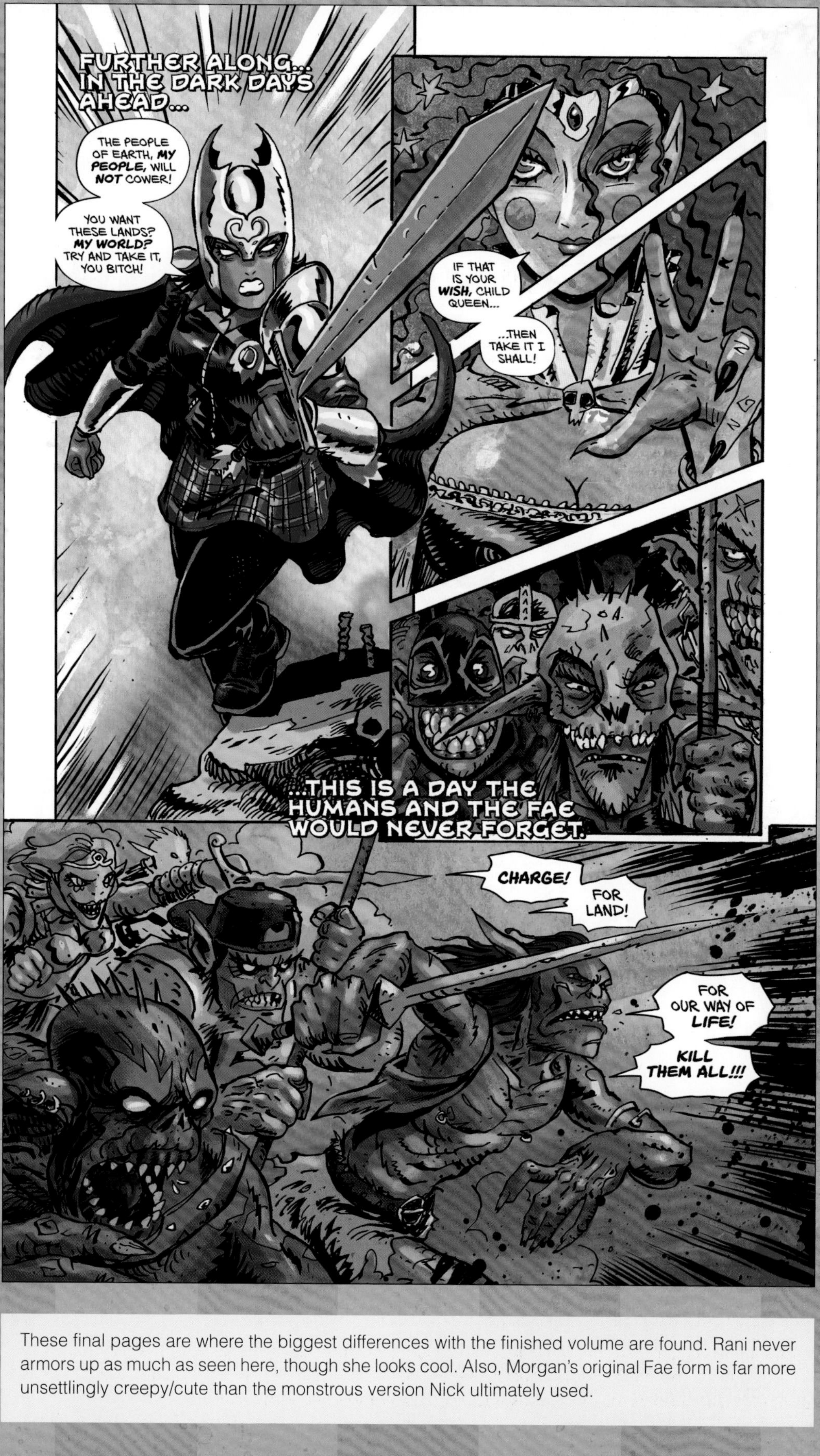
FURTHER ALONG... IN THE DARK DAYS AHEAD...
THE PEOPLE OF EARTH, MY PEOPLE, WILL NOT COWER!
YOU WANT THESE LANDS? MY WORLD? TRY AND TAKE IT, YOU BITCH!
IF THAT IS YOUR WISH, CHILD QUEEN...
...THEN TAKE IT I SHALL!
...THIS IS A DAY THE HUMANS AND THE FAE WOULD NEVER FORGET.
CHARGE!
FOR LAND!
FOR OUR WAY OF LIFE!
KILL THEM ALL!!!

These final pages are where the biggest differences with the finished volume are found. Rani never armors up as much as seen here, though she looks cool. Also, Morgan's original Fae form is far more unsettlingly creepy/cute than the monstrous version Nick ultimately used.

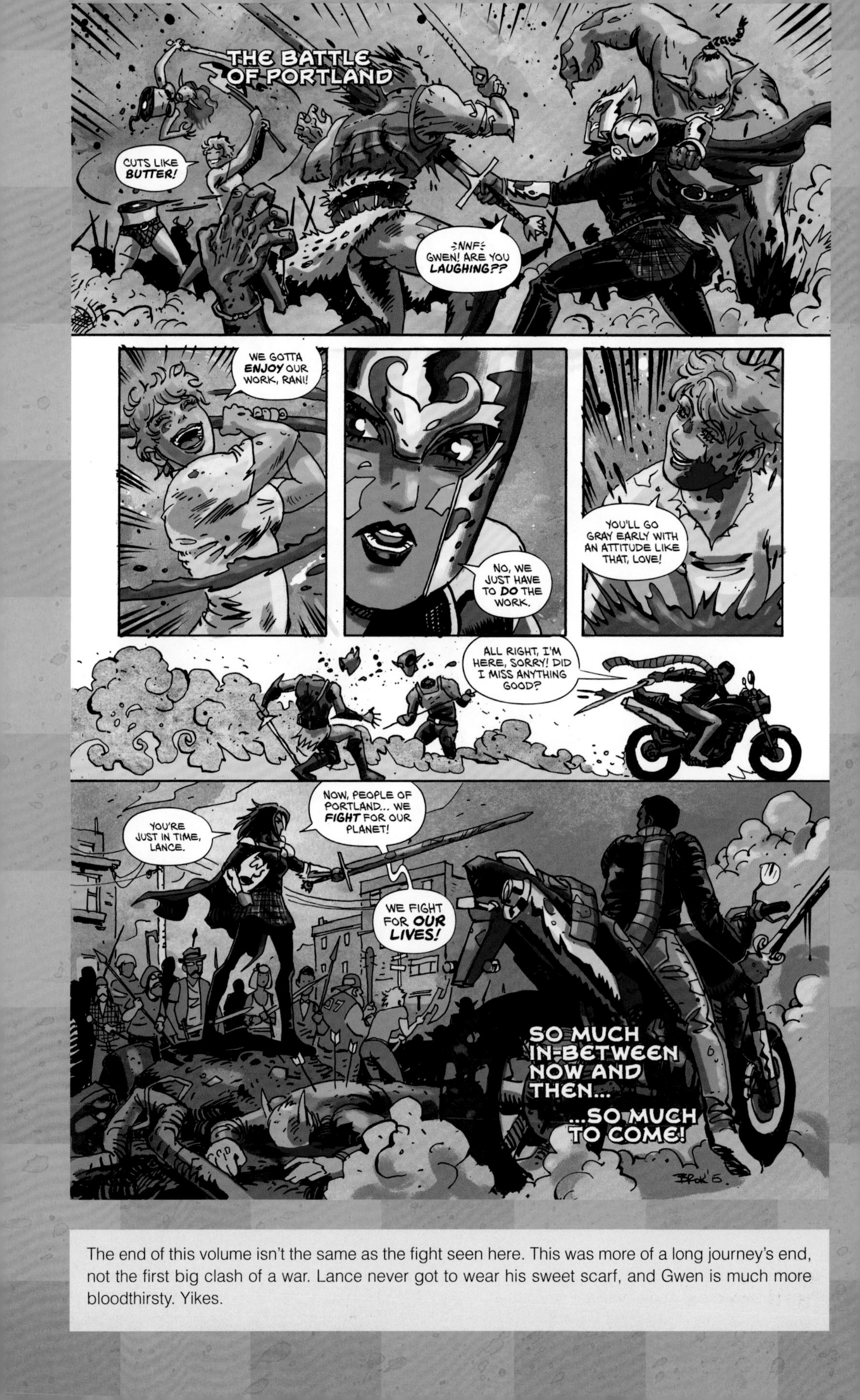
THE BATTLE OF PORTLAND
CUTS LIKE BUTTER!
NNF! GWEN! ARE YOU LAUGHING??
WE GOTTA ENJOY OUR WORK, RANI!
NO, WE JUST HAVE TO DO THE WORK.
YOU'LL GO GRAY EARLY WITH AN ATTITUDE LIKE THAT, LOVE!
ALL RIGHT, I'M HERE, SORRY! DID I MISS ANYTHING GOOD?
YOU'RE JUST IN TIME, LANCE.
NOW, PEOPLE OF PORTLAND... WE FIGHT FOR OUR PLANET!
WE FIGHT FOR OUR LIVES!
SO MUCH IN-BETWEEN NOW AND THEN...
...SO MUCH TO COME!

The end of this volume isn't the same as the fight seen here. This was more of a long journey's end, not the first big clash of a war. Lance never got to wear his sweet scarf, and Gwen is much more bloodthirsty. Yikes.

MORE TITLES YOU MIGHT ENJOY

ALENA
Kim W. Andersson
Since arriving at a snobbish boarding school, Alena's been harassed every day by the lacrosse team. But Alena's best friend Josephine is not going to accept that anymore. If Alena does not fight back, then she will take matters into her own hands. There's just one problem . . . Josephine has been dead for a year.

$17.99 | ISBN 978-1-50670-215-5

ASTRID: CULT OF THE VOLCANIC MOON
Kim W. Andersson
Formerly the Galactic Coalition's top recruit, the now-disgraced Astrid is offered a special mission from her old commander. She'll prove herself worthy of another chance at becoming a Galactic Peacekeeper . . . if she can survive.

$19.99 | ISBN 978-1-61655-690-7

BANDETTE
Paul Tobin, Colleen Coover
A costumed teen burglar by the *nome d'arte* of Bandette and her group of street urchins find equal fun in both skirting and aiding the law, in this enchanting, Eisner-nominated series!

$14.99 each
Volume 1: Presto!
ISBN 978-1-61655-279-4
Volume 2: Stealers, Keepers!
ISBN 978-1-61655-668-6
Volume 3: The House of the Green Mask
ISBN 978-1-50670-219-3

BOUNTY
Kurtis Wiebe, Mindy Lee
The Gadflies were the most wanted criminals in the galaxy. Now, with a bounty to match their reputation, the Gadflies are forced to abandon banditry for a career as bounty hunters . . . 'cause if you can't beat 'em, join 'em—then rob 'em blind!

$14.99 | ISBN 978-1-50670-044-1

HEART IN A BOX
Kelly Thompson, Meredith McClaren
In a moment of post-heartbreak weakness, Emma wishes her heart away and a mysterious stranger obliges. But emptiness is even worse than grief, and Emma sets out to collect the pieces of her heart and face the cost of recapturing it.

$14.99 | ISBN 978-1-61655-694-5

HENCHGIRL
Kristen Gudsnuk
Mary Posa hates her job. She works long hours for little pay, no insurance, and worst of all, no respect. Her coworkers are jerks, and her boss doesn't appreciate her. He's also a supervillain. Cursed with a conscience, Mary would give anything to be something other than a henchgirl.

$17.99 | ISBN 978-1-50670-144-8

MAE
Gene Ha, Paulina Ganucheau
When Abbie was young she discovered a portal to a new world and has had great adventures there. But when she turned twenty-one it all came apart and she decided to return home. Her sister, Mae, has had no idea what happened to Abbie, and Abbie's tales are too hard to believe—until monsters start to cross over to our world.

$17.99 | ISBN 978-1-50670-146-2

MISFITS OF AVALON
Kel McDonald
Four misfit teens are reluctant recruits to save the mystical isle of Avalon. Magically empowered and directed by a talking dog, they must stop the rise of King Arthur. As they struggle to become a team, they're faced with the discovery that they may not be the good guys.

$14.99 each
Volume 1: The Queen of Air and Delinquency
ISBN 978-1-61655-538-2
Volume 2: The Ill-Made Guardian
ISBN 978-1-61655-748-5
Volume 3: The Future in the Wind
ISBN 978-1-61655-749-2
(Available September 2017)

THE SECRET LOVES OF GEEK GIRLS
Hope Nicholson, Margaret Atwood, Mariko Tamaki, and more
The Secret Loves of Geek Girls is a nonfiction anthology mixing prose, comics, and illustrated stories on the lives and loves of an amazing cast of female creators..

$14.99 | ISBN 978-1-50670-099-1

THE ADVENTURES OF SUPERHERO GIRL
Faith Erin Hicks
What if you can leap tall buildings and defeat alien monsters with your bare hands, but you buy your capes at secondhand stores and have a weakness for kittens? Faith Erin Hicks brings humor to the trials and tribulations of a young, female superhero, battling monsters both supernatural and mundane in an all-too-ordinary world.

$16.99 each | ISBN 978-1-61655-084-4
Expanded Edition | ISBN 978-1-50670-336-7

ZODIAC STARFORCE: BY THE POWER OF ASTRA
Kevin Panetta, Paulina Ganucheau
A group of teenage girls with magical powers have sworn to protect our planet against dark creatures. Known as the Zodiac Starforce, these high-school girls aren't just combating math tests—they're also battling monsters!

$12.99 | ISBN 978-1-61655-913-7

COMING SOON!

SPELL ON WHEELS
Kate Leth, Megan Levens, Marissa Louise
A road trip story. A magical revenge fantasy. A sisters-over-misters tale of three witches out to get back what was taken from them.

$14.99 | ISBN 978-1-50670-183-7 (Available June 2017)

THE ONCE AND FUTURE QUEEN
Adam P. Knave, D.J. Kirkbride, Nick Brokenshire, Frank Cvetkovic
It's out with the old myths and in with the new as a nineteen-year-old chess prodigy pulls Excalibur from the stone and becomes queen. Now, magic, romance, Fae, Merlin, and more await her!

$14.99 | ISBN 978-1-50670-250-6
(Available November 2017)

DARKHORSE.COM
AVAILABLE AT YOUR LOCAL COMICS SHOP OR BOOKSTORE | TO FIND A COMICS SHOP IN YOUR AREA, CALL 1-888-266-4226
For more information or to order direct: • On the web: DarkHorse.com • Email: mailorder@darkhorse.com • Phone: 1-800-862-0052 Mon.–Fri. 9 AM to 5 PM Pacific Time.

Alena™, Astrid™ © Kim W. Andersson, by agreement with Grand Agency. Bandette™ © Paul Tobin and Colleen Coover. Bounty™ © Kurtis Wiebe and Mindy Lee. Heart in a Box™ © 1979 Semi-Finalist, Inc., and Meredith McClaren. Henchgirl™ © Kristen Gudsnuk. Mae™ © Gene Ha. Misfits of Avalon™ © Kel McDonald. The Secret Loves of Geek Girls™ © respective creators. The Adventures of Superhero Girl™ © Faith Erin Hicks. Zodiac Starforce™ © Kevin Panetta and Paulina Ganucheau. Spell on Wheels™ © Kate Leth and Megan Levens. The Once and Future Queen™ © Adam P. Knave, D.J. Kirkbride, and Nick Brokenshire. Dark Horse Books® and the Dark Horse logo are registered trademarks of Dark Horse Comics, Inc. All rights reserved. (BL 6041)

DARK HORSE COMICS

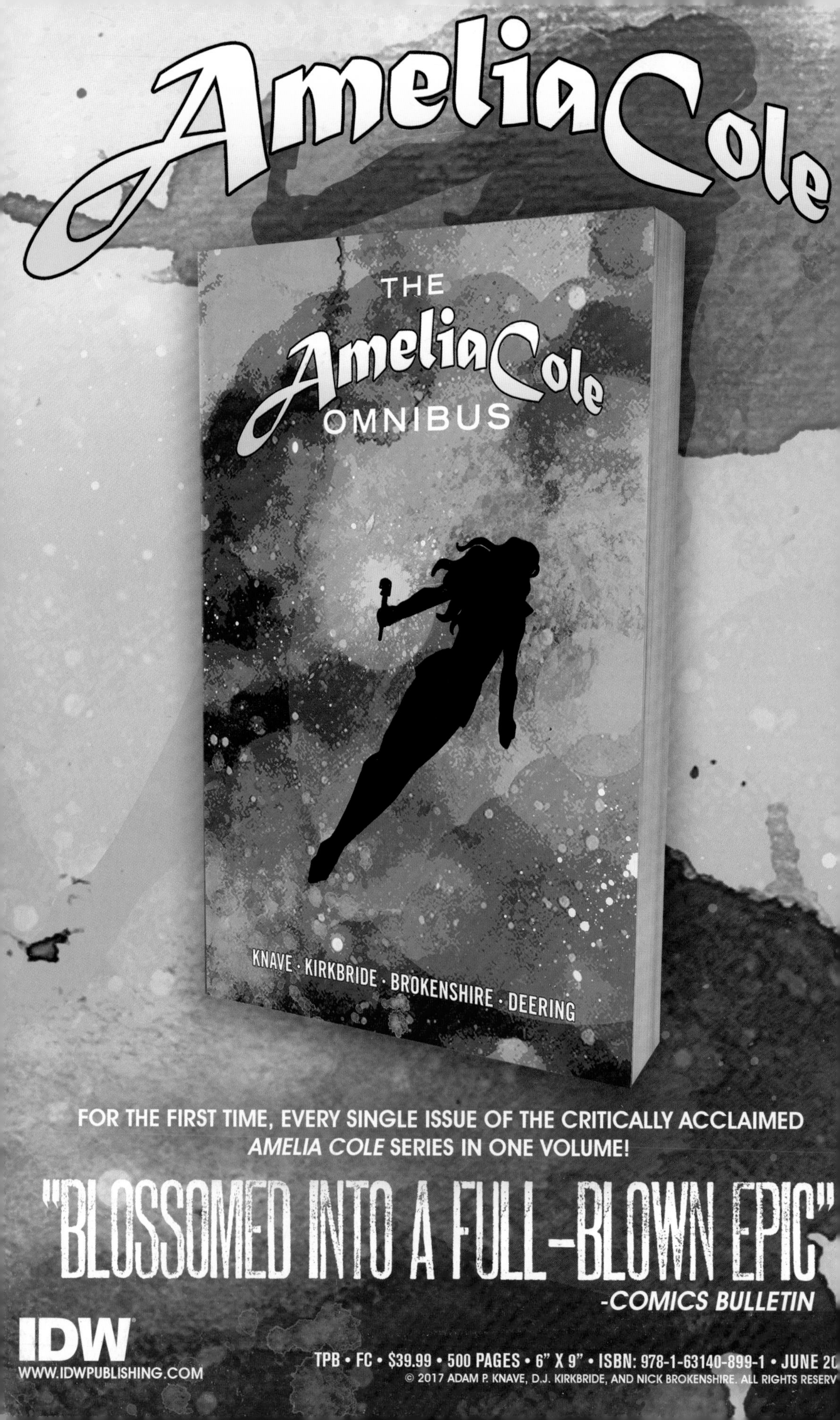
Amelia Cole
THE
Amelia Cole
OMNIBUS
KNAVE · KIRKBRIDE · BROKENSHIRE · DEERING
FOR THE FIRST TIME, EVERY SINGLE ISSUE OF THE CRITICALLY ACCLAIMED *AMELIA COLE* SERIES IN ONE VOLUME!
"BLOSSOMED INTO A FULL-BLOWN EPIC"
-COMICS BULLETIN
IDW
WWW.IDWPUBLISHING.COM
TPB • FC • $39.99 • 500 PAGES • 6" X 9" • ISBN: 978-1-63140-899-1 • JUNE 20
© 2017 ADAM P. KNAVE, D.J. KIRKBRIDE, AND NICK BROKENSHIRE. ALL RIGHTS RESERV